LIVING WITH ZOM

CONTRIBUTIONS TO ZOMBIE STUDIES

White Zombie: *Anatomy of a Horror Film*. Gary D. Rhodes. 2001

The Zombie Movie Encyclopedia. Peter Dendle. 2001

*American Zombie Gothic: The Rise and Fall (and Rise)
of the Walking Dead in Popular Culture*. Kyle William Bishop. 2010

*Back from the Dead: Remakes of the Romero
Zombie Films as Markers of Their Times*. Kevin J. Wetmore, Jr. 2011

*Generation Zombie: Essays on the Living Dead
in Modern Culture*. Edited by Stephanie Boluk and Wylie Lenz. 2011

*Race, Oppression and the Zombie: Essays on Cross-Cultural Appropriations
of the Caribbean Tradition*. Edited by Christopher M. Moreman
and Cory James Rushton. 2011

Zombies Are Us: Essays on the Humanity of the Walking Dead.
Edited by Christopher M. Moreman and Cory James Rushton. 2011

The Zombie Movie Encyclopedia, Volume 2: 2000–2010. Peter Dendle. 2012

Great Zombies in History. Edited by Joe Sergi. 2013 (graphic novel)

Unraveling Resident Evil: *Essays on the Complex Universe
of the Games and Films*. Edited by Nadine Farghaly. 2014

"We're All Infected": Essays on AMC's The Walking Dead
and the Fate of the Human. Edited by Dawn Keetley. 2014

Zombies and Sexuality: Essays on Desire and the Living Dead.
Edited by Shaka McGlotten and Steve Jones. 2014

...But If a Zombie Apocalypse Did *Occur: Essays on Medical,
Military, Governmental, Ethical, Economic and Other Implications*.
Edited by Amy L. Thompson and Antonio S. Thompson. 2015

*How Zombies Conquered Popular Culture: The Multifarious Walking
Dead in the 21st Century*. Kyle William Bishop. 2015

Zombifying a Nation: Race, Gender and the Haitian Loas on Screen.
Toni Pressley-Sanon. 2016

*Living with Zombies: Society in Apocalypse in Film, Literature
and Other Media*. Chase Pielak and Alexander H. Cohen. 2017

LIVING WITH ZOMBIES

Society in Apocalypse in Film,
Literature and Other Media

Chase Pielak *and*
Alexander H. Cohen

CONTRIBUTIONS TO ZOMBIE STUDIES

McFarland & Company, Inc., Publishers
Jefferson, North Carolina

ISBN (print) 978-1-4766-6584-9
ISBN (ebook) 978-1-4766-2792-2

LIBRARY OF CONGRESS CATALOGUING DATA ARE AVAILABLE

BRITISH LIBRARY CATALOGUING DATA ARE AVAILABLE

Front cover illustration by Anna Pagnucci

Printed in the United States of America

*McFarland & Company, Inc., Publishers
Box 611, Jefferson, North Carolina 28640
www.mcfarlandpub.com*

For Isaiah, Kira, Nathaniel,
and Isaac.—Chase Pielak

For Dion, for teaching me to use insanity
to stay sane.—Alexander H. Cohen

Acknowledgments

We are grateful to a horde of scholars who have heard, read, and commented on various portions of this book. Kyle William Bishop, Angela Tenga, Dawn Keetley, Katherine Bishop, Katherine Schutte, Jennifer Harbour, and the anonymous readers at McFarland and Rutgers deserve particular mention for reviewing chapters of the manuscript, for their helpful comments, and for encouragement.

We appreciatively acknowledge *Modern Language Studies* for allowing the reprint of an edited version of "Yes, But in a Zombie Apocalypse," *MLS* 43.2 (2014); the Mid-Atlantic Popular & American Culture Association for allowing the reprint of an edited version of "Growing Up Walking," *The Mid Atlantic Almanack* 23 (2014); and *Midwest Quarterly* for allowing an edited reprint of "Archiving the Apocalypse," *MQ* 57.3 (2016).

Table of Contents

Acknowledgments   vi

Introduction: Living with Zombies   1

1. Approaching the Apocalypse   17
2. Parsing Apocalypses   35
3. Apocalyptic Temporality   71
4. Apocalyptic Causes (by Matt Lewerenz, Chase Pielak and Alexander H. Cohen)   102
5. Apocalyptic Living (by Chase Pielak and Fanny Ramirez)   124
6. Curing the Apocalypse   140
7. Archiving the Apocalypse   156

Conclusion: Yes, but in a Zombie Apocalypse   171

Chapter Notes   183

Works Cited   189

Index   197

Introduction:
Living with Zombies

A simple Google search demonstrates what we all already know: zombies are everywhere. Over the past decade or so, boosted by the success of such films as *28 Days Later* (2002), *Warm Bodies* (2013), and *Pride and Prejudice and Zombies* (2016), television shows such as *The Walking Dead* (2010–), and books such as *Zone One* (2011) and *Feed* (2010), zombies have become a hot commodity, and scholars have turned a cottage industry of zombie criticism into a booming intellectual stock exchange.[1] The primary point of departure for analysis is often the same: many of these articles start with constructions like "Zombies are everywhere," "The walking dead are upon us," and "Zombies are inescapable." Yes, zombies are here. Now what do we do with them? Or, more appropriately, how do we live with them? Why do we need them? And what can the walking dead say—or groan—to us about our present circumstances as a living species?

The Cultural Zombie

Zombies hold a uniquely relevant place in contemporary Western culture. Elena Gomel asserts that "if every culture has its signature monster, ours is the zombie" (31), and follows Franco Moretti in describing our monster as a metaphor "that express[es] underlying fears and anxieties of [our] culture" (32). Kyle William Bishop treats them as "metaphorical icons" (*How Zombies Conquered Popular Culture* 12) or vessels for making meaning, arguing that they are "perfect figures to explain an apparently inexhaustible host of natural occurrences, social interactions, technological advances, psychological and physiological anomalies, economic structures and relationships, political dynamics, and more" (*How Zombies Conquered Popular Culture* 6). Bishop concludes his argument: "people see in zombies what they *need* to see" (*How Zombies Conquered Popular Culture* 17, emphasis original). Zombies reflect the culture that creates them. And, in our present social and historical context, they are an ideal way to access relevant cultural concerns.

With this frame in mind, we make two suggestions. First, zombies are intimately cultural and populate imagined worlds that are reflections of our own. As Shaun Mason, one of two protagonists of the zombie novel *Feed*, reveals: "I've spent my whole life imagining worlds other than the one that I was born in. Everybody does" (519). Second, zombies are relatively easy to defeat. Shaun's job is, after all, to poke zombies and record the close encounters. So, together, zombies help us imagine ideas and possibilities that would be too challenging otherwise to consider.

It is important to note at the outset that our definition of "zombie" is broad and inclusive, particularly since the zombie body becomes a device for making meaning rather than a line of demarcation. In other words, it can be meaningful that some things look, or act, or groan like zombies. We, therefore, include several other zombie kin that might otherwise be excluded but that are interesting and meaningful nonetheless, as, for example, the *draugr* of *Dead Snow* (2009) and the vampiric zombies of the most recent film version of *I Am Legend* (2007).

This inclusive gesture is neither intended to flatten the cultural possibilities of the Norse treasure-guarding monsters in *Dead Snow* any more than it is to artificially conflate creatures that don't belong together.[2] Rather, we take these monsters as they are reflected through American culture and seek to identify what they mean for viewers. When we speak of the creation of these monsters, we identify two levels where meaning is encoded—that of the creator (producers, studios, writers, actors, etc., responsible for bringing about the creature) and that of the observer (the audience or reader). That our methodology might apply to other creatures read as zombies opens possibilities for further discussion rather than ignoring key differences that audiences observe even while laying a zombie filter over the creatures.

But everything gross and vaguely human is not a zombie (nor are all zombies gross, in fact). And zombies are not simply anything that was formerly-human. As we discuss in much greater depth in Chapter 2, most zombies are characteristically gutted of the essence of self but nevertheless retain some trace of their former visage. Furthermore, and perhaps most critically of all, zombies are no longer considered alive. As soon as this distinction fails, we are forced to reevaluate what it means to be alive and human, and what it means to be zombie. Nevertheless, a small selection of zombies are interesting because they *do* retain a sense of self, but they eat brains. Regardless of where precisely zombies fall on the spectrum of zombie characteristics (speed, relative intelligence, reason vs. stimulus response, relative contagion, etc.), critically, we group such creatures together under the auspices of this text because they register as zombies for the American reader, function in the same way, and participate in the cultural expectations common to the zombie genre.

This book is not strictly a study of the zombie itself. Rather, we are primarily interested in the socio-cultural conditions from which zombies arise and are seen, how these conditions and the corresponding creatures operate, and any possible means of altering or ending the particular version of the end of the world as it was known into which the zombies arose. These conditions are particularly interesting because they tell us about our anxieties, our fears, and our hopes regarding the trajectory of society and the state of humanity. Our analysis is linked closely to the idea of apocalypse, in that it is under apocalyptic conditions that zombies arise.

The overall aim of this book, then, is to trace the zombie apocalypse, as seen in cultural artifacts, from cause to cure, in totality, as a reflection upon the state of our civilization. We argue that zombies exist in mainstream culture in that they represent a more-or-less recognizable figure, present in films, books, and zombie runs. They have ostensible bodies that can be read for meaning.[3] Yet they also function as signifiers, standing in the physical gap for something metaphorical: they are the walking dead and the physical locus or representation of some other, otherwise inaccessible, fear. Zombies have become the readily accessible scapegoats for us all to imagine and insert into our fantasies when the conditions of the world as we find it aren't working, so that when we kill the zombie, we can pretend that we're excising the real problem by shooting it in the head. As Max Brooks, author of *World War Z*, puts it, "You can't shoot a financial meltdown in the head—you can do that with a zombie.... All the other problems are too big" (Doug Gross). These giant fears are often of schism or rupture.

Ultimately, each of these metaphorical referents—these bodies that have risen for our viewing and reading pleasure—point to the fact that operative law, both normative and juridical, exists in a state of exception.[4] The stable basis for our society has eroded, which is exactly what we fantasize as we watch zombie films and read zombie novels. The rules for society are not working, and it's severe enough that the world as we knew it has somehow ended; we call this a "state of apocalypse" following Agamben's theory outlined in *State of Exception* (2004) discussed below, but which focuses on juridical rather than normative law.

Apocalypse occurs in the context of social collapse into an exceptional state. State here refers both to conditions of existence and the physical state, the locus of the zombie occurrence. Thus, in our cause-to-cure analytical model, we move from various causal concerns (what creates the zombie that populates any particular representation)—to a cure, (the means by which humans attempt to excise the metaphorical problem and its physical representation.[5] Our vantage is interdisciplinary, seeking to honor the vast array of work already done on the subject. This is a philosophical, political, literary, and cultural exploration. And while our critical analysis of zombies is novel in some respects, it is grounded in a number of intellectual currents with their own established and rich traditions.

Literary analysis, for instance, has long been fascinated with the idea of the "monster." Scholars of letters, drawing, music, and performance have always been acutely aware that art is a representation of the culture that creates it. So, too, with zombies. The discipline of animal studies has grown substantially in recent decades as well, and its questions of animal subjectivity and human/non-human boundaries abound in zombie criticism. The affinity between animal studies and zombie studies is clear, and while we don't necessarily need to approach the question of the animal here, we approach the corresponding question of the human.[6] The decay of the domestic social space, and of the living human body, together shape critical responses to zombie hordes. Building on literary criticism prevalent in the last two decades, as well as posthuman criticism of the last ten years, we argue that our culture is continually undergoing a remaking of cultural subjectivity, one that presently calls for a reinvigoration of the zombie figure.

Defining Apocalypse

Remaking cultural subjectivity is no more or less than apocalyptic. However, significantly, it is a key premise of this book that "apocalypse" need not be cataclysmic. Rather, apocalypse represents a shift in the world, ideological or otherwise, toward a new relationship between its inhabitants and each other, and the inhabitants and the world at-large. We imagine the possibilities of the coming event of the end of the world as we know it, the beginning of the end, in order to inoculate ourselves against the possibility, even while paradoxically demonstrating the already extant conditions for the dissolution of the thin veneer of present stability.

Jacques Derrida posits that we exist in a twilight state, demanding a simultaneous consideration of both the time in which we live and what will come after (Jacques Derrida and Elizabeth Rudinesco ix). One needs look no further than the *Divergent* novels (2011–2013), the *Hunger Games* novels (2008–2010), and the *Twilight* novels (2005–2008), and their corresponding films, to say nothing of the plentiful iterations of zombie apocalypse, to observe an unprecedented interest in our twilight state. Derrida's questions of the time in which we live and what might be to come after (*avenir*, a future that is not foreordained) become of critical importance. Consideration of this *avenir* requires reflecting upon two important ideas. First, we must think about where or who we might be now. Second, we must consider our actions and decisions in the present twilight, as these will bring about whatever it is that might come next.

Stories of the apocalypse focus our attention on both of these considerations; they are necessarily revelatory as a genre, exposing the state of the culture telling the story, and the coming of the end of the world *as we know it*. Raymond Brown discusses the biblical apocalyptic, a literary genre with its nominal exemplar in *The Book of Revelation* (also known by the transliteration of its Greek name, *The Apocalypse*). Brown asserts that apocalypse reveals some form of transformation "from this world to a world or era to come…. The vision of the supernatural world or of the future helps to interpret present circumstances on earth, which are almost always tragic" (775). The revelatory nature of biblical apocalyptic literature that Brown identifies becomes characteristic of apocalyptic literature in broad form: a human is engaged in a transitional vision of the future that reveals deep social fears about the consequences of our current conditions of existence. Apocalyptic narrative structure takes shape as revelation, from a human observer who witnesses a transformation from present circumstances to some generally tragic future, who then paints iterations of apocalypse, particularly as they expose social fears that bring about tragic outcomes. Apocalypse, therefore, need not be cataclysmic but is a consistently revelatory transitional state.

5

Apocalypse, as we understand it, is as much a descriptive term as a destructive one. We can understand our present state as one of apocalypse, despite its apparent leisure, relatively stable economy, and feeling of comfort, in terms of the relationship between law and our present circumstances. If indeed law decreasingly applies (as opponents of the PATRIOT Act and internment of flagless "combatants" at Guantanamo Bay would argue), then we are vulnerable to abuses of power that are often relatively ignored by society at large.

The erosion of law in imagined pre-apocalyptic worlds parallels that in our own world in at least three key ways. First, there is no apparent recourse or defense for the acts of terror resulting from ideological conflict that, in fact, are perpetrated by those espousing an apocalyptic worldview, and which seem to increasingly plague civilized society; meanwhile, the techniques historically used to enforce territorial borders and state sovereignty continue to degenerate. Second, the possible responses, including ambiguously targeted war with severe consequences for civilians, arming the American populace with conceal-carry weapons, or even charitable giving, all require the redefinition of traditional legal structures, precisely acknowledging the state of exception in which the West finds itself. Finally, increasing economic disparity in the West empowers the richest citizens through vague tax laws and lax enforcement while evidently disproportionately eluding those who could most benefit from increased wealth (see the biting commentary of Robert Reich, former Secretary of Labor, for example). These examples are symbolic of myriad instances that document a state of relative suspension of law for those capable of eluding the system.

The films and texts that we address herein all threaten to become apocalyptic, precisely because the society that they depict has become infected with the possibility of apocalypse, which we see as revelation, and further as revelatory of the society that creates and then views the texts. So, even when society is apparently functioning normally around an outbreak of the infected, as in the scene in *Dead Alive* (1992) when the hero visits the park with his zombie baby wreaking havoc on all of the other astonished parents who are out for a day at the park with their very human babies, apocalypse is at work. It both threatens imminent destruction through the possibility of cataclysm, and works more insidiously through the failure of current conceptions of law to operate properly.

Further, we do not mean to claim here that all zombie movies are traditionally apocalyptic. Not all zombies physically end their worlds. Even *Night of the Living Dead*, the genre's exemplar, clears up the outbreak by morning, allowing anyone left alive to return to the world as it had been. What we mean by apocalypse, then, is that there has occurred a fundamental ideological shift in the world creating the film so that it can no longer exist as it had been; the world as it was known is effectively over, even if the world of the film returns to its evidently static, pre-outbreak state, as in *Night*. We hold that this reconfiguration of the world (and thereby word, apocalypse) occurs along the lines specifically of a failure of law as Giorgio Agamben explores in his seminal *State of Exception* (2004).

State of Exception

The ideological shift is toward exception, and we are, as Giorgio Agamben argues, living in a state of exception, a time outside the expression of law. However, we are not culturally aware of our state, except as it is represented, in part through the recent and overwhelming interest in zombies. That the Gothic has reemerged at times of ideological struggle is a key premise of Kelly Hurley's *The Gothic Body*. Gothic literature, with its interests in portraying a redefined subject existing in a dangerous and threatening world, came of age as a late eighteenth- and early nineteenth-century literary genre contending with the political discomfort embodied in the French Revolution and enlightenment uncertainty. It reemerges in the later nineteenth century in the contexts of uncertainty surrounding the state of the human embroiled in a debate over Darwin, and in the context of the emergence of pre–Freudian psychology. This lineage is picked up in American noir literature surrounding and following World War II, and again as zombies begin their shambling progression into mainstream media in the latter half of the twentieth century. While the shape of the destabilizing figure has changed, the Gothic figure emerges consistently during periods of cultural ideological struggle as a means of interacting with a subjectivity-threatening shift that would otherwise be too terrible to engage.

In short, we mask many of our real fears with Gothic bodies, which are most recently expressed as zombie faces. After all, the zombie is a fundamentally Gothic figure. In most portrayals, the figure lacks, by definition, subjectivity, the ability to decide, which is precisely what is at stake in

Gothic literature, coupled with the overwhelming destabilization of culture and class systems that structure society during the period. To see the Gothic as a reaction to the trauma of loss is also nothing new, particularly when that trauma constitutes the unmaking of the subject, living in an ambiguous relationship to social power structures and human relationships, which somehow both constitute and trouble the possibilities of self. That stable conceptions of the self are unmade is a central premise of posthuman criticism.

But the apocalypse, too, occupies a central point in our narrative. While the zombie itself is a fascinating figure laden with cultural meaning, the *zombie apocalypse* is an entity in itself. In an apocalypse, an end of life as it has been known has taken place. The apocalypse is a radical end that itself produces a new *telos*, a new ending. The post-apocalyptic world is new, replete with new rules, which entails a remaking of society. And since apocalypse is a distinct possibility, given that humanity has, for the first time in its history, acquired the potential to destroy itself, whether it be through bombs or germs or resource depletion, it is important to understand what a theoretical zombie apocalypse tells us about our current circumstances as human beings, societies, and civilizations.

The most recent representations of zombie apocalyptic states feature a profound reimagining of life together with zombies in familiar geographic locations but with new political praxes and radically new structures for both power relations and human relations, including ethics. While it is tempting to see this as a simple engagement with taboo, in other words

Columbus (Jessie Eisenberg) rewrites rules for an apocalyptic society in *Zombieland*. Pragmatically, cardio is essential.

as contrasted against a present systems of ethics and behavior, it is really a more radical reimagining of the possibilities of living and living together. Apocalypse denotes, therefore, the creation of both a new political power structure and a new set of forms of life. A post-apocalyptic world entails a new state of being. Even if we argue that the zombie itself is an extant being, just gutted, the new human living in the apocalyptic state is a new being. A posthuman being, perhaps.

These are the bones of our narrative: zombies, our human fascination with undeath, the cause of the contagion, and a prevailing interest in curing the apocalypse. None of these can be taken at face value, for much like the pallid and decomposing visage of the zombie horde, they mask deeper fears. While this is not an exercise in horror, it is fair to say that, in zombies, we see the worst of ourselves, and in the apocalypse that surrounds them, we see an ending that enthralls because it so repulses. Yet, as we will find, the generation of artists and authors who have crafted these zombie representations place the culpability for such a terrible end squarely in our hands. And through their eyes we wonder, too, if a cure for the apocalypse can exist. If it exists, can it succeed? And would such success mark the end of the time—*our* time, at least—as some cure for the human condition?

These are crucially important questions to consider, and this mode of zombie inquiry wrestles with the guts of teleology. And while this is analysis on a grand scale, we approach interpretation through broad critical strokes and with close examinations of exemplary individual texts. It is our hope that our readings might equip our readers to make meaning from not only the zombie texts we address but also the raging horde surely to come. We hope that what we have produced is agile, accessible, and can say something to everyone, regardless of academic background and discipline. Of course, this assumes that those attempting to read have eyes that are not rotting out of their skulls.

From Cause to Cure: A Blueprint for Apocalypse

We begin with a chapter providing a meta-analysis of the state of critical zombie literature. Rather than attempt an exhaustive representation of zombie critical texts, which has become virtually impossible, we instead focus on interdisciplinary approaches that lend themselves to critical analysis of both the zombie body and its metaphoric role in Western culture. Specifically, "Approaching the Apocalypse" explores several discrete applications of the concept of the zombie. This chapter may serve as a primer for those interested in critically approaching zombies from a trans-disciplinary perspective. It highlights several important faces of the academic study of the zombie. We bridge critical distinctions between zombies used as a mirror for the human condition, as figures for contemporary social issues, as pedagogical tools, and as one-dimensional tools for modeling/demonstrating/labeling ideas (such as tax code concerns and employees who do not think for themselves). Bringing together disparate criticism opens the possibility of cross-disciplinary uses. This further reveals the extent of interest in the zombie as a framing principle as well as the many forms that this analysis can take.

In turn, this helps us all understand what these scholars already know: that the fascination with the zombie—a popular culture phenomenon that has taken on increased prevalence in the post–9/11 world—is more than just blood, gore, and T-shirts. It has spawned legitimate intellectual responses and dialogues. Furthermore, by providing several critical responses early in the book, readers are equipped with critical methodologies and lenses to apply to the primary texts that we address through the rest of the book. In later chapters, we offer our own critical methods and fill some gaps in this early dialogue by critiquing specific aspects of the zombie and the itinerant apocalypse to further explore what these human creations can tell us about ourselves and our state.

We move on to a chapter considering differences in zombie representations that nevertheless help to shape the cause-cure frame we apply. Significantly, "Parsing Apocalypses" presents an interpretive model through which to assess common traits linked to zombies, and to model the expression of these traits, particularly when they seem to be in conflict with those that would traditionally exclude the creature in question from zombie status. For example, the film *Warm Bodies* (2013) features a self-aware, dead-but-recovering main character, who, nevertheless, has a penchant for eating human brains and is otherwise apparently still a zombie. The film is without question a zombie film; clearly the task of defining the zombie needs to be addressed now more than ever. Furthermore, the meaningful differences represented in zombie films act on alternate sets of audience fears to produce markedly different effects. This chapter parses both physical (appearance and perceived appearance, relative speed, strength, and means of dispatch) and cognitive (social ability/ability to organize, reason, empathy) differences from the perspectives of the fears represented and the effects on the audience. This is fundamental to considering the representation of these films within a cause-cure frame. Furthermore, we give primacy to the physical characteristics of zombies, developing a rotten aesthetic theory that upends our relationship to these films.

We treat another interesting effect, temporal distortion, presented in virtually all zombie films, in its own chapter, "Apocalyptic Temporality." These temporal distortions inform our understanding of both the causes and the cures of apocalyptic iterations. Herein, we coin the term relative nostalgia, by which we describe the more or less nostalgic relationship to the pre-apocalyptic world held between the survivors in zombie films after the apocalypse. We also treat the forward-looking hopes for the future that inevitably arise alongside zombie apocalypses. This is fundamental to the possibility of cure, both within zombie representations and of the cure for the social cause that initially gave rise to the representation. Characteristics addressed in Chapters 2 and 3 begin to shape a system to organize apocalyptic films and suggest interpretive similarities (due both to cause—from whence, and effect—our reading of the representations) that shape much of our experience with zombie representations. This system lays out the central differences in zombie films that shape the cause-cure response that we undertake to develop through the rest of the book.

Having considered important differences in zombie representations, we move on to a chapter considering causes of the apocalypse, "Apocalyptic Causes." This chapter effectively bridges the world before the apocalypse in which we presently live, and the apocalyptic world. It lays out the trajectory from cause to cure through representative films like *I Am Legend* and *Warm Bodies*. We categorize types of causes and illustrate cultural effects, both within the representative films and in terms of the social phenomena that spawn the apocalypses represented in this chapter and begin to relate the causes to the world of the audience.

Removing the zombie mask from larger social fears leads us to "Apocalyptic Living," which focuses on the individual, tracing the development of the human as a result of the possibility of becoming a zombie. This chapter examines Carl Grimes, a character in the AMC show *The Walking Dead*, growing up in a world in which zombification has become not only a possibility but a certainty. The show plays with the possibility of becoming zombie, paradoxically in a world in which everyone already is. But the inhabitants of the walking world maintain the essence of their humanity, their agency, the ability to make decisions and a sense of responsibility. This turning drama foregrounds another drama of agency, that of the coming of age of a young boy who seems poised to become the show's hero. Living in light of the reality that the survivors of the walking apocalypse have already become zombies except for the moment of the final turn—in the presence of and in constant confrontation with death as the end of the self—changes the coming of age story, the *Bildungsroman*, into the *Bildungstod*. What is really at work in the coming of age story is "the integration of a particular 'I' into the general subjectivity of a community, and thus, finally, into the universal subjectivity of humanity" (Marc Redfield 38). Coming of age is about becoming human. But in a world in which humanity has already become something other than human, characters must gradually learn to become zombie subjects who nevertheless maintain their essential humanity. The threat of becoming a zombie is that, rather than the simple end of self upon death, the self (or some version of the self) will come back ready to destroy the community. This, in turn, separates the community from its general subjectivity (the ability to make responsible decisions, legal and otherwise) and thus humanity itself. The stakes for viewers mirror those reflected in the show as we, too, learn to live in a walking world. This chapter intimately ties the potential cures for apocalypse to our own world, asking how do we live in a walking world?

In "Curing the Apocalypse" we finally consider a means of moving forward as a society living with zombies in a state of apocalypse, through representations of the cure. A small but vital subset of zombie films fixate on the possibility of curing the zombie apocalypse. In each manifestation, the apocalypse takes place in a "state of exception" in which the world, under a sovereign agent, operates outside governmental and social law. Yet despite the apparent efforts to subvert catastrophe, the cure for the zombie contagion requires reproducing—and thus affirming—the pre-apocalyptic power systems in the absence of law that led to the state of exception. The cure brings humanity full circle: it reproduces the ideological conditions that created and spread the zombie contagion in the first place. Considering the cure to the zombie apocalypse, no matter what form it takes, demonstrates how the state of exception has become the rule, which explains, in part, our horrified fascination with representations of zombie apocalypse. Exemplary representations of apocalyptic cures flesh out the shape and practices for curing the apocalypse.

We explore one version of a cure in "Archiving the Apocalypse." It is possible that the means of moving beyond apocalypse might develop in response to the archive, some sort of lasting record of what exactly it meant to be human in a pre-apocalyptic context. This is perhaps one of the few ways to resist the apocalypse and develop a distinctly human voice that might speak from beyond the grave.

The possibilities of a cure lead us to ask how we might expand the zombie conversation beyond this text, and what questions are essential for the conversation. We address this idea in "Yes, But in a Zombie Apocalypse." By looking at how zombies can be used to stimulate conversation in the classroom and compel young people to address important societal questions, we demonstrate how zombies help both instructor and student contemplate questions of responsibility, agency, and the ends of our own humanity in society at-large. We begin from the premise that, in a zombie apocalypse, all bets are off. Exploring the uncomfortable feeling of survival outside the boundaries of human society compels students and teachers to consider the responsibility resulting from our choices—that which makes us human. It also underscores the crucial link between the ability to influence events in a meaningful way and the feeling of being human, as well as the possibility of denying this ability to others. Finally, it exposes the mask obscuring larger social fears that are so often what we really mean when we populate our nightmares with zombies, and invites the removal of the mask. These observations lead to a framing of the question of what constitutes the human that underlies our analysis and so much cultural exploration.

State of Emergency

It might seem a strange place to start, but the low budget 2011 movie *State of Emergency* exemplifies our interest in the zombie genre. Neither original, nor particularly novel, the film nevertheless manages to capture much of what is most interesting in recent film and sets the tone for the rest of our book, precisely because it engages a state of exception. It begins with an emergency broadcast, effectively wordless, parading stereotypically through images of absence and lack. These are images of apocalypse, as the landscape mirrors the lack or reassessment of self-subjectivity demonstrated in apocalyptic works. The film captures the state of post-apocalyptic life first through its interest in lack of language. Language itself has failed and become post-apocalyptic. It is barren, neither representational nor referential, transcending the extent of human experience. The story is told through flashback and disconnected image as much as through the eventual interaction between the very small group of survivors.

Caused by an apparent explosion at a chemical plant, the apocalypse in this film is limited to those directly affected by a mysterious chemical. The chemical plant is never explicitly identified as a biological weapons manufacturer, but it seems to have been producing some sort of biological weapon for the military; the film is satisfied to identify it as a chemical or viral airborne agent, "most likely one that was engineered." Late in the film, a group of soldiers extricates the survivors from their warehouse in the nick of time. It is clear both during the rescue and in the careful containment that follows that this apocalypse represents a diseased military response to an unnamed terror that appears, at least, to have been caused by efforts toward developing biological weapons. There has been, clearly throughout the film, a basic disregard for life and law, evident in the creation of a biological weapon, the failure to contain it, and then in the military response that contains the survivors.

The characters in the film resist the placelessness that accompanies living in a state of apocalypse. They attempt to uphold social stereotypes within their heteronormative partnered pairs. When Scott (Scott Lilly), one of the two male leads, complains of his wife, "even in the apocalypse she's got me doing chores" and the men investigate strange sounds in the warehouse hideout only after sending the women to the relative safety of the office upstairs, the audience hears the echoes of social place and hearkens back to a time before the apocalypse—one that feels distinctly untenable.

There is an even more interesting facet of the film, though: its zombies talk. At one point, toward the middle of the film, one of the zombies that has been creepily lurking outside the warehouse comes to the windowed-door and begins to vigorously knock and demand to be let in. The infected woman (Vickie Earley) keeps repeating, "Where's my daughter? Have you seen her?" When she begins to become aggressive and breaks the window glass, she is shot. The audience cannot help but to identify the zombie mother as the possible mother of one of the survivors Ix (Tori White), who has recently indicated that she has lost her parents. This clearly humanized, but nevertheless red-eyed and flesh-eating female zombie forces us to confront the state of the human even as we mourn her loss. We must ask ourselves if zombies could talk, what would they say? Would they sing "Hit Me Baby One More Time" like the Britney Spears fan zombie in *Scouts Guide*? The *State of Apocalypse* mother zombie clearly holds dear the connection to her daughter, perhaps the most human relationship possible: that of parent and child. That separation from this relationship would be difficult and not enacted until the final abandonment of the human form is reassuring, even in a world that no longer seems to have other rules that uphold our state of humanity and the rules for living together.

Iterations of apocalypse raise the possibility of, at least, different ends of the human. To recall the etymology of apocalypse as revelation (the Greek word *apokalypsis* literally means an uncovering), the versions of apocalypse we create are revealing. The word certainly carries the dual connotations of revelation and cataclysm. Each meaning deserves consideration, but they also deserve consideration together in that they represent the aspects of humanity that, when taken together, cause the most anxiety for our human condition. What will end us? Which apocalypse will create a posthuman world? The answer must be all of them. Even as imagined possibilities, they shape the world as we know it, reflecting both the fears and hands of the apocalyptic creator (our collective society), and the collective desire to overcome our own end. That we live in a state of apocalypse, in which the suspension of law demands that we imagine our destruction, must not necessarily end us; we must seek to cure the conditions that lead to apocalypse as we find them.

1

Approaching the Apocalypse

"Have you heard about Pacific Playland? There are no zombies there."—Little Rock (*Zombieland*)

In order to adequately explore the modern significance of the zombie—and the dramatic cause-to-cure arc that is our primary analytical focus—as well as to offer those coming to zombie studies from other disciplines a deeper understanding of the scope of responses already at work in the discipline, we offer first a typology of how zombies are used by scholars and practitioners in a variety of fields. By understanding the many ways that zombies are used *by* us, we can better understand how they affect us. This is central, in turn, to unlocking the cultural anxieties expressed in their evocation, which, we later argue, can be voiced in the creation of apocalypse and the eventual remedy in a cure (if one exists).

This is an important endeavor in fulfilling one of the primary goals of this book: to move toward a cultural analysis of the appropriation of the zombie. Yes, zombies are everywhere, including in Pacific Playland. While this is true, past this fact lies a fascinating and often overlooked meta-narrative. Just as zombies are everywhere, so too are responses to their existence. Some of these take the form of scholarly work; others are focused on practical use of the zombie to achieve some communicatory goal or teach some lesson. In order to understand how zombies explain the state of exception in which we find ourselves, we must examine our own collective responses to the object (zombies in culture), rather than just analyzing the object itself. These responses may be viewed along typological dimensions. This chapter, then, highlights several important faces of the study of the zombie, in an effort to better understand why studying zombies is, indeed, a worthwhile investment. Furthermore, it begins to set the scope of available representations of the creature that we call "the zombie." Almost as difficult a term as "the human" or "the animal," the zombie carries so much linguistic and historico-cultural baggage and applies to so many disparate iterations of deadish creatures (mostly but not always human) that really we are confronted with overlapping choices: to speak of zombies, or *a zombie* (as in that one, that particular creature), foregoing the definite article as it fails to apply.[1] This chapter aids in parsing this complexity by presenting scholarly perspectives from a variety of disciplines.

Others have done a fantastic job laying the groundwork for this analysis by focusing on the object of the zombie film, and a few deserve particular mention. Peter Dendle deserves recognition for his creation of the *Zombie Movie Encyclopedia*, Volumes 1 (2010) and 2 (2012), which analyze the near-totality of the zombieverse on the big screen (and direct-to-DVD, of course). Other critics have taken on a similarly analytical task, including, for example, Ozzy Inguanzo with *Zombies on Film: The Definitive Story of Undead Cinema* (2014). In this chapter, we frame some of the burgeoning criticism to establish how and why zombies matter to modern scholars, an important first step in our overall analytical arc.

Zombies as a Mirror into Human Condition

Scholarship is, of course, rife with iterations of zombies used as mirrors of the human condition. By gazing at the partially decomposed faces of loved ones, experiencing the horror of undeath, and watching the shambling hordes tear our beloved civilization to dust, we can reflect on the nature of life, existence, and all the intangibles that make us human beings. In many ways, this is the simplest evocation of the zombie because it is the most straightforward: the mirror into the self.

Like Dracula, Frankenstein's creation, and Grendel, the zombie is a monster, a creature of paradoxical excess and lack. The critical analysis of literary monsters is firmly established as an academic discipline, and is readily applicable to the zombie. Like all monsters, zombies are human constructs that, consciously or unconsciously, highlight or explore some aspect of our humanity or existence that is inherently frightening. In an effort to better understand *what* we fear, scholars have analyzed a number of ways that zombies provoke fear (an effort to which we contribute with this book).

Angela Tenga and Elizabeth Zimmerman offer a particularly interesting contrast by comparing the modern zombie to the modern vampire in "Vampire Gentleman and Zombie Beasts." This repeats, to some extent, the gist of Julia Lupton's 2011 "Re-vamp: A Response" (in the flagship literary journal, *PMLA*). In popular depictions, vampires more frequently are lonely and tragic creatures, so enamored with or ashamed by their own lost humanity that they deliberately avoid drinking human blood. For instance, Louis, the protagonist in Anne Rice's novel *Interview with the Vampire* (1976), feeds largely upon rats, in contrast to his creator, Lestat, who delights in killing. Many of the vampires in HBO's popular *True Blood* (2008–2014) and the *Twilight* film franchise (2008–2012) ardently avoid feeding on humans—though, interestingly, they are usually contrasted with a more violent and wild version of the vampire who, like Lestat, simply loves to kill. But these antagonists—who form the counter-point to the idea of the peaceful vampire—have nuanced views about the world around them, and their own loss of humanity. Most of all, like their protagonist brethren, these vampires are sexy, forlorn, lonely, and sympathetic—even Lestat ultimately transforms into a hero and takes center-stage to save humanity from an even more destructive incarnation of the vampire. Later, he comes to deeply love several human beings. Zombies, on the other hand, are generally clear antagonists, though there are notable exceptions in *Warm Bodies* (2013) and *Fido* (2006) in film, for example, or *iZombie* (2015–) on television, and even in Dan Simmons' novella *This Year's Class Picture* (1992). Despite these anomalous depictions of relatively friendly monsters, and even including initial reactions to their featured monsters, the walking dead evoke a specific set of human fears ripe for critique.

Perhaps most explicitly, zombies evoke the terror of death. This evocation can be very primal and visual—the zombie is often literally flesh decomposed (as Kyle William Bishop, for example, discusses). Not only do zombies remind us that death is always lurking in the wings—that one day, we will all be nothing but desiccated guts and bones—but that human civilization, too, may one day be reduced to dust. In psychoanalytical terms, zombies may be regarded as chilling evocations of the human "death drive," a concept developed primarily by Sigmund Freud (in *Beyond the Pleasure Principle*), who, in accounting for the human tendency toward destruction, postulates that we instinctively seek death as a return to a time before the emergence of existence. For Freud, many human compulsions with negative and self-destructive consequences are linked to this primal, biologically hard-wired tendency towards death (very much mirroring what physicists regard in more general terms to be the universal trend of all matter in the universe towards entropy).[2] Later psychoanalysts like Jacques Lacan and scholars like Slavoj Žižek would associate this death drive with culture rather than biology (e.g., as noted in Žižek, *Living in the End Times* 72).

Religion, for instance, is often interpreted as a social construct built to contend with the fear surrounding the potential for nonexistence. There is, therefore, a correspondingly significant sub-genre of zombie theological criticism developed by Kim Paffenroth, for example, and in the notable "Zombies in the Sacred" segment of Christopher M. Moreman and Cory James Rushton's *Zombies Are Us*.

The important point here is that the inevitable drift towards the consideration of, and ultimately subjugation to, death, is beyond the conscious control of the individual: the "death drive" is, like zombiism, an infection. Ola Sigurdson cleverly reminds us that the zombie mythos—in particular, the Romero canon—is constructed around a consideration of the human condition, as well as the social context that surrounds it. In this respect, zombies remind us that death is a part of who we are, and force us to confront this reality, just as we always have. It is an evocation of the self not unlike the Mexican Day of the Dead, a social and spiritual practice in which humans walk the streets clothed as skeletons, which serves to remind us of what always lurks around the corner. Zombies fill this same role by tying death to our own humanity, and forcing us to face it, albeit in a disguised fashion.

Zombies also remind us of other frightening aspects of our humanity. They often lack self-control, reflecting our own fears of lacking agency. For instance, in many depictions derived from its Haitian origins, zombies have been portrayed, quite literally, as slaves to a higher power (we discuss this move briefly in Chapter 2). In this conceptuality, zombies are beings who are directly under the control of some sort of puppeteer typically imbued with magical powers. Extensive criticism on the Haitian origins of the zombie, including that by Chera Kee, segments in Deborah Christie and Sarah Juliet Lauro's *Better Off Dead*, Moreman and Rushton's *Race, Oppression and the Zombie*, and many others, including a forthcoming work by Dawn Keetley. While these depictions were a reaction to the realities of slavery in the Caribbean, they do reflect an even older tradition of thought, in which humans (both living and dead) can be used as pawns to those in power. In fact, Jim Kline convincingly traces the idea of zombification to a "god-force responsible for ... manipulation" in *The Epic of Gilgamesh*, in which the god Enlil threatens to eliminate mankind by opening the underworld and letting loose an army of the dead (471).

Some recent depictions of zombies, rather than focusing on enslavement before a higher power, have regarded zombies as enslaved by human vice. In the space opera *Serenity* (2005), for instance, the zombic monsters known as Reavers have entirely given in to their carnal desires to kill and rape. While Reavers, like so many other creatures recognized as zombies, are not strictly undead, in that death does not take place prior to their transformation, Gerry Canavan situates these creatures within the zombie canon. In other depictions, such as the very mobile zombies of *28 Days Later*, zombies operate with purpose and rapidity for one reason: they want to consume flesh, gluttonously, without the possibility of ever being fulfilled. This overwhelming need to consume is cleverly reflected in Romero's choice of setting in *Dawn of the Dead* (1978), which takes place in a shopping mall.

Another fear evoked by zombies is the lack of individuality. They often appear in hordes and move without distinct purpose, reflecting deep fears of depersonalization—fears that are often accentuated by the increasingly globalized and technologized nature of our world. Zombies are anonymous, which suggests an absence of empowerment; it is, perhaps, due to the frightening nature of the term that the hacktivist group Anonymous has appropriated the term as tool to evoke fear in its enemies.

Nevertheless, zombies also remind us of what is good about our nature. If zombies are a mirror into the self—the enemy *within*, so to speak—then the act of surviving zombies can highlight what is truly best about our humanity. We see this positivity in some, but certainly not all, zombie films. Notable examples include *Zombieland* (2009), *Warm Bodies*, *Shaun of the Dead* (2004), and in some choice moments, *The Walking Dead*. Significantly, while the conditions of the apocalypse are seldom reversed and the infection seldom cured, protagonists find friendship, community, love, morality, and other satisfying human joys. While we are all born and will one day face the cold inevitability of death, there is plenty of warmth in between, and even in using zombies to explore and codify our fears, we may also observe other, more positive aspects of our humanity. Thus, while the zombie is very much a reflection of our fears, the zombie story can also be a narrative of our hopes—which, altogether, reflect the human condition.

Zombies as Lenses into Contemporary Societal Issues

Just as zombies can help us reflect upon our humanity, they can help us understand contemporary societal issues. Such scholarship tends to analyze systems of human interaction, with focus on themes of oppression, identity, imperialism, and community. Key recent collections exploring such themes are Dawn Keetley's *"We're All Infected": Essays on AMC's The Walking Dead* and Stephanie Boluk and Wylie Lenz's *Generation Zombie: Essays on the Living Dead in Modern Culture*, and Kyle William Bishop's *How Zombies Conquered Popular Culture*.

In particular, scholars have extensively explored such broad themes in AMC's *The Walking Dead* and George Romero's canon. Romero's earlier films delve into racial issues that plagued America (which, of course, remain relevant today in the wake of cultural events like the Michael Brown and Trayvon Martin shootings, the dismissal of Clippers owner Donald Sterling, and the "Black Lives Matter" movement). In *Night of the Living Dead*, Barbra, a white woman, is saved by Ben, a black man. However, they never become romantically engaged, even though they are paired together as survivors with a rapidly deteriorating situation and must work together to overcome certain doom—circumstances that, in film, seem to automatically produce such couplings. The film's refusal to accept romance highlights the racial divide still broiling throughout American society in the late 1960s—one rendered particularly salient amidst the tail-end of the Civil Rights movement and, specifically, the battles against segregation in the Jim Crow south. However, *Night of the Living Dead* also hints that interracial relationships are a genuine possibility, no longer entirely inconceivable in the popular imagination. While Barbra and Ben may not become romantically intertwined, they do work together with a semblance of equity, a theme seldom portrayed in films of the era.

Nearly a decade later, Romero's *Dawn of the Dead* caps the 1970s on a more hopeful note: Fran, a white woman, and Peter, a black man, escape into the sunset, presumably to preserve the human race through love and, more instrumentally, reproduction. Here, Romero reflects changes in the social fabric of American life that occurred between *Night* and *Dawn*:

while racial equality has not been definitively achieved, love between the races—and, indeed, individuals of two different races—is a real possibility.

Justin Ponder reads Zach Snyder's 2004 remake of *Dawn of the Dead* as a continued commentary on race. In one particularly poignant moment in the film, a zombie child is born from an infected mother. Ponder finds this moment particularly interesting. The child's status as a zombie mirrors the status of interracial children; the thing is half-human, half-zombie, and faces an uncertain future as the conflicting attributes of both will make for a difficult, if not impossible, life.

At times, the zombie itself is used as a symbol of oppression or slavery, which often connects directly to its conceptual roots in African and Caribbean mythology. For example, Rebecca Romdhani argues that in the 1998 speculative fiction novel, *The Girl in the Ring*, the zombie is used to symbolize "black people's history of oppression, exploitation, and demonization," and also the "consequential shame that members of the African-Caribbean diaspora may experience from a legacy of oppression, which,

The setting for *Dawn of the Dead*, directed by George Romero, is a shopping mall. Through this choice, Romero highlights the parallel between the zombie and Americans in contemporary culture: the need to consume. Zombies consume humans for no other reason than they, apparently, feel compelled to do so; human beings are merely a commodity for which zombies "shop." This is, to Romero, at least, role reversal. In a typical shopping mall, it is the humans who shamble down the corridors, lifelessly choosing what clothes to purchase, and who bang against the front doors in a great horde on Black Friday.

significantly, includes internalizing a white Western perception of their African and Caribbean cultural inheritance" (72). In such works, the zombie itself—rather than the human protagonists or the context that surrounds—are the key figures in understanding race relations in the Western world.

Race has not been the only social concept examined in the zombie canon. Again, Romero has been instrumental here. His *Dawn of the Dead* is a vehicle that powerfully critiques American consumer culture. In it, Romero was eager to point out that our human tendencies to consume may well be consuming us (see, for example, Denise Cook). The film, which tellingly takes place in a shopping mall, is populated with dead-eyed zombies who wander long corridors and department stores in search of human prey; to the zombie, the living are nothing more than a mere commodity for consumption. Zombies are allegories for the human shopper who, enslaved by advertising and the promise of better material life, is compelled to wander malls on weekends and black Friday, searching for happiness amid the possible possessions that line racks and shelves, driven to consume just as compulsively as zombies. The message is simple: consumerism is killing us. As Jim Kline puts it, "the relentlessness with which many people pursue money and the compulsion to obtain as much money as possible in a lifetime reflect the zombie pursuit of human flesh" (472).

Romero is certainly not alone among zombie film-makers in providing societal commentary. Nicole Birch-Bayley has identified a streak of post–9/11 "millennial zombie films" that delve into other social issues (1139 ff.). Here, the zombie contagion is frequently an allegory for the costs of globalization. First, in a world long organized by the Westphalian state-system (at least, according to realist paradigms of international relations), many iterations of post-apocalyptic zombies are significant in that they are truly stateless (although, some prominent examples such as *Warm Bodies* must be set aside here). We speak, here, of the mindless zombie hordes that populate *The Walking Dead, World War Z, and 28 Days Later.* Such zombies have no flag; they do not respect borders or the laws of the international order. Moreover, unlike religious or cultural movements that, in their initial stages, transcended state borders without any or only partial state sponsorship (such as Ba'athism, nineteenth-century anarchist and communist movements, or present day renditions of radical Islam), most zombies do not have any sort of political, ideological, or spiritual beliefs (setting aside, for example, *iZombie* here). The extent of their needs and wants, usually, is to simply eat flesh, not unlike bacteria: like bacteria their incessant reproduction and the spread of infection is ancillary to their hunger. For Birch-Bayley, such zombies personify many of the arguments made against the proliferation of ideas, people, and products that come with political and technological globalization: such transformations in global structure promote sameness, destroy cultural distinctness, and eliminate the relevance of existing power structures. Indeed, often, the proliferation of the zombie hordes cause the collapse of the state-centric world system (as in *World War Z*).

Moreover, zombies are often products of globalization. The initial infection is often *caused* by the increased connectivity between nations. In *The Omega Man* (1971), the advance of technology coupled with ever-growing closeness between great powers (in this case, the cultural antagonisms between capitalism and communism) drove humanity to create the contagion as a weapon. In other depictions, globalization has opened the door for greater power amongst transnational corporations, who, not bound by the laws of any central power, are able to conduct pernicious experiments that lead to the creation of zombies, such as the aptly named Umbrella Corporation in the game *Resident Evil* (1996). In these ways, the millennial zombie mythos helps explore the fears and anxieties created by an increasingly globalized world.

Steven Pokornowski offers another example of the connection between zombie films and fears of globalization: that the zombie narrative often highlights the global, homogenizing force of the international medical régime, embodied by the United Nations and World Health Organizations, and the imperializing undercurrents that run through even fictitious perceptions of and responses to the spread of contagion. Much like the International Court of Justice is inept at halting genocide and limiting humanitarian atrocities, the global medical bureaucracy is usually portrayed as woefully unable to contend with a zombie apocalypse, particularly as the world grows closer together. After all, globalization increases the ability of the zombie infection to spread easily, not unlike the spread of diseases like H1N1 and SARS. This, in turn, echoes fears of the internationalization of contagions like Ebola and Zika. While these fears have found expression in the "millennial zombie film," such evocations are really just new twists on old terror surrounding globalization. As Boluk and Lenz point out, accounts of plagues and epidemic can be traced all the way back to Herodotus, and they contend with common themes of global interconnectivity—a trend particularly pronounced, at least in the Western canon, in British fears associated with early mercantilism. When London became an unofficial capital of the world where cultures from all around the globe suddenly collided with traditional English sensibilities, anxiety abounded. Such accounts mixing fears, globalization, and disease can be found in Ben Johnson's *The Alchemist* and Daniel Defoe's *A Journal of the Plague Year*. In this way, zombie contagion engages far older intellectual discourse.

Relatedly, other zombie films use the global catastrophe of apocalypse as a window through which to critique the media and other information-senders. Romero's *Diary of the Dead* (2007), for instance, focuses on how the media can distort, misuse, or obscure important information (see Birch-Bayley 1146). In many ways, this mirrors fears in other "virus literature" like Steven King's novel *The Stand* (1978), in which information about a cataclysmic contagion is deliberately hidden from the public. In *The Stand*, the motivation intriguingly has nothing to do with public safety: those who are responsible for creating the virus that nearly wipes out humanity refuse to acknowledge its existence or their complicity even as the world ends, going so far as to execute "false flag" operations in which they deliberately spread the virus to Europe, in order to preserve a positive image of the United States government—even after that government, and potentially all of its citizens, are nothing but dust. More than twenty years after King's opus, technology has given those with the power over information an even more pronounced ability to distort and control messaging (hence *Diary of the Dead* takes place through the eyes of independent documentarians). Margaret Atwood's *Oryx and Crake* (2003) offers another haunting take on this concept as genetic engineering eradicates the world and a copy-writer narrates to the reader. In our world, one needs look no further than the case of Edward Snowden to see the saliency of this discussion in public discourse, and so it is unsurprising that these find voice in zombie films.

Zombies have been used to explore tensions other than race relations and the externalities of globalization, of course. For instance, scholars of Alzheimer's disease have noted that the zombie stigma is often affixed to Alzheimer's patients (see, for example, Aquilina and Hughes and Behuniak). As Susan Behuniak aptly puts it: "*Alzheimer's Disease: Coping with a Living Death* (Woods 1989) and *The Living Dead: Alzheimer's in America*

(Lushin 1990) clearly link patients with ghouls. The destruction of the person and the animation of the corpse is another theme: Cohen and Eisdorfer (1986) referred to the 'death before death,' Smith to the 'funeral that never ends' (1992: 49) and Fontana and Smith (1989) to the 'self that unbecomes'" (71). Those who suffer the disease are additionally disadvantaged by the social construction of their circumstance as zombified, which leads to fear and marginalization.

That zombies evoke such variegated feelings should not be surprising. Like any cultural artifact, they sublimate our fears and allow us to confront that which we would otherwise be unable to face. They are, as Cari Keebaugh reminds us, like fairy tales; they "serve as ciphers through which we can deal with the issues that plague us" (599). Or, as Max Brooks—author of *World War Z* and son of legendary comedian Mel Brooks—puts it: "You can't shoot a financial meltdown in the head—you can do that with a zombie.... All the other problems are too big. As much as Al Gore tries, you can't picture global warming. You can't picture the meltdown of our financial institutions. But you can picture a slouching zombie coming down the street" (Doug Gross). That slouching zombie opens an interpretive gateway.

Zombies as Pedagogical Tools

Millennials acutely feel the cultural impact of the zombie. In film, video games, iPhone applications, comic books, television, and other media, they are continually driven to engage with this monster. Consequently, interesting scholarly work explores the utility of capitalizing upon this trend and using the zombie as a pedagogical tool.

In political science, for instance, Robert Blanton offers us a general guide to integrating zombies into international relations coursework that draws heavily on *World War Z*. Combining popular methods of international relations pedagogy—popular culture, simulations and active learning, and counterfactual analysis—Blanton offers some modest suggestions about how to use zombies in class. For instance, *World War Z* can be used at the individual, national, and international level to explore ethics (exploring Brooks' the Redekker plan and the celebrity bunker), crisis decision making (the Iran-Pakistani conflict), bureaucratic behavior (the Battle of Yonkers), and the relationship between policy and régime type (Cuba v. North Korea). *Fido* is used to explore identity. Suggestions to integrate these into coursework include discussion questions, breakout groups, and simulations of events from the book.

Derek Hall presents an interesting account of how to use *28 Days Later* and *Wild Zero* to teach comparative political economy. He argues, among other things, that the origin of the Rage virus in *28 Days Later* maps nearly perfectly atop Ellen Meiksins Wood's *The Origin of Capitalism*, that the conclusion of the movie more or less precisely mirrors the rise and fall of the USSR, and that director Danny Boyle invokes Rosa Luxemburg, famed early twentieth-century Marxist, when Major Henry West (Christopher Eccleston) ruminates on a zombified former companion chained in the backyard of his fortified mansion: "He's telling me he'll never bake bread, plant crops, raise livestock. He's telling me he's futureless." Similarly, Hall explains that *Wild Zero*, which is essentially a film about a Japanese punk band that winds up fighting zombies by making their heads explode and destroying their spaceship (they are, it turns out, alien zombies), can be interpreted as "an account of the post–1985 dynamics of the Japanese political economy and its engagement with Asia" (1). While both films obviously deal with human themes that tangentially relate to political factors, no evidence exists that the creators of either work sought to make such compelling, deep, and, shall we say, "convenient" connections to these courses of study. To his credit, Hall acknowledges (2) that neither Danny Boyle nor Takeuchi Tetsuro sought to make films that so neatly fit these theses, and Hall is pleasantly tongue-in-cheek through the entire affair as he attempts to convince the reader that he is, in fact, a sane and productive academic and not a madcap graduate student poking fun at the entire peer-review system. Significantly, his point is valid: these films offer sufficient complexity to be used as interpretative tools, almost like *Rorschach* blots. Hall then argues that these films can engage, teach, and enlighten students about esoteric and otherwise less accessible lessons in comparative political economy. Scholarship here underscores an important point: zombies are here and so we might as well use them. And scholars *are* using them this way, even if it means drawing parallels between zombie-propagating spaceships and the economic assistance offered to firms by a highly interventionist Japanese state. After all, this is, in Hall's words, a "relatively easy" connection to make.

William Struthers engages the theological and philosophical implications of the apocalypse, arguing that millennials might do the same by using zombies to explore philosophical, theological, and moral issues:

"zombies can elicit a primal response that offers a unique opportunity to engage in philosophical and theological questions about human agency.... 'Are zombies moral agents? Do they have souls? Does the absence of a soul define what it means to be a zombie? Are human beings really just zombies that don't eat brains?'" (195). He suggests that directed essay writing pushes students to engage these complex questions.

Zombies, apparently, also have something to teach us about calculus. In *Zombies and Calculus,* Craig Williams uses an encroaching zombie apocalypse as a skeleton through which to teach calculus, largely by showing how calculus can help survive the apocalypse. They can also be instructive tools in understanding the human brain from a neuroscientific standpoint (as Zombethics convincingly proves).[3] In *Do Zombies Dream of Undead Sheep? A Neuroscientific View of the Zombie*—a titular play on Philip K. Dick's *Do Androids Dream of Electric Sheep*, which was in turn the basis for the Ridley Scott film *Blade Runner*—Timothy Verstynen and Bradley Voytek use the premise of the zombie as a launchpad for exploring the neuroscientific changes necessary for the human brain to become "zombified." And they can teach us about acting, as Gerald Large demonstrates in his discussion of using the zombie to help students of theater learn how to unlock unique physicality of their bodies in the performance of classic plays like Ibsen's *A Doll's House* and Tennessee Williams' *The Glass Menagerie.*

Even lawyers have gotten in on the game. Thomas Simmons, for instance, draws on a large literature that touches on how zombies can meaningfully be integrated into curriculum in law schools. Many of his own techniques, he argues, are simple but effective: instead of using the classic legal reference points of "A," "B," and "C" to reference individuals, he utilizes characters from AMC's *The Walking Dead.* For example, he populates a legal scenario with characters from *The Walking Dead*: "Rick Grimes makes a gift in trust to Shane Walsh as trustee to pay to Rick's wife, Lori, for life, remainder to son, Carl. The point here is that the remainder gift to Carl, while a completed gift and vested interest, would not qualify as a present interest for annual exclusion purposes" (730–31). Again, here we see the utility of the zombie as a valuable analytical construct that engages students. Simmons is not alone in this approach of using zombies as a tool to teach and explore the law. Adam Chodorow, for instance, uses zombies to play with estate and income tax laws, and Simmons points to a number of other interesting cases.

Finally, one does not need to look hard to see examples of zombie-themed events at universities, such as zombie walks and human vs. zombie games, which often connect to Freshman orientation or are employed to teach students some important lesson about the university community.

These accounts are telling because they signify a small but identifiable trend in education to utilize a popular construct—the zombie—to teach lessons of import. This in itself is not new, of course, as good teachers are willing to do just about anything to access and inspire their students. We discuss this in greater detail in our concluding chapter.

Zombies as a Practical Conduit for Improving Public Health

As the cultural relevance of the zombie has increased, some medical scholars have used the zombie to refine, advertise, and analyze larger social discussions regarding public health and disease. Some of this work integrates the zombie as an entertaining hook into an exploration of best practices for citizens and health professionals during any epidemic or natural disaster. For instance, The Office of Public Health Preparedness and Response at the Centers for Disease Control offers a number of resources to help individuals and families prepare for the zombie apocalypse, which includes a zombie blog, a depository of zombie-themed classroom materials, posters, and a novella. The OPHPR's website notes the somewhat surprising effectiveness of the campaign: "As it turns out what first began as a tongue in cheek campaign to engage new audiences with preparedness messages has proven to be a very effective platform. We continue to reach and engage a wide variety of audiences on all hazards preparedness via Zombie Preparedness" ("Zombie Preparedness"). Likewise, *The Journal of Clinical Nursing* features a piece (by David Stanley) on briefing nurses regarding handling a zombie epidemic. While this article is obviously tongue-in-cheek, a zombie epidemic poses an interesting analogy for whatever unknown contagion might next be unleashed upon the health care system. Because, one supposes, one never knows what lurks at the microbial level.

Further, the use of the zombie as a "disaster proxy" has trickled into postsecondary education, where the theatrical nature of a zombie apocalypse offers a model for real disaster response. At the Michigan School of Public Health, for instance, faculty, staff, and students recently engaged in a live zombie invasion, wherein participants spread infection via a sticker (Natalie McGill). Participants and observers were asked to consider responses to the spreading disaster.

While considering a zombie apocalypse is a satirical way to teach about disaster preparedness, quantitative epidemiologists have also subjected a zombie contagion to mathematical modeling as a means to understand how other diseases spread. Caitlyn Witkowski and Brian Blais use logic statements and Bayesian modeling via Markov Chain Monte Carlo simulations to generate models for both *Night of the Living Dead* and *Shaun of the Dead*, then apply these models to Google Trend data on influenza epidemics. While the use of zombies is admittedly entertaining, it "present(s) a straightforward method for handling real-world disease epidemics" (12).

While zombies are not real, treating them as potentially real-world problems has provided health care scholars and professionals a tool with which to pursue their research and policy agendas. Zombies act as an ideal laboratory through which to model real-world disease and disaster precisely because they are not real. They allow us to explore real threats without actually confronting the threat itself. Perhaps they act like a vaccine, in this respect, denatured, but provoking the same immune response as the real thing.

Thinking Zombies/Unthinking Humans

Philosophers have used zombies to explore the philosophical constructs of consciousness and cognition and to re- (or un-) think what it means to be human (see, for example, Daniel Dennett, David Chalmers, Declan Smithies, Robert Kirk, and Fiona MacPherson). For questions of consciousness, perception, and existence, the *idea* of the zombie makes a useful petri dish for scholars. Many of these treatments delve too far into formal philosophy to enjoy a fair treatment here, but they are part of a complex intellectual discourse among philosophers that demonstrates the conceptual utility of the zombie.

A group of bioethicists and neuroscientists have likewise used the undead as windows to explore discipline-specific issues. According to the

"Zombethics" subdivision of the University of Emory's neuroethics blogs, the 2013 "Zombies and Zombethics" conference explored, among other things, "the place and 'use' of zombies in the Academy," "the ethics of defining brain death," and "the portrayal of disability in the horror genre" ("Zombethics").

Similarly, scholars of organizational management have considered the concept of zombies in the workplace. Here, the traditional attributes of the zombie are used to understand how and why individuals disengage and do not participate, and how they drag down all around them (see, for example, Stephen Hacker). Such works frequently draw on fictitious accounts of zombies in discussing how to cure such organizational tendencies. Zombies, after all, classically act without feeling or thinking, tendencies that are dangerous for an innovative enterprise and which can be encouraged or discouraged by management.

Feminist scholarship has used the zombie novel as a prism through which to explore contemporary gender relations. Jessica Murray, for instance, offers an analysis of two teen zombie novels: *Deadlands* and *Death of a Saint*. Here, she explores how upheaval caused by a zombie apocalypse offers alternative constructions of gender relations while also reinscribing traditional patriarchal norms and beliefs.

Scholars have also used the zombie as a commentary on similar frightening characteristics infecting modern Universities. One pair of Australian scholars, writing the enticingly brutal article "Invasion of the Aca-zombies," suggest:

> Universities are increasingly populated by the undead: a listless population of academics, managers, administrators, and students, all shuffling to the beat of the corporatist drum.... In this bleak landscape the source of the zombie contagion lurks in the form of bland, mechanical speech ... peppered with affectless references to citation indices, ERA rankings, ARC applications, FoR codes, AUQA reviews, and the like.... Many zombies appear incapable of responding meaningfully to the tyranny of performance indicators, shifting promotion criteria, escalating workload demands and endless audits, evaluations and reviews. Try as they may to resist, zombies merely acquiesce to the corporatist line [Joseph Gora and Andrew Whelan].

Such critiques are not unique, suggesting that many in the Academy have been infected, if not irredeemably. As Suzanne Ryan points out, the zombie metaphor aptly captures the woeful inability of academics to resist the seemingly ever-rising tide of standardization, workload, governance, and political agendas, even as wages and job security continue to erode.

The Zombie Diaspora

Significantly, as academics of all stripes become increasingly aware of the ever-growing zombie fetish in academia, a discernable desire to experiment sneaks into some published work. Tying one's course of study into the cresting zombie wave becomes an intellectual exercise—a valid one, we would argue—prompting zombie scholarship to materialize in places where we would least expect it. For instance, in reflecting on the North American James Joyce conference, Richard J. Gerber notes that "people seem fascinated by zombies lately" (222), highlights interesting work tying *The Dubliners* to the zombie/vampire dichotomy of evil from the outside vs. evil from the inside, and remarks how the Facebook pages of dead loved ones—growing collections of memorial postings—resemble digital zombies. Along an equally literary vein, Robert Yeates provides a re-examination of Toni Morrison's book *Beloved,* using a zombie lens to make statements about slavery, prosthetics, and the African and Caribbean roots of the book that, in his eyes, have received scant attention.

Astronomers have also begun using the zombie nomenclature in their taxonomy of astronomical events. Galaxies have traditionally been thought to live relatively human lives: they start young, grow old, and die, exhibiting apparent characteristics that coincide with their age. However, some galaxies apparently do not stay dead: hence, "zombie galaxies," another example of the prevalence of this nomenclature in an unlikely branch of scholarly literature.

Finally, and naturally, anthropologists continue to use culture-specific evocations of zombies as lenses through which to better understand those cultures (see Isak Niehaus, for example, as well as Bishop's recent work). This scholarship is particularly prevalent in the South African context, where folk tales of zombies and witches in the *veldt* are part of popular culture. There are analogies here, too, of course: Jean Comaroff and John Comaroff give an interesting account of how modern day zombie sightings in rural South Africa are symbolic for the horrors of capitalism. Of course, it would be impertinent to claim that the success of the zombie in Western media has driven this scholarship. We simply note the coincidence.

Conclusion

Clearly, zombies are everywhere—and not just in theaters, on television shows, and in novels. They have penetrated intellectual discourse in meaningful ways. At times, they are a useful subject of study in themselves, as they shed some light on those aspects of human nature that sometimes lurk in the darkness. Of course, the broad range of responses collected here is a representative tip of the iceberg. However, each of these responses illustrates that zombies are ultimately an artifact of culture and readily reflect the social and political tensions emanating from the cultures that create them. Such perspectives are important to understand, as understanding societal, social, and technological problems is important to solving them (in our parlance, thereby "curing the apocalypse"). And zombies are a helpful intellectual prism through which to explore these problems. Throughout the remainder of this book, we synthesize this rich range of critical response in all its disparate incarnations to offer our own voyage through the zombie hordes and the battered cityscapes in which they reside. In the next chapter, by way of departure, we begin by examining the construct most central to the intellectual energy discussed here: the zombie itself. In order to understand the potential causes of the apocalypse, the creature itself must take center stage.

2

Parsing Apocalypses

"How can I describe my emotions at this catastrophe, or how delineate the wretch whom with such infinite pains and care I had endeavored to form?"—Victor Frankenstein (*Frankenstein*)

All zombies do not rise equal. Differences in zombie representations, aesthetic, behavioral, and ontological affect how we see zombies. After all, different zombie evocations evoke altering sets of feelings, fears, or hopes. In other words, each zombie can mean something different, and these gradations of meaning are tied to its attributes. This chapter provides an interpretive model through which to assess common variant traits traditionally linked to zombies, and to analyze the expression of these traits, particularly when they seem to be in conflict with typical expectations. As we earlier argued, the gesture of including a panoply of border-zombie creatures in our analysis allows an investigation into the ways that culture invigorates the zombie representations that return to plague it. In order to understand the cultural forces at work in causing apocalypses, we first need to parse zombie characteristics. In doing so, we acquire a better understanding of what these shambling (or sprinting) creatures *mean* to us, which is crucial in parsing apocalypses that takes place later in the book.

A particularly interesting, and divergent, incarnation of the zombie can be found in the film *Warm Bodies*. R (Nicholas Hoult) is a self-aware zombie protagonist who has a penchant for eating human brains. R is certainly presented as a zombie to the audience, at least at the film's start. Yet even though the audience is told that R is a zombie—and given no reason to disbelieve this classification within the narrative framework—R exhibits characteristics that are distinctly un-zombielike. He thinks; he considers; he reasons. The movie's first lines are first person narration from R's perspective. Yet he is still biologically a zombie, within the logic of the film.

R thus fails to exhibit the key lack of self that characterizes the classic zombie figure popularized by Romero. Yet *Warm Bodies* is without question a zombie film. This is a fascinating divergence reflecting a growing and meaningful ambiguity in zombie films. This ambiguity further plagues films like *Freaks of Nature* (2015) and the show *iZombie*, each of which capitalize on the storytelling power of a self-aware zombie protagonist to interest audiences. In these cases, zombies clearly reflect their human counterparts, and yet they are still distinct. Significantly, making zombies protagonists rather than antagonists is not as simple as slapping a 'zombie' symbol around a pretty performer's neck; these zombies, while easier to empathize with than a gruesome, flesh eating skull-creature, nevertheless *do* exhibit believable zombie characteristics, to various degrees. This creates a problem and demonstrates the usefulness of the taxonomy presented here: how are we to delineate the wretches that we have formed?

Clearly, the task of parsing the divergent attributes of zombies still needs to be addressed. We are particularly interested in the fears evoked by these differing attributes; after all, these creatures are designed to summon fear and dread, at least on some level. Even when mixed with comedy or satire, *fear* remains a crucial part of the idea of the zombie. Using this as a prism, we can see that zombies exhibit meaningful differences, which act on alternate sets of audience fears to produce corresponding effects. Each of these effects tells us something important about the zombie as a construct, and ourselves as a society. This chapter attends to both physical and cognitive differences from the perspectives of the fears represented and the effects of these fears; we address zombie sight, faces, bodies, relative speed and strength, the source of life and means of dispatch, rot, the ability to reason, zombie relationships, and communication. We offer a few exemplary films to illustrate the impact and breadth of these distinctions, which will inform our model for interpreting future iterations of apocalypse.

What Is a Zombie?

Our point of departure for understanding zombies and their component parts is Kevin Boon's complex taxonomical model, developed in "And the Dead Shall Rise" and in more detail in "The Zombie as Other: Mortality and the Monstrous in the Post-Nuclear Age." In these chapters,

Boon describes nine types of zombies, with the understanding that the central definition is that "the original self has been altered in a way that guts its essence" ("And the Dead" 7). His nine types, which frequently overlap and are not necessarily mutually exclusive, are:

> (1) *zombie drone*: a person whose will has been taken from him or her, resulting in a slavish obedience; (2) *zombie ghoul*: fusion of the zombie and the ghoul, which has lost volition and feeds on flesh; (3) *tech zombie*: people who have lost their volition through the use of some technological device; (4) *bio zombie*: similar to tech zombies, except some biological, natural, or chemical element is the medium that robs people of their will; (5) *zombie channel*: a person who has been resurrected and some other entity has possessed his or her form; (6) *psychological zombie*: a person who has lost his or her will as a result of some psychological conditioning; (7) *cultural zombie*: in general, refers to the types of zombie we locate within popular culture; (8) *zombie ghost*: not actually a zombie, rather someone who has returned from the dead with all or most of his or her faculties intact; and (9) *zombie ruse*: sleight of hand common in young adult novels where the "zombies" turn out to not be zombies at all ["And the Dead" 8].

In many ways, one might read this chapter as complementary to Boon's work, as it serves to clarify some of the apparent contradictions in typology at work through these overlaps. However, we are not restricted to this typology. We go on to argue that all zombies and zombie-kin (whether they are called "zombie" or not) are cultural representatives and they all serve culture, and they (and the differences between them) are worthy of study.

The cultural impact of the zombie has long been inflected by a submerged (one might say legendary) origin story. As Chera Kee documents, the notion of the zombie is inherited from West Africa prior to the penetration of European influences (10ff.). And though the etymological genesis of the term is unclear, connections to the French or Arawak languages have been suggested, as well as to the creator god of the Bantu people *Nzambi*, and several other African deity figures (see Jeanine Gauthier and Hans Ackermann for an excellent etymological history of the term). A common thread in these myths is that those risen from the dead inherit superhuman powers. There is general agreement that the concept of the zombie and its itinerant cultural meaning was imported to the Western world via the importation of slaves, and that our modern Western understanding of the zombie was initially framed by Haitian voodoo culture.[1] Here, the zombie is generally recognized to be a soulless body, often enslaved or under the control of a practitioner of voodoo. This idea

While not strictly a zombie film, Robert Wiene's *Das Cabinet des Dr. Caligari* draws on themes of control, domination, and the loss of the self that are reflective of later, more zombified work. Above, the insane Dr. Caligari (Werner Krauss) demonstrates his control over a chronic sleepwalker (Conrad Veidt), whom he uses to commit murders. The film, which was made during the Weimar Republic, is often regarded as presaging the rise of Naziism in its treatment of the loss of the self, and with Dr. Caligari seen as a symbol for the totalitarian state. The similarities between Cesare, the sleepwalker, and early manifestations of the zombie seen in *Magic Island* and *White Zombie* are striking: the zombie is mindless and without self-control. The theme of control by an outside party also resonates with the Haitian conception of the zombie and its allegory to plantation slavery.

appears to be rooted in the psychological horror of plantation slavery, where imported African laborers toiled in fields without any sense of agency (Kee 13–14). Chris Vials traces a direct lineage from the U.S. occupation of Haiti in 1915 to the cultural preoccupation with the zombie in American culture (42).

It is also clear that zombies began increasingly to consume international popular culture in the early twentieth century, certainly by the time of Victor Halperin's *White Zombie* (1932). The stage for the zombie's popularity on the silver screen, however, may have been set by a pre-zombie film composed amidst the frenzy of the early Weimar Republic. *Das Cabinet des Dr. Caligari* (1920) features a murderous carnival hypnotist (Werner Krauss) who controls a somnambulist, Cesare (Conrad Veidt), who commits a number of murders while under the doctor's control. The film's powerful effect comes from the possibility that one might control another sufficiently to eliminate self-control and therefore suppress one's humanity. Not only does this idea presage the rise of fascism in Europe, *Dr. Caligari* and its themes of lost control are central to early conceptions of the zombie figure. Though the film finally resists when Cesare cannot murder the lovely Jane (Lil Dagover), the frame narrative ultimately dissipates the possibility of self-control as all of the film's characters are revealed to be housed in an asylum and with no more (apparently actually less) control of their faculties than the murdering somnambulist. Other early influential work includes William Seabrook's 1929 book, *The Magic Island*, popularized the concept of the zombie as a product of Haitian voodoo. Thus thematic follow-ups such as *White Zombie* and Jacques Tourneur's *I Walked with a Zombie* (1943) continued to regard the zombie as a reanimated shell that is mindless, shambling, and enslaved.

Over the last half century, however, the idea of the zombie has morphed in imaginative ways. George Romero's *Living Dead* film series (beginning with *Night of the Living Dead*) were particularly powerful transformative agents. Zombies were no longer necessarily the manifestation of enslavement or exploitation, but rather more overt reflections of a more diverse set of pressing contemporary social tensions. For Richard Matheson, in the novel *I Am Legend* (1954), the creation of zombie-like creatures was the end product of Cold War pressures exploding beyond containment.[2] For Romero, zombies reflect rising social tensions. In *Night of the Living Dead,* they are a lens through which to explore materialism. In *Dawn of the Dead*, they critique materialism. *Day of the Dead* (1985) uses zombies to explore the loss of interpersonal communication. *Land of the Dead* (2005) examines the potential for totalitarianism, which is framed around zombies and humans that are equally powerless.

Each of these rich manifestations of the zombie—the classic "voodoo" zombie, the risen corpse intended to horrify, the purposefully satirical device, and onward—is worthy of considerable examination. We attempt to do so here, focusing on the attributes of various incarnations of the zombie, and the differences between them.

Parsing Zombies

Perhaps no attribute enables more ready identification of a zombie than its image and presence, which are both repulsive and attractive, in various degrees, depending on the representation. Zombies are attractive because they used to be human; they can be mourned, remembered, and even loved by humans, but can also be repulsive because they portray a distorted, ruined image of what *was*.

When we think of zombies, it is the image of the creature that first leaps into the forefront of imagination. This image appears in widely varied media forms, from video games, to movie posters, book covers, T-shirts, posters in college dorm rooms, and even several different editions of zombie-themed Monopoly games. It is emulated in zombie walks and on Halloween. The physical characteristics of zombie bodies are particularly significant because despite their marked inhumanity, they retain some aspect of the human visage. Jacques Derrida identifies three characteristics of the "thing" perceived in the specter that apply no less surely to the zombie; the first of these is its connection to radical mourning:

> It consists always in attempting to ontologize remains, to make them present, in the first place by identifying the bodily remains and by localizing the dead (all ontologization, all semanticization-philosophical, hermeneutical, or psychoanalytical-finds itself caught up in this work of mourning but, as such, it does not yet think it; we are posing here the question of the specter, to the specter, whether it be Hamlet's or Marx's, on this near side of such thinking). One has to know. One has to know it. One has to have knowledge.... Now, to know is to know who and where, to know whose body it really is and what place it occupies-for it must stay in its place. In a safe place. Hamlet does not ask merely to whom the skull belonged ("Whose was it?" the question that Valery quotes). He demands to know to whom the grave belongs ("Whose grave's this, sir?"). Nothing could be worse, for the work of mourning, than confusion or doubt: one has to know who is buried where-and it is necessary (to know-to make certain) that, in what remains of him, he remain there. Let him stay there and move no more! [*Spectres of Marx* 9].

Parsing zombies is an attempt to know who confronts us and the submerged paradoxes therein: the zombie is dead but undead, a figure of present absence that nevertheless manages to look at us. The zombie can engage the observer in mourning even as it grapples to kill the mourner. Mourning, the distinct sense of loss accompanying the loss of a known subject, afflicts humans suffering death and other separation. The zombie body represents the loss of humanity that may be mourned. For instance, one might recall the awful scene in the first season of *The Walking Dead* when Morgan Jones (Lennie James) is forced to put down his turned wife, Jenny Jones (Keisha Tillis), or perhaps the gut punch when Beth Greene (Emily Kinney) dies in Season 5. These apocalyptic evocations of mourning define us as human even as they set us apart from the creatures who have lost the ability to mourn their own losses.

Still, the remnant of life, held in the zombie visage, engages the viewer in the Freudian paradox of the familiar that has become uncanny: an "intellectual uncertainty whether an object is alive or not, and when an inanimate object becomes too much like an animate one" (Freud, "Uncanny" 8–9); "Dismembered limbs, a severed head, a hand cut off at the wrist, feet which dance by themselves—all these have something peculiarly uncanny about them, especially when, as in the last instance, they prove able to move of themselves in addition" (Freud, "Uncanny" 14). The zombie body retains some element of the familiar that has clearly changed into something other. Nevertheless, zombies are not simply reducible to the status of object, in part because of this familiarity.

Glenn (Steven Yeun, left) and Rick (Andrew Lincoln, right) from *The Walking Dead* smeared with gore and toting dismembered limbs in order to avoid detection by the nearby zombies. The stunt blurs the distinction between zombies and humans pretending to be zombies by wearing dead human parts.

These characteristics, furthermore, act in film in specific ways. Zombies are particularly well known for their engagement with the horror genre. They essentially feature gore, with relatively more or less substance. There is a certain magnetism at work in the presentation of the zombie creature that engages the viewer. We are drawn to watch even as we are thankful that our real situation is really not like the carnage-blasted zombie world. For Akira Lippit, who writes of animal magnetism in *Electric Animal*, magnetism works through simultaneous drawing-in and rejection (166–69).

This inevitably requires consideration of the body of the animal, for Lippit, and, we argue, of the zombie. Zombies perform the simultaneous draw and rejection characteristic of animal magnetism as they call us even while repelling the viewer, which also inevitably destabilizes the human. Are we, the watchers, somehow dehumanized? We choose to watch, and in the process remake ourselves, in part, in relation to the zombie, making its boundary somehow less than clearly defined from our own. Therefore, by misidentifying the boundary between human and zombie, or by pointing to a failing boundary, perhaps, we attempt to escape responsibility, to evade the consumption that marks the zombie genre, the consuming of the self, and the becoming void of humanity. Innocent evasion (and perhaps fraught evasion of the human, as viewers seek to both escape the grasping hordes and the image of their own visage staring back at them from the screen) becomes a technique of freeing the human from its own zombie nature. As Stephen King suggests: "The mythic horror movie, like the sick joke, has a dirty job to do. It deliberately appeals to all that is worst in us. It is morbidity unchained, our most base instincts let free, our nastiest fantasies realized ... and it all happens, fittingly enough, in the dark.... For myself, I like to see the most aggressive of them—*Dawn of the Dead*, for instance—as lifting a trap door in the civilized forebrain and throwing a basket of raw meat to the hungry alligators swimming around in that subterranean river beneath" ("Why People Crave Horror Movies" 463). We look to the physical zombie with extraordinary interest both because, as King suggests, it allows us to take a roll in the grass with our subconscious, but also because we cannot look away. We choose and we fail to choose at the same time; we exhibit self and we succumb to the control of self simultaneously.

So, whether we see in zombies conscious images of ourselves, reflections of human ends, or social disaster, what we see matters. No matter how an author or director or producers conceive their horde, even when they are romanticized, there is *something* awful about zombies. They reflect what we have always suspected: "Man is an invention of recent date. And one perhaps nearing its end…. If some event of which we can at the moment do no more than sense the possibility—without knowing either what its form will be or what it promises—were to cause them to crumble, as the ground of Classical thought did, at the end of the eighteenth-century, then one can certainly wager that man would be erased, like a face drawn in sand at the edge of the sea" (Foucault, *The Order of Things: An Archaeology of Human Sciences* 387). The horror that we experience when viewing zombie representations is recursive to our own nature; if it were not, it would not be horror. Yet different apocalyptic manifestations evoke different sensations of horror, which are in turn linked with different manifestations of our own characteristics. Our sensations of horror are reflected explicitly through the cause/cure model and implicitly through the physical characteristics of the horde. Each possibility serves, in turn, as another depiction of the event that promises, as Foucault suggests, to erase the human characteristic that has been drawn in the sand. There has ceased to be an unassailably human characteristic; zombies specifically attack these characteristics even as they threaten to consume the flesh of the unwary victim. As each depiction effaces what is human it paradoxically writes our story. And this story is written on the faces of the horde.

Faces

The retention of human appearance is perhaps the most complicated of the physical traits presented by the living dead. What, after all, makes a zombie recognizable as human? It is clearly appearance. They are bipedal, at least until appendages are removed by rot or chainsaw. They have (or have had) heads. While they may lose flesh or even limbs in undeath, zombies typically do not grow *new* physical features like the fangs of the vampire or the beard of the lycanthrope. They are recognizably human, and yet they are distinctly not.

The physical process of decomposition presents some notable concerns for zombie texts, particularly when they take place over a period of time as in serialized shows like *The Walking Dead*. While a novel like *Feed*, for example, has the relative luxury of arguing that its zombies do, in fact, decompose and lose much of their freshness in the wild, sharing this idea with Seth Grahame Smith's novel *Pride and Prejudice and Zombies* (2009), it is not forced to depict the creatures.[3] There is perhaps also some room for the suspension of disbelief as zombie bodies exist in our imagined worlds as the horrifying mirrors of self, not particularly needing an embedded end. We return to this discussion below in the discussion surrounding relative rot.

For the moment, it is enough to consider the relative range of decomposition of the face highlighted in *Warm Bodies*, in which there is a dichotomy between the relatively human zombies (called "corpses" in the film), amongst which the protagonist counts himself, and the "bonies," zombies which have lost all semblance of their humanity except their musculo-skeletal structure. Bonies have lost or removed the skin, apparently beginning with the peeling-off of the face as the audience is graphically shown, followed by the remaining soft tissue that would otherwise cover the recognizably human body. They have, therefore, the structure of a face without the actual features that would otherwise mark the creature as human. And the face—in its varying degrees of decomposition and considering its relationship with other zombie attributes—is a key to understanding the meaning of the zombie.

It is important, then, to consider what it means to have a face (perhaps not as differently construed from Derrida's idea as it might seem). Derrida dialogues with Levinas in *The Animal That Therefore I Am* about the significance of having a face. Zombies are no more animal than human, but the affinity between non-human animals and posthuman zombies is extraordinary. While famously responding to his cat looking at him, Derrida writes:

> As with every bottomless gaze, as with the eyes of the other, the gaze called animal offers to my sight the abyssal limit of the human: the inhuman or the ahuman, the ends of man, that is to say the bordercrossing from which vantage man dares to announce himself to himself, thereby calling himself by the name that he believes he gives himself. And in these moments of nakedness, under the gaze of the animal, everything can happen to me, I am like a child ready for the apocalypse, I am (following) the apocalypse itself that is to say the ultimate and first event of the end, the unveiling and the verdict. I am (following) it, the apocalypse, I identify with it by running behind it, after it, after its whole zoology [*The Animal That Therefore I Am* 12].

The problem here arises in confrontation with the other. Derrida's supposition that he is following the apocalypse is really a means of situating himself in relation to the apocalyptic creature; it becomes, in fact, a means of situating us in relation to the creature. It is this situation that interests us: what is the creature against which we must be situated in the apocalypse? Derrida's abyssal cat is no longer responsible for delimiting the limits of the human. The naked human, under the gaze of the zombie, becomes food, meat, animal. To the extent that we follow the apocalypse, we seek it and come after it. We seek the apocalyptic creature and seek to represent ourselves as living. That which is culturally dead (for its engagement with the taboo of cannibalism) and which is physically dead, even while retaining animation, becomes the figure against which we seek to name ourselves as human: we live, we avoid taboo. We place ourselves in a complex zoology, seeking the living amidst the dead, seeking whatever it might be that makes us alive. And with this, we settle on the face, on the zombie face that no longer can see except to see the barest distinction between food or irrelevant. The register of appetitive consumption is not lost in the parsing of this definition, for the mouth remains a key feature of the face. In the face of its creature, we witness the character of the apocalypse. It is the event, that which is utterly surprising, which could not have been anticipated. We see in the zombie gaze the death of the self that cannot really die and really isn't dead.

In parsing the meaning between various incarnations of zombies, then, there are two questions that we must then consider. The first is whether or not zombies can have faces. The next is whether or not they do actually have a face. The philosophical and perceptual problem presented to us by an author, director, or video game designer, is whether or not the zombie is looking back at me. The metaphor of having eyes, and therefore, a face, is essentially that of consciousness: zombies may or may not have consciousness and, therefore, they may or may not look back as an other existing outside the shaping gaze of the viewer. The viewer must choose to imagine whether consciousness exists, an exercise tied into the face itself. So while they may or may not literally have a face (as it may or may not have rotted off), zombies may also have or fail to have consciousness beyond that of, say, a falling apple or a floating sardine can. Falling apples and floating sardine cans move, though they distinctly lack consciousness.

So, then, can at least some zombies have faces? We would argue that they can, though whether they *do* is tied to a combination of makeup and behavior. After all, to have a face is to have the ambiguity of life, a key theme in zombie representations. Zombies may or may not be able to stare back at the viewer. Some zombies clearly do have faces that can, independently of the viewer's expectation, stare back. Despite the rot so commonly disfiguring what we recognize as zombie faces, walkers generally have not lost their eyes. In the aforementioned confrontation in Season 1 of *The Walking Dead*, for instance, when Morgan Jones confronts the question of whether his zombified wife meandering in front of his house is indeed conscious, viewers are forced to wonder whether or not Jenny Jones is staring at her former home with some hint of recognition, staring at the door in some dim memory of long lost-family dinner, or merely shuffling along randomly, like her counterparts. The face—and the unknowable synaptic connections within—are keys to answering this question.

Perhaps the best critical model for reading zombie faces comes from animal studies. Consider, for instance, the worm, the human, and the idea of *vileness*. Janelle Schwartz identified images of the worm as centerpoints of aesthetic disruption in the nineteenth century both for the worm's inability to be classified taxonomically and for its location at the border of the human: the site of decay, the place at which the human ceases to become the human (*Worm Work*). This situation thus opens the vile as a new aesthetic category, one which simultaneously draws and repulses us, destabilizing all the while. Sure enough, the zombie functions not unlike the worm in this capacity; it engages the vile precisely because it disrupts human aesthetics. One needs look no further than Zombie Burlesque, a relatively new, sexy-but-dead show in Las Vegas. The disruptive presence of zombie bodies destabilizes our ability to make aesthetic judgments, diminishing our capacity to say what is human, what is beautiful, and where the human ends.

This interruption of the vile is the location of a specific loss of self for the human viewer. As the viewer sees her or his own reflection on the face of the zombie that was human, she or he can no longer find a stable understanding of the self reflected back. The human has ceased to have the ability to say, or to even define what is human, because of the presence of the shockingly vile face before it. The human self, therefore, deteriorates in the face of the zombie. If we hold that agency of voice—the ability to say, the ability to make judgments that classify and interpret—is inherently human, then the reflected zombie that was once human but is now both human and inhuman becomes logically problematic. It is for this reason that there is so much interest in zombie taxonomy: our zombies, ourselves. If we can understand the zombie face, we can assimilate the disturbing wound to our selfhood. It is, therefore, the first step toward a cure of the apocalypse; once we have differentiated what is not human from that which is, we can begin to respond. The act of differentiation is, itself, a response to apocalypse; a cure for what ails us, the voicelessness echoed in the zombie groan; humans must be able to say.

Thus, all zombies *can* have faces, and some *do*. There is a distinct difference between the sentient zombies in *Warm Bodies, Ahhh! Zombies, Fido, I Am Legend, Freaks of Nature, This Year's Class Picture,* and the like. These zombies maintain disruptive individuality represented as having a face. Romero's zombies, those in *The Walking Dead,* and those in *World War Z,* on the other hand, represent the much larger body of zombie representations that are evidently not distinguishable as irreplaceably singular. These zombies are far less human; they are a simple dot among the nameless horde. However, the question of whether or not even zombies of the latter type might retain the disruptive point in their visage remains. Can those creatures with a zombie face that are not themselves irreplaceably singular, through the visage, still disrupt me—as, say, Benjamin's original auratic image might, or as Barthes' *punctum*?[4] The answer seems to be a resounding yes. This is the character of the zombie face, regardless of the relative sentience of the creature it represents. So, then, all zombies do have faces, though whether they reflect deeper consciousness is a third question.

This observation conjures the vital point: while only some zombies can recognize people, and people can only recognize some zombies as unique from the horde, all zombies can cause people to recognize their own humanity (both as an extension of the need for survival and as a reaction to horror), through a complex process of disruption theorized alternatively by Lacan and Barthes and Benjamin as the point of disruption present in the gaze.[5] The self is constituted at the point of disruption realized in the gaze and against the recognition of the othering zombie.

Aside from the critical necessity to see their prey, zombie eyes maintain the semblance of human form more substantially than any other aspect. Derrida, following Lacan, suggests the necessity of, and perhaps the inevitability of forgetting—the abyssal dispossession of the other from the self. The eyes, and the face that surrounds them, reminds us not only that zombies were once human, but that they still reflect some essential

Penny Blake (Kylie Szymanski) from *The Walking Dead*. Her father, The Governor (David Morrissey), brushes her hair.

attribute of our humanity, one that cannot be erased even as flesh melts to mush. The process of memorialization, that is both a remembrance of one dead and a forgetting of the individuality of the one now dead (since the dead one is carried forward only in the context of a remembering self), postdates the human now zombie, and is carried on in the memorial of the zombie face.

This memorial is meaningful, and can be explored through two common instances in which zombies appear to have a face that suggests some underlying memory of the past has survived. In the first, zombies demonstrate some resemblance to their human lives: they recall a profession, or a lost love, or draw the human viewer to wonder what they might have been categorically. The vast collection of zombies in the airport in *Warm Bodies* demonstrates this category; Romero's townspeople in *Land of the Dead* offer another exemplary collection. In the second set of instances, particular zombies are in some way confused with their former individual selves; they take on the characteristics, even if only in the mind of the viewer, that they held while alive. They appear to be what they once were. Key examples of this type include, in *The Walking Dead*, the Governor's Daughter, Penny Blake (Kylie Szymanski), Sophia (Madison Lintz), and the aforementioned Jenny Jones, whose soulful eyes haunt her husband; R in *Warm Bodies* fits in this category; Fido (Billy Connolly) does, as well. Here, it is the face that reminds us most of what has been lost in death.

There is considerable ambiguity between human and inhuman differentiation in some representations. In *28 Days Later*, a soldier is infected, then chained as a research experiment. Private Mailer (Marvin Campbell) awaits starvation while chained in the yard, though he continues to wear his military uniform and retains his human visage, relatively undamaged. It is this character who eventually wreaks havoc on the soldiers when the film's hero, Jim (Cillian Murphy), frees him in order to help rescue the film's heroine, Selena (Naomie Harris), who is being held captive by the rest of the soldiers. Private Mailer, therefore, blends both categories and both retains vestiges of his former appearance and some fighting capabilities of his former self. However, he is distinctly not human and exists as a figure manipulated by Major Henry West first, in an experiment to see how long it takes to starve to death, then by Jim as his fighting automaton.

In every case, zombies retain some aspect of the human face. This has the effect of destabilizing the boundary between the living humans and their zombie counterparts. It is at the heart of posthuman criticism—we are in the period during which there is a much less distinct means of distinguishing ourselves from others and in which we have begun to see our own faces in the eyes of non-human creatures staring back at us. This marks a fundamental identity crisis from which we have yet to emerge and which is the most disturbing aspect of human fears present in these films. The loss of a stable foundation for self is that of which we are really afraid.

Apocalyptic Bodies

Beyond the face, zombies have broader shape and form, and can resemble anything along a continuum from an intact human with glowing eyes to a lump of rotting flesh retaining only the slimy residual of human flesh and teeth. Almost always, zombies have teeth. While advances in movie makeup and computer generated graphics have changed the expected features of zombies since Romero's first blood smeared corpses, a common aesthetic sensibility shapes their representations.

Returning to *Worm Work*, we find another place for Schwartz's suggestion of the possibility of a vile aesthetic leading toward the disruptions inherent in the abject. In the Romantic period, during which the literary Gothic takes shape and the impulse to categorize and classify other living creatures as against the human, it is perhaps not surprising that interest often turns toward the lowly worm. The creature is disruptive, inevitably collapsing hierarchy (after all, we fat ourselves for maggots) and notoriously difficult to classify.[6] A corresponding interest in aesthetics, that which constitutes the beautiful and who gets to say so, places the worm at the ideal intersection of the vile. It is disruptive, repulsive, and nevertheless inescapable. The worm's ability to signify the borders of the human that nevertheless collapse as it ingests our bodies make it an ideal prefiguration of zombie aesthetics, which similarly engage the abject.

Julia Kristeva theorizes the idea of the abject, a term which describes that which we cannot assimilate or confront linguistically. The abject both repulses and compels us, and ultimately disrupts the distinction between the subject and the object. Exemplary instances of the abject, for Kristeva, include curdled milk, clipped fingernails, filth, wounds, and the corpse (2–3). These exemplars contrast the living perceiver against what it is not, what it has thrust off in living, that nevertheless demand from the viewer attention. Her essay, *Powers of Horror*, begins like this:

> There looms, within abjection, one of those violent, dark revolts of being, directed against a threat that seems to emanate from an exorbitant outside or inside, ejected beyond the scope of the possible, the tolerable, the thinkable. It lies there, quite close, but it cannot be assimilated. It beseeches, worries, and fascinates desire, which, nevertheless, does not let itself be seduced. Apprehensive, desire turns aside; sickened, it rejects. A certainty protects it from the shameful—a certainty of which it is proud holds on to it. But simultaneously, just the same, that impetus, that spasm, that leap is drawn toward an elsewhere as tempting as it is condemned. Unflaggingly, like an inescapable boomerang, a vortex of summons and repulsion places the one haunted by it literally beside himself [1].

The zombie apocalypse operates as one of these instances during which revolts of being occur as a direct confrontation with the disruption of the trajectory of life and death. Apocalypse challenges our conceptions of what constitutes the accepted bounds of human life, ending the self as we know it. We are caught in the vortex of summons and repulsion, unable to look aside from the apocalypse even as it horrifies us. The zombie corpse is the agent of this apocalypse. Its carefully constructed self is just that: carefully constructed. Filmmakers and authors have shaped this class of beings in order to engage this disruption. The zombie body matters. Zombie bodies are vile not because they are ugly, though perhaps they are, but they are vile because they confront us with ourselves and expose that which we would rather seek to hide: human frailty and wounding.

Replete with wounds in even the most aesthetically pleasant incarnations, as R from *Warm Bodies* and the cast of Zombie Burlesque demonstrate, the zombie body has nevertheless come to magnify the process of rot and decay. Gaping wounds are one physical manifestation of trauma, specifically trauma that resurfaces bringing the human into conflict with itself, quite literally its inner self, and therefore with mortality. Wounded bodies signify the trauma of confrontation with the apocalyptic. This wounded body becomes synonymous with the abhuman, the body suggested by Kelly Hurley in *Gothic Bodies*. Hurley argues that "constructs of human identity" undergo periodic remaking through changing conceptions of the Gothic (3), and the Gothic figure she would identify as abhuman. "The abhuman subject is a not-quite-human subject, characterized by its morphic variability, continually in danger of becoming not-itself, becoming other" (Hurley 3–4). In apocalyptic literature, this definition becomes dangerously close to describing not only the zombie body but that of the supposedly human characters as well. We return to this possibility in Chapter 5.

This problematic dissolution of the self, occurring at the site of the wound, the body, begins as an act of defamiliarization. Hurley suggests convincingly that there is a set of strategies that "enact the defamiliarization and violent reconstitution of the human subject" (4). For the zombie, which acts as a more recent incarnation of the terror of the Gothic, there is certainly a set of strategies that defamiliarize and reconstitute the human subject, specifically across the boundary of death. Thus, Hurley's characterization of the Gothic figure seems epitomized in the zombie; it is "between species: always-already in a state of indifferentiation, or undergoing metamorphoses into a bizarre assortment of human/not-human configurations" (10). If late nineteenth-century Gothic literature imagined degeneration into social chaos and barbarity (Hurley 10), the zombie narrative adopts and notably extends this fear. We might turn to Seth Grahame Smith's *Pride and Prejudice and Zombies* as an obvious example of this extension, as it rewrites Jane Austen's nineteenth-century classic with a heroine who is as skilled in the arts of combatting the undead as playing the pianoforte. The zombie represents a cultural overflow of the abject, of something that needs to be cast out, the human that isn't human, the abhuman. The zombie body is the physical manifestation of this representation.

One of the key elements adopted into the zombie genre from the literary Gothic is a sense of dreadful pleasure, due, in part, to a shared vile aesthetic. Anne Radcliffe's bodies (real and wax), Matthew Lewis' monastic horrors, and Horace Walpole's crushing helmets draw and suspend us despite their repulsiveness. And long before Kristeva and Freud sought to explain such things, humans have been fascinated with that which repulses us. Edmund Spenser's gobbets of flesh in *Faerie Queene* (1590), spewed from Errour's foul mouth, illustrate the effect:

> Therewith she spewd out of her filthy maw
> A floud of poyson horrible and blacke,
> Full of great lumpes of flesh and gobbets raw,
> Which stunck so vildly, that it forst him slacke
> His grasping hold, and from her turne him backe [1.1.20].

Even while we are repulsed right along with the back-turning Redcrosse Knight, like him, we desire to charge ahead anyway. Gobbets of dead, rotting flesh are essentially vile. In the confrontation with dead flesh, with dead bodies, life is nevertheless affirmed. Confrontation with death reminds us not only of our own inevitable march toward our fate, but that we are alive in the meantime. It is with this in mind that the zombie body undertakes the vile confrontation.

Furthermore, it has become tasteful to be a zombie connoisseur. Taste, the designation of relative fitness for consumption and perception of relative pleasantness to the palate, and who gets to say, is culturally constructed, ever rooted in ideology.[7] How do we account, then, for our taste for zombies? Why must they fill our shelves, screens, and cover our bodies (at Halloween, on zombie runs, and in the proliferation of live action role playing [LARP] games collaborating with Nerf)? A submerged zombie aesthetic, both vile and pleasant, disruptive, as set against both the human floor (as of the worm) and as against the sublime (which often serves as a ceiling for the human), the zombie aesthetic differentiates parallel creatures.[8] We are insulated from the real zombie (as it remains a fictitious creation, art, perhaps) and it acts as a site of appreciation of the mirrored self and creating world, but there is, in zombie aesthetics, clearly an end in sight. We look to the zombie because it operates from the causes incubated in our own anxieties and with the understanding that in it we might find the cure for what ails us, as well as for the temporary pleasure of imagining our own fears as irreal—written on the bodies of imagined creatures. We consume the creature, therefore, with an eye for reality: we want the most real fictitious representation available. We demand the one that, if we didn't know better, we would swear was actually risen from the grave. Taste dictates that while we can engage in an occasional B-movie representation of the undead, or a mass-marketed show/trade paperback/game a real zombie purist must know of and appreciate the classics, before technological augmentation differentiated the creature from its creator. A glance back at Romero's zombies illustrates their similarity to Barbra rather than to *Warm Bodies'* bonies.

Relative Speed

Despite the significant and pervasive rot often affecting zombie hordes, they occasionally, paradoxically maintain superhuman qualities, including speed, manifested in the ability to run to pursue victims. The nature of this speed is twofold. First, zombies may simply be faster than

Gerry Lane (Brad Pitt) flees from an extremely fast zombie in the movie rendition of *World War Z*. In contrast to Max Brooks' books, which featured very slow moving, shambling zombies, the motion picture boasts zombies that run, jump, and hunt with extraordinary speed.

human beings, such as those infected with the Rage Virus in *28 Days Later*. Or zombies may be fast simply because they do not get tired, as in *Z Nation*. These two manifestations are not mutually exclusive, of course: hordes can run, relentlessly, tirelessly in pursuit of human victims. The cultural idea that these creatures are out to get us is made tangible by the possibility of literal pursuit.

Speed is significant; it suggests inescapable motility that demands confrontation. Though not impossible to evade fast zombies, it rarely happens that survivors can outrun them. Humans tire. Further, the zombie problems cannot be left to end themselves; they continuously threaten to at least destabilize, or at worst end the possibility of life. Fast zombies force confrontation. Examples of fast zombies include those in *Scouts Guide*, *28 Days Later*, Zach Snyder's 2004 remake of George Romero's *Dawn of the Dead*, *I Am Legend* (2007), *28 Weeks Later* (2007), and *Quarantine* (2008). The film version of *World War Z*, however, depicts an exemplary fast zombie. The earliest encounters with zombies in the film appear like tsunamis of racing action; humans are cast against the rising tide of the apocalypse. There is no slow reveal, no exposition to the idea of infection. The infection is presented as fact, and Gerry Lane (Brad Pitt) and family are forced to run—and run fast in order to preserve their lives. They soon tire, failed by their car, and are forced to hide. All the while, their asthmatic daughter contrasts human frailty with the apparent omnipotence of the horde. Though the Lane family escapes the immediate initial assault through a miraculous governmental intervention, hordes of fast zombies threaten to consume the planet and humans must react quickly or perish.

Later in the film, we watch as these zombies hurtle towards the walls built to protect Israeli territory like a tide of swarming insects. Through their tenacity, they eventually scale these barriers, presumably destroying everything inside. For Jew and Palestinian alike, just like for the family in the initial apartment into which the Lane family took refuge, hiding only delayed the inevitable. These zombies do not waste time shambling or groaning, and like those infected by the Rage virus, they run, they kill, and then run some more. Fast zombies, therefore, demand, even as they threaten, the possibility of human agency and individuality. Through forced confrontation, they demand response, reasoned, thoughtful, or decidedly not. Representations of fast zombies accompanied by the increased ability of the creature to reason and problem solve leads human survivors to work together to accomplish particular tasks, as in *I Am Legend* and *Land of the Dead*. In *World War Z*, this results in international collaboration, significantly led by the same Gerry Lane, a former United Nations investigator. Collaborative response (specifically contrasting the film's depiction of the isolationist Israeli approach) is the only hope for humanity, and the nearest approach to the cure for apocalypse.

Of course, not all zombies are fast. Relative speed exposes which of two different potential threats are at work in the representation. Fast zombies act to directly, physically threaten potential victims and demand an immediate fight or flight response. Slow zombies act collectively (even while often demonstrating the inability to act collectively) to capitalize on human inadequacy with paradoxically little that can remedy the threat. The relatively immediate nature of the former contrasts the relentless nature of the latter to situate the nature of the threat posed by each type. Many retain a shambling lack of speed and some have no legs at all with which to pursue, yet even these remain dangerous: the image of the biting torso proliferates in zombie representations. Memorably in *Z Nation*, Brandon Doyle (Richard Sloniker), abandoned in a lab, rots into a pile of flesh that simply can't die. Even static, relatively immobile creatures are dangerous in numbers and devotion to eating flesh, and require a different set of solutions. This collective nature, set against the inability to act collectively (intentionally) except in blind pursuit of human flesh, makes this version of the zombie dangerous. Whereas fast zombies tend to destroy the societies that surround them relatively quickly, slower zombies offer civilizations an opportunity to consider a collective response, resulting in a referendum on the utility of humanity, and ultimately on the state of apocalypse. The inevitably ineffective human response to the slow apocalypse mirrors the creation of the particular apocalypse, repeating the conditions that led to the apocalypse, which has itself become apparently unavoidable.

Slow zombies have, since *Night of the Living Dead*, also exposed the catastrophe of human error. After all, when zombies are slow, they can be very, very slow. In Romero's film, the slowly closing circle of the dead establishes itself as a zombie trope. When Ben (Duane Jones), Tom (Keith Wayne), and Judy (Judith Ridley) exit the fortified house, Tom makes the first major mistake in the face of the slowly encroaching horde as he attempts to pump gas. Spraying gas everywhere, he manages to light the escape truck ablaze. A slow, measured response, mirroring the zombies' approach, would have been successful. Tom is, however, so disrupted and disorientated by their approach that he can't manage the simple act of pumping gas into the car. His own human error, rather than any particularly successful move on the part of the zombies, results in his death. This is the telling move. He is burned alive in the truck moments later and then eaten by the horde. The closing circle of the horde immediately threatens to overwhelm the speechless Ben who has been watching this incredible spectacle. The constricting circle casts a pallor of anxiety over the film that extends until it ultimately ends the lives of all of the film's major protagonists. Highlighting human error and the inevitability of constriction make the slowly encroaching zombie horde feel hopeless even as its members offer themselves as relatively easy fodder.

Slow zombies figure the inevitability of encroaching death. They overwhelm rather than directly pursuing specific victims. They diminish human individuality in that they have not chosen a specific victim but roll across the landscape like a tide of destruction. They represent, therefore, a hopeless sense of human impotence. The slow march of the relentless horde removes the possibility of human agency in the face of apocalypse. In effect, they create mirrored versions of themselves in the human victims that they overcome.

Perhaps the most striking incarnation of slow zombies comes from Max Brooks' *World War Z* (the book, not the film, in which the zombies are inexplicably transformed to be scarier to moviegoers). Brooks' zombies are fascinating in their relative lack of superhuman characteristics. They are difficult to kill, do not rest, and do not feel pain, but they cannot run faster or farther than humans. In fact, they do not run. They are a slavish tide that, on a one-on-one basis, can be relatively easily dispatched with a shovel or club. *Freaks of Nature* seems to play on this type of zombie image to create creatures that are distinct for their subhuman qualities. For Brooks, the real danger of the zombie apocalypse isn't the zombies, *per se,* but how the living *react* to the zombies. These zombies are almost a backdrop: in *World War Z*, humans cause and continue to cause their own trouble. Nuclear strikes are fired out of panic, loved ones harbor zombies and refuse to acknowledge the realism of infection and prevent quarantine, opportunistic smugglers move the infection across borders, gangs of thugs take over the Sears tower to make a new kingdom for themselves, and so on. The slow-moving nature of the zombie horde is significant because it draws our attention to the inevitability of destruction, of death, even, that lurks beneath all the promises of modernity. The problem lurks within the human.

Relative Strength

Physical strength, here, is defined as the ability to push, lift, or otherwise move objects, or specifically to engage humans in hand to hand combat. This is encoded onto zombie bodies as a remnant of power; it is inconsistently applied, and oftentimes disproportionate to the relative strength possessed during life. The recent film *Cooties* (2014) features a horde of child-zombies, ridiculously strong relative to their comparative human stature and age, for example. And when zombies burst through windows in *Scouts Guide* and throw humans, they are clearly stronger than they were in life. While *Scouts Guide* zombies are fairly sentient, zombie power need not necessarily contradict the relative lack of agency or authority attributed to the creature; instead, like the physical drive to consume flesh that can no longer be resisted, it is often an ambient or latent power, as in *Dead Alive*, for example. There is no control to be applied.

As one might imagine, there is often an affinity between strong zombies and fast zombies, and they can at least occasionally demonstrate reason alongside these features. In the film version of *I Am Legend*, for example, the zombie-creatures are both fast and strong. Similarly, in *Warm Bodies*, the creatures (both corpses and more notably bonies) are at least occasionally both fast and strong. In both films they perform superhuman (notably not subhuman) feats of destructive strength that specifically act against human defenses.

Thus zombie power works in several ways: first, as an overwhelming collective force, as when a horde overwhelms a target, giving amusing new meaning to the adage that many hands make light work. Second, as a singular individual feat. In yet another notable example, Dale (Jeffrey DeMunn) is overwhelmed in hand-to-hand combat on *The Walking Dead*. Or, third, as some combination of both, such as in the laboratory scene in *I Am Legend* when each member of the horde manifests significant personal strength, which is used in collective fashion to destroy the walls of the lab.

Strong zombies are a problem in themselves: left in a room alone with a strong zombie and armed with a baseball bat, a victim will invariably become lunch within moments. While strong zombies offer exemplary individual and personal threats, they function critically to highlight the problem at-hand in the apocalyptic iteration. For example, in *I Am Legend,* the problem at-hand is whether humanity can remain relevant in

A zombie child from *Cooties*, ready to infect the playground.

the face of massive social and evolutionary change. In *Warm Bodies,* we are asked to question whether it is better to love and be vulnerable, or to be remorseless and void in the name of self-preservation. In *Serenity* and *28 Days Later,* strong zombies are the evocation of our base desires. In *Cooties,* strong zombies represent the fear that children will eventually overtake their teachers, who will have inevitably become irrelevant.

Yet, as with slow zombies, zombies lacking increased physical strength provoke a different set of problems. Again, Brooks' *World War Z* is exemplary. Zombies are slow, stupid, and no more strong than the average human (though their inability to feel fear or pain certainly magnifies their edge). But the problem of the book is not that this sort of zombie is unbeatable, it is that humanity must adjust to find a solution. This is the same impetus that drives Mira Grant's *Feed,* with its relatively weak zombies that nevertheless demand a massive-scale social response, the premise on which the book turns. Grant invites the reader to view the zombies not as the primary threat in the novel, though they certainly are a threat, but rather to understand the human villain, Governor David Tate, as the real threat. It is Tate, a corrupt politician whose radical ideas cause him to abandon the well-being of the people in favor of pursuing an agenda of rigorous safety that eradicates potential threats and a certain view of monolithic American greatness justifying whatever means necessary. Ultimately, as in Brooks' *WWZ, Night of the Living Dead,* and others, this zombie character tends toward defeat, or not, based on the use of a combination of bureaucratic organization, government efficiency, planning, and good-old-fashioned 'Merican firepower: all factors that existed before the apocalypse, but required the exigent conditions of the apocalypse to force humanity to remember its ability to adapt, govern, and live together.

This is a crucial point of disjuncture between Brooks and the creators of the stronger zombies highlighted above. When zombies are strong, they are enemy. Certainly, resisting them requires a reaffirmation of some essential element of our humanity, such as science, innovation, or love. But such zombies embody what is wrong—the thesis—which is emphasized by their prowess. For Brooks, though, what is wrong is not the zombie apocalypse. This is the table he sets for an exploration of the real problems: living in a human society in an interconnected world where we are all wired together the next disaster is hard to predict. That Brooks tells his stories through the testimonies of survivors, some of which are villainous, affirms this intent: *we* are the antagonists. We are more willing to sacrifice others, we live powerless before the government having lost our voice, and we allow suspension of the law.

The Speed of the Change

At times, there is a distinct waiting period between being bitten or otherwise harmed by a zombie, essentially the moment of infection, and the ultimate transition into the ranks of what we mean when we say zombie. This time period varies rather widely, apparently partly for the sake of dramatic effect. In *Feed*, the protagonist Georgia Mason is infected, and she has enough time to write a final blog post as she transforms: "They [members of the government] are lying to us. They are willfully channeling research away from the pursuit of a cure for this disease…. I don't know who 'they' are. I didn't live long enough to find out" (517). Her use of language literally degenerates by the end of the post until it is unrecognizable: "cant do this jhjnfbnnnn mmm…" (517).

In films like *Dead Alive* and in texts like Grahame Smith's *Pride and Prejudice and Zombies* that showcase these very slow alterations, there seems to be a more significant point at work. In *Dead Alive*, Mum (Elizabeth Moody) is patient zero in the film, and the hero's mother; she hosts a dinner party even as she begins to change. Skin nearly rips from her face as she prepares for her guests, but her dutiful son helps her to glue the dangling swatch of flesh back into place. During dessert, she eats her own ear, which has fallen into the custard. That the guests could not readily tell that Mum had mostly changed into a zombie is clear social critique. That we might be willing to keep silent in the name of decorum, even as someone eats their own ear, sounds farfetched, but it is nevertheless a commentary on the human condition, one of such aggressive inarticulacy that we might somehow be indistinguishable from the zombies we purport to fear so much. It is further worth noting that once Mum eventually does become fully undead, her son cannot seem to be rid of her. Even at her funeral, rather than mourning her loss, Lionel (Timothy Balme) is instead engaged in attempting to continue to tranquilize her body so that she cannot rise from her coffin during the ceremony. Unfortunately, he is unable to do so and they burst through a glass wall during the funeral; excision from humanity is virtually impossible.

A similar point is at work in Grahame Smith's *Pride and Prejudice and Zombies* as readers and Lizzie Bennet watch poor Charlotte Lucas' transition into a zombie before our eyes.[9] This happens literally; the illustrations in the book help us along. Charlotte's shocking and very slow transformation is used with effect as her husband refuses to notice the fact that she has been a zombie for virtually their entire time together. Mr. Collins is certainly intended to be read as a mockery of human existence, as he highlights when comparing himself to his stricken zombie bride: "There is in everything a most remarkable resemblance of character and ideas between us. We seem to have been designed for each other" (171). But he nevertheless also stands in as a less wise version of the reader, oblivious to surroundings, the possibility of apocalypse going on around us.

The Source of Life and Dispatch

Finitude is central to humanity. Humans live and must eventually die. This is precisely what zombies cannot share with humans (and, therefore, perhaps what most clearly marks the transition of R in *Warm Bodies* from inhuman zombie back to human). This is shared between humans and animals, and one possible means of distinguishing what constitutes what we call animal from what we call zombie. However, while zombies cannot die, per se, they can cease to be zombies. They can be converted to inanimate piles of flesh. There are various ways to accomplish this, and each tells us something not only about the zombie, but the humans who create, consider, write about, and reproduce them.

Virtually all recent representations of zombies exhibit a quintessential weakness: they cease to function when exposed to traumatic brain injury, most often delivered by a head-shot or a more violent and immediate obliteration through blunt force weapons. The means of delivery matters, it seems, for the head-shot allows and often takes place at a distance; the immediacy of blunt force weapons (ranging from the popular shovel and amusing cricket bat to the spike-augmented aluminum bat wielded in the SyFy show, *Z Nation*) as the means of dispatch forces itself a site of confrontation during which the human violently ends the independent functioning of the zombie permanently. It becomes a site of choice, of catharsis, perhaps, in which the trauma of destruction underlying the apocalypse is repeated on an individual basis and in which, nevertheless, self-preservation wars with the destruction of whatever remnant of life and self animates the now smashed brain of the zombie.[10]

This weakness to the head shot is paradoxically precisely what makes zombies ambiguously alive in the first place. Whatever it is that animates the differing representations of corpses, it seems to occur in the brain, the location that we presently recognize as the seat for the human self, the place of the humane, and the location from which consciousness originates.[11] This is exploited interestingly in *The Walking Dead*, for example, when the group meets Dr. Jenner at the CDC only to discover that his wife has already succumbed. To end the recording of her transformation, the bullet pierces the screen as it pierced her head—shocking the audience with its brutality. That human motor control is facilitated by our brains certainly necessitates the destruction of the infected brain. Nevertheless, that it is also the seat for our conceptions of self problematizes the head shot as a means for dispatch. It is associated with a sense of finality and irredeemability. Whatever hope for the recovery of the self may have existed, it is forever destroyed by the head trauma.

The importance of the head as differentiating a moving zombie from a rotting corpse is unsurprising; just as the face is the prime marker of humanity, what lies behind the face is essential to orchestrating the actions that make up life (or, in the case of the zombie, performing the simulacrum of life). It would make little sense for a zombie to die because an arm has been lost, or a toe severed. Here, in the zombie, we see a sideways reaffirmation of what makes us human. There are occasional exceptions in which zombies march forward without a head, but these are relatively unusual.

Yet, the head-shot is not the only way that zombies cease to be zombies. In some cases, zombie flesh continues to decay, despite undeath. In *World War Z*, for instance, the walking dead grow weaker and weaker as they, quite literally, fall to pieces. *Warm Bodies* addresses the eventual decay by producing a subset of zombies (bonies) as the most extreme form of zombification. Bonies have lost virtually all of their flesh as a visual metaphor for their increasingly lost humanity. They are far gone, indeed. The natural decay of the zombie body as a means of dispatch is occasionally fantasized but relegated to the background in favor of facing the creatures as a more immediate threat. The temporal possibility of zombie decay is only achievable when the humans in question have already survived the more immediate threat of the present zombies.

Rot

Relative rot, then, must be considered against the zombie animus. Zombies literally rot in front of their human counterparts in the very vast majority of representations (*I Am Legend* is a notable exception, here, as its creatures not only maintain their bodies but seem to thrive). This can certainly be excused, as they are, after all, dead. This rotting nature is particularly interesting in serialized shows like *The Walking Dead* in which the time lapse between apocalypse and the theoretical present in which the characters operate in the most current season grows by the year. The zombies ought to literally rot into non-existence. *World War Z* and *Warm Bodies* both explicitly address this phenomenon in telling fashion. The former suggests that they will eventually rot, and the latter offers the threat of becoming bonie to its partial zombies if they are not cured soon enough.

In these models, the zombie does not continue to generate the forces (or fluids) necessary to maintain the body. Undeath is a temporary condition, just like life, and zombies must reside within a life cycle that is relatively unexceptional. Regardless of how they behave, they are "born" in that they have a definite beginning, a moment of turning; and they will eventually die (even if they carefully avoid chainsaws and spearguns). Again, as with the head-shot, we see the reaffirmation of the basic human condition: we begin, we eventually confront the certainty that death is inevitable, and we all fall apart. The horror of the zombie is compounded by the horror of their human similarity.

The zombie is, in part, problematic in that it cannot die and therefore cannot be held to be a singular, irreplaceable other. While they can cease to exist, death has already occurred. It is only through the possibility of death, and possibly through the apprehension of the imminence of death, that a thing can rise to the significance of an other. Consequently, zombies cannot be suitable others because they virtually always fundamentally lack this ability to die. The iterations of zombies wasting away that occasionally populate zombie representations are therefore far more significant than simply that there might be an end to the threat of the zombie if humans can simply wait it out. The decay of the ubiquitous corpse actually resolves the philosophical problem of the possibility of the replaceable uniformity of the zombie creature that cannot die: these zombies can die and therefore can be singular and therefore contain the disruptive face of human singularity. These zombies, like their human counterparts, can die and therefore have at least the appearance of a face. Whether they can apprehend death, the other qualification of irreplaceable singularity, remains to be seen.

Nevertheless, in some iterations zombie decay is not inevitable. The zombies of *I Am Legend* and *The Omega Man* have no such constraints. They are free to continue living, presumably immortal, unless they run into Will Smith or Charleton Heston. Notably, these zombies maintain human culture and relationships—these zombies evoke fear of change, of our own limitations as human beings, and remind us (quite verbally, in the case of *The Omega Man*) that we have failed as a species and are destined to be replaced. To such zombies, we are dinosaurs. And when one considers the plagues that we inflict upon the environment and each other, one is compelled to consider that this might be true.

The Ability to Reason

The essence of the self that tends to be gutted from zombies most often includes the ability to think, to reason. It encompasses the ability to choose from options that are not preprogrammed (really the ability to choose at all), the possibility of exhibiting agency, and therefore the ability to respond as outside of basic preprogrammed response to stimuli, which can occasionally manifest in the ability to work together. Typically, whether they are fast or slow, weak or strong, decayed or just decaying, zombies lack the ability to reason. They generally cannot problem-solve. In many iterations, zombies may be relentless in search of prey, banging on doors and barricades in order to devour their victims, but they fail to purposefully move obstacles, use tools, or otherwise do anything other than shamble from point A to point B. (Some choicer versions of zombies, as discussed shortly, might manage tool-use, reason, and even organization ability, though these evoke different fears.) In *World War Z*, for instance, zombies remain stuck within automobiles, unable to release their safety belts despite the proximity of savory living flesh. In AMC's *The Walking Dead*, zombies may push at doors or fumble with knobs, but they lack the cognition to complete such a simple act. These lacking creatures exaggerate (perhaps) human fears of lack of agency, powerlessness, and the need to consume that trumps all else.

Stimulus response, or taxis—the innate drive to move toward or away from a stimulus—guides most zombies individually, and perhaps most zombie hordes. Derksen and Hick distinguish between the zombie guided by simple stimulus response and the "agent" zombie, effectively one that reasons. While all zombies may be drawn to eat human flesh, only agent zombies can reason around obstacles to accomplish this drive. When we face agent zombies, Derksen and Hick argue, we are faced with the uncanny, the inability to categorize the ambiguous object of which we are frightened (16). Yet the fears we face are located more deeply than in uncertainty about the object of the fear, and certainly are worse than that of death, consumption, or contamination (though these certainly locate a portion of our fear). Neither is the fear of ultimately becoming zombie, though that may be yet another locus of fear. The agent zombie is frightening because the threat ambiguity is rather that we cannot distinguish the creature from the fearing self; we are already zombies, fearing that the distinction will be unable to be upheld outside of language.

Zombies have occasionally exhibited mental processes recognized as human, including the ability to empathize (or perhaps to sympathize), the ability to act together, the ability to alter or to perhaps act outside an ideologically inflected system such that the conditions of power implicit in the system might not apply. Zombies apparently exhibiting some of these behaviors appear in *Land of the Dead, Fido, Warm Bodies,* and *Ahhh! Zombies,* each depicting representations of the zombie figure that has not lost the cognitive characteristics that would ordinarily only be applied to humans. When, for example, in *Fido,* the titular zombie determines to save rather than to eat Timmy, he appears to enact empathy as well as the choice to act in an unpredictable fashion.

Starting with the first zombie (played by S. William Hinzman) in George Romero's *Night of the Living Dead* (1968), a significant population of walkers maintain some ability to reason. In Romero's film, the zombie that answers the classic threat, "They're coming to get you Barbra," manages two significant cognitive feats. First, Hinzman's zombie moves around the car that is shielding the film's female protagonist, Barbra, effectively moving further from her, in an attempt to more easily access her. The ability to generate and attempt alternate methods to accomplish an objective fits a classic understanding of reason. This act, of trying first one door then moving around the car to try the next demonstrates at least some cognitive ability.

Further, on finding that door similarly inaccessible, Hinzman's zombie then picks up a large stone and throws it through the car window. Later in the film, tool use becomes more extreme as zombies apparently collaborate to break down the wall of the fortified house using chair legs, large stones, and other items. In the most striking instance of tool use (perhaps in all zombie movies taken together), a young girl turned zombie, Karen (Kyra Schon), picks up a trowel (a literal tool) and uses it to stab her mother to death. It is unclear why Karen chooses not to eat her mother, but the viewer might surmise that she's already full after snacking on her father. At any rate, the ability to use tools is a particularly frightening zombie characteristic, since, in addition to increasing the directly threatening capacity of the creature, it also diminishes the distance between the human and its deadish simulacrum.

In the frightening Norwegian zombie film, *Dead Snow* (2009), characters we read as zombie Nazis, though they are actually *draugr*, as Kyle William Bishop clarifies, use all sorts of tools (knives, binoculars, helmets, etc.) in order to pursue treasure stolen from the local population. The grossly outnumbered students on vacation in Oksfjord who find and appropriate the pilfered treasure as their own are brutally massacred for their theft. That the zombies in this film use tools to accomplish a complex objective (retrieval of their pilfered loot) and that the zombie Nazis are retrieving the loot that they stole from the vacationing students who stole

The *draugr* of *Dead Snow* share several affinities with Nazi zombies.

it from them highlights the similarity rather than the difference between the zombies and other humans. This comparison is particularly unflattering since, while it would be terrible to be a zombie, it surely would be worse to be a Nazi zombie. This sort of zombie, tool using and somehow set against a population of equally bad humans, also occurs in *Land of the Dead*, in which the zombies organize (again using all sorts of tools) to finally lay siege to the town run by the evil (human) Kaufman. While Kaufman is not a Nazi, his classist, hierarchical ideology is clearly under attack in the film. Perhaps the most amusing tool using zombie occurs in *Scouts Guide to the Zombie Apocalypse*, in which not only do the zombies open doors and fire weapons, they also sing along to Britney Spears. The zombie that is capable of rational tool use has not been gutted of its entire self; the inability to control the appetite for flesh (still the singular drive in each of these aforementioned zombies) is at odds with the ability to use tools to accomplish rational objectives (or not, as in the case of singing along to Britney Spears, which apparently serves no purpose in this film or perhaps any film).

The distinction between tool-using, reasoning zombie and human is minimal indeed. And when the distinction erodes, we are faced with a horrifying vision of ourselves. These deadish zombies remove the veneer of distinction and confront us much more directly with the underlying causes of apocalypse; it is perhaps with this in mind that direct confrontation with traditional power structures hallmarks these films. While zombies like Hinzman and Fido are clearly exceptional, Matheson's *I Am Legend*, as well as its various film adaptations, and *Warm Bodies* together exemplify another subset of zombies that can not only reason and think, but that have created a sophisticated culture replete with rituals.

Zombie Relationships

One defining characteristic of the zombie is, generally, the complete lack of emotion with which they approach their daily task of eating the living. Zombies are, for the most part, robotic, operating on preset priority queues that usually involve only grunting and eating. They kill impassively, without hesitation, and with an almost artificial enthusiasm towards the act of rending flesh. Significantly, this lack of emotion extends both to the human victim as well as the fellow zombie. Zombies will step on one another—even trample one another—in pursuit of quarry. They do not interact with one another in any meaningful way, by forming cliques, demonstrating affection, or forging rivalries. As Paffenroth puts it, "zombies are essentially... without, or without much, reason and intellect.... They are completely self-centered, showing no concern for their fellow zombies or mercy to their human prey" (11–12). This sort of flat-affect zombie is a reflection of our fears of loss of connectivity with one another, or worse, that our perceived ability to communicate is, in fact, only illusion. This fear only grows more acute as we increasingly rely on digital measures of interpersonal communication.

Of course, the exceptions to the rule tell us a great deal. Some zombies exhibit the means for organization and operation in a complex social fashion, in which emotion appears to dictate behavior. Both corpses and bonies collaborate in *Warm Bodies*, respectively defending and attacking human populations (and each other), zombies stemming from Matheson's book (in *The Omega Man* and *I Am Legend*) work together to accomplish common objectives, and seem to uphold complex organizational structures around lead figures, and *Ahhh! Zombies* features a small group of zombie protagonists working together to investigate their own circumstances and to bring about a new, zombie inflected world. *This Year's Class Picture* imagines its students in just such an emotionally connected relationship with their teacher, Mrs. Giess. The students depend on their teacher for protection, cooperating at the least to avoid mutual destruction. It seems that when operating as a collective, despite the suggestion that emotion might prevail and connect us even after death, the intentional herd figures an insidious possibility. The collective herd that cooperates engages our fears of an overwhelming force operating in the world that might invalidate human individual capacity to resist. But if the apparent herd simply acts in response to common stimulus, already invalidated, zombies engage fears of deep seated incapacity and the loss of responsibility; this is the same fear that underlies most zombie representations, perhaps with the added dimension of multiplicity that itself threatens to overwhelm. Somebody slips into unstable subjectivity in the herd, whether the individual member in the horde that can't resist the pull of the collective, or the survivor. Either way, ultimately, the viewer is placed into an unstable relationship with the world around as a perceiving self that may individually respond. That we cannot tell the status of the zombie threatens the deciding self who views it. We become the sacrifice before the horde.

Further, some zombies can even maintain the possibility of friendship, which Derrida suggests is possible only in light of the consideration of death. It seems clear that virtually all zombies can distinguish live (or at least recently living) flesh from dead flesh; they are not ghouls, after all. They can apprehend death, though perhaps not the death of the self that accompanies bodily death. And yet, in *Land of the Dead*, *Fido*, and *Warm Bodies*, at least, zombies recognize the death of other zombies, but only in *Warm Bodies* do they face the immediacy of physical decay accompanying the transition to death. The irony is, obviously, that most zombies are already dead. This subset must therefore fear a second death, an utter end to their existence. It is perhaps most sensible that this possibility has developed since we seem to fear that we are living a zombie existence already. We may be virtually dead, lacking the ability to choose and to reflect our own agency; even more frightening, perhaps, we might have already lost even that vestige. Most frightening of all, then, if these zombies reflect ourselves as we go on to argue in our conclusion, is that even a zombified existence seems to be better than the alternative, the utter end of the self.

There is also something to consider as herds move collectively without the apparent need for communication. Herds are often collections of individuals moving toward a stimulus, of course. There remains some aspect of stimulus memory, as the shot of the zombie horde continuing on after a departing car (headed into the sunset, no doubt) runs rampant in zombie representations.

Communication

While a few specific zombies speak, including the aforementioned Britney Spears fan zombie in *Scouts Guide* and the mother zombie in *State of Apocalypse*, most do not. Most zombies that operate together engage two paradoxical, competing fears. First, they very often work together without apparent communication. We read telepathy, like that which ants appear to exhibit, as an unconscious threat to humanity, toward our communication-based existence. That there might be communication going on beyond the range of our sensory perception is frightening. That zombies might work in a way that is utterly foreign to us might mean that humans can operate in a way that is utterly foreign to us, and this is rightly frightening. When we encounter elements of the world that operate beyond our apparent range of understanding, we seek to systematize and explain so that we can reincorporate the disparate elements into our coherent understanding of the world. Thus we invent conspiracy theories to explain significant events that might otherwise shock our stable understanding of the world, like the assassination of JFK, the fall of the Twin Towers, and the shooting at Sandy Hook. We are bombarded with extraordinary popular narratives on YouTube and elsewhere suggesting that these events are contrived: because we understand corrupt governments and secret societies but we cannot understand the horrifying events as expressions of real humans operating according to their own social standards that do not reflect our own. Zombies, then, take this especially frightening possibility of the utter loss of self that occurs in death and near-death and dramatize the possibility that the human might exist (or at least appear to exist) outside of its faculties. If, at least, the herd cooperates, then it might fit within our existing understanding of groups of humans operating according to their own social standards that do not reflect ours. If they are not communicating but still responding to stimulus, then humans have really been reduced to a state of incapacity, to a state in which they do not have control. This we have much more reason to fear than an inability to defeat an overwhelming combatant force.

The tremendous range of zombie characteristics already envisioned inevitably speaks to the range of virtually unintelligible human characteristics; more particularly, it identifies fears that arise in zombie literature and film. Variegated zombie representations shape both the viewer's understanding of the cause of the apocalypse and the effects of the cause on the expression of the apocalypse. It is these characteristics of expression that necessitate particular iterations of cure. These variations, therefore, demonstrate the need to revisit the evolutionary model so frequently suggested as a means of articulating the development in zombie representations. The creatures with which we populate our worst fears speak volumes about us, their creators. There are clearly other causes at work that affect the expression of zombie traits. Before we can begin to consider the causes themselves, we need to consider the temporal setting for apocalypses, as it is the connective tissue that relates the extant time of the viewer and the vision for the world that is reflected in the particular representation. Only then can we move toward the particular causes that necessitate particular cures dictated by the present fear that shapes the representation.

3

Apocalyptic Temporality

"But vastness blurs and time beats level. Enough! the Resurrection."—G. M. Hopkins

Thus far we have focused on the expectations and interpretive frameworks applied to the zombie and the particular characteristics and meaning of the zombies represented within various iterations. With this basic frame in mind, we turn to the core of our analysis: the cause to cure arc that is the focus of this book. We begin by exploring the temporal relationship between the zombie text and the viewer.

The experience of time in apocalyptic literature is necessarily distorted. The horrors characterizing the existence of living outside the reach of normative social and judicial law are too shocking, traumatizing, and disturbing to process and assimilate. Film representations of apocalypse, therefore, maintain alternate relations to linear temporality as a means of escape from the apocalyptic present. This becomes more complex when we consider that the alternate temporality of viewers runs alongside that within the imaged apocalyptic world.

Connecting the pre-apocalyptic past to the apocalyptic present also serves characters well; maintaining (or even forging) some relationship with the past and future appears crucial for survival. Characters (and always alongside them, viewers) use two strategies to live in the apocalyptic world: they engage in nostalgia, remembering the past. They also look toward the end of apocalypse, imagining a future to come. Both are fraught strategies, revealing more about the present conditions of existence than either the past or the possibilities of the future. It is further necessary to divide apocalyptic representations into three relations to the present, which control the setting of the world, but which are rather temporal than geographical; these are pre, mid, and post-apocalyptic worlds. This situates the time from which the characters look back or forward.

iZombie's protagonist, Liv Moore (Rose McIver), working as a medical examiner.

Zombie representations shiver between iterations of pre-apocalyptic visions, those in the midst of cataclysmic apocalypse, and those featuring survivors in a post-apocalyptic world. *Fear the Walking Dead* (2015–), in its second season, frames this apocalyptic confusion through Celia's (Marlene Forte) proclamation: "this is not apocalypse. This is our beginning, Nicholas. The end of death itself. Life. Eternal." This chapter argues along Celia's lines. In zombic time, despite the pervasive characterization of the worlds represented in zombie films as defined by their relationship to cataclysm, the apocalypse has already become possible in these worlds. Whether or not cataclysm has occurred (and most would argue that in *FtWD* it has), the worlds are apocalyptic, altered irreparably by a new beginning.

The opening sequence of *iZombie* sets the stage for a complex look at the way that time functions in an apocalyptic world. We term this apocalyptic temporality. *iZombie's* protagonist, Liv Moore (Rose McIver), a cardiac surgical resident, opens with the Dickensonian statement "this was my life before I died" and proceeds to save the life of a near-death patient. Later in the episode she dies, an early victim of an "inexplicable zombie outbreak" that occurs before the show moves into its opening credits. Caught up with the fictive present, the viewer then engages the aftermath of her becoming zombie for the rest of the series to date. The formulaic introductory look back at life before contagion is hardly shocking or aweing. Shots of the camera panning across the divide before an apocalypse and after effectively function as an introductory nostalgic survey; this survey has become *de rigueur* in zombie representations ranging from *Pride and Prejudice and Zombies,* to Max Brooks' set of origin tales *The Zombie Survival Guide: Recorded Attacks.* The experience of nostalgia, of looking back fondly toward a time before an apocalyptic event (one which ends the world as we know it), situates apocalyptic narrative, and thus the apocalyptic mode of storytelling, in its relative relationship to the temporality of the particular apocalyptic vision.

We understand cataclysmic apocalypse as the physical destruction of the world at large, as opposed to the understanding of apocalyptic, which we would describe as the destruction of the world as we know it. This might seem a minor point, but cataclysm implies a physical destruction that isn't necessarily always represented in zombie films and texts. For example, while the world ends in Grahame Smith's *Pride and Prejudice and Zombies,* previous social forms still substantially continue. Few would argue that this isn't cataclysmic as there are roving hordes of zombie hunters, regular attacks, and pits in which zombies are burned lighting the night sky. However, in *iZombie,* the world has hardly ended for the protagonist, let alone the average Joe. Citizens are kept blissfully unaware of the occurrence of apocalypse, in part because of the protagonist's efforts to thwart the malicious efforts of various zombies intent on spreading their condition.

Dead Alive is another film in which the average citizen can sit at the park despite the already started apocalypse. Evidently even the shock of seeing a zombie baby is not enough to disrupt their understanding of the stable world. Generally speaking, this is characteristic of mid-apocalyptic tales. However, cataclysm is not always necessary in order to figure apocalypse. Apocalypse can, instead, end the social systems and living conditions of the world as we know it. Whether or not every citizen is engaged in some sort of physical destruction becomes unimportant. *Night of the Living Dead* created a new world, and even though order is restored at the end of the film, the disruption evidently cured (suppressed?), the post-apocalyptic filmic world is no longer what it once was, and perhaps neither is the real world that we inhabit. This is no less true because worldwide destructive cataclysm has apparently been averted.

Thus when apocalypse is prevented or cured or otherwise subverted within the filmic world, the apocalypse becomes possible and inescapable. It is the underlying premise of existence for the culture represented in the narrative world. And using narrative worlds as a prism, apocalypse is thus also made possible in our own culture. Through the imaginative creation of apocalypse, it is made possible in our own culture as the one that has imagined the narrative representation in which we engage. It is, therefore, no longer impossible, but imagined and extant. As we have already begun to argue, we live in a state of apocalypse, in which not simply the cataclysmic apocalypse but the everyday reimagining revelatory apocalypse, that suggests instead a suspension of cultural and authoritative law, is already our condition of existence. The culture that can imagine itself in an apocalyptic world is already there (or perhaps then), for as Sartre tells us, "no development of the image can surprise me, whether I produce a fictitious scene or one of the past. In both cases the preceding moments with their contents serve as means of reproducing the following moments considered as ends" (*The Imaginary* 132). The imagined image and the one experiencing it are constructed together, as is their occupied time outside of time, reflecting the real but necessarily irreal. In order to flesh out the functioning of time in this constructed vision, we begin with relative nostalgia.

Relative Nostalgia

To begin, we must look back. A contrasting effect presented in virtually all zombie films has to do with the relative state of the pre-apocalyptic world as perceived after the apocalypse, an effect we'll call relative nostalgia. The dis-temporality or, perhaps, anachronism of relative nostalgia, connects to the end of the zombie, and the particular teleology of the zombie apocalypse. We are ever, as viewers, looking forward to possible ends and back to a time when life was simple, before we perceived the possibility of the end.

With regard to the look back, using memory, Steven C. Schlozman returns to nostalgic etymology reminding his readers that "nostalgia literally means the pain of imagined homecomings" (21). However, these homecomings in apocalyptic worlds aren't really homecomings: they are the comings home into a world that is no longer home. Freud identifies the unhomelike feeling, the interruption of the past into the present, which is akin to déjà vu, in his "Uncanny" essay: "That factor which consists in a recurrence of the same situations, things and events, will perhaps not appeal to everyone as a source of uncanny feeling. From what I have observed, this phenomenon does undoubtedly, subject to certain conditions and combined with certain circumstances, awaken an uncanny feeling, which recalls that sense of helplessness sometimes experienced in dreams" (10). Apparent recurrence, whether pleasant or not, of a time or set of circumstances past, is indeed uncanny. The world that had been familiar has become unfamiliar, and memory serves to connect the discontinuous present with the expired past. Perhaps the connection to imagined worlds is more relevant, as apocalyptic representations are imagined instances of where home isn't any longer. For example, this appears when Rick (Andrew Lincoln) first returns home in *The Walking Dead* to find Carl (Chandler Riggs) and Lori (Sarah Wayne Callies) absent or when Alexandria, which seemed so homelike, is utterly violated at the end of Season 6. Since its beginning, the siege on the home, the space characterized by safety and familiar relations, has been a hallmark of the zombie genre. This is very likely carried over from its cultural antecedent, the Gothic, in which novels like *The Castle of Otranto*, *Wuthering Heights*, and *Dracula* all figure prominent violations of a home space that ought to be safe but proves to instead be precisely the scene in which threat overtakes the protagonists. *Night of the Living Dead* firmly entrenches the trope in the zombie genre as its farmhouse sanctuary is violated at the end of the film, first by the zombie horde then by the bullet of a militia sniper.

Still, Rushton and Moreman notice that "not all zombie texts bother to lament the world we have lost" (5). The hope of a reformed government, they suggest, is not hopeful for those who had been already excluded and oppressed before the apocalypse. And yet, even in the hopeless case of the one who had been excluded and will not lament for the world lost, there may yet appear nostalgia for the world before. As Schlozman notes, "survivors of the cataclysm recall the world before its fall through quintessentially rose-colored glasses" (25). The distortion across the boundary of the apocalypse makes it seem as if the world was, in fact, pleasant before the apocalypse.

And yet, one of the few consistent markers of the zombie genre has indeed been the permanent dissolution and reimagination of social order. This often happens along the lines of the artificially positive imaginative reconstruction taking place through the nostalgic recreation of the world. We find, thus, apparently idealist leaders like Murphy in *Z Nation* and Rick in *The Walking Dead*; potentially inclusive societies, as in *Night of the Living Dead* and *Scouts Guide*; and social inclusion, as in *Warm Bodies* and *Freaks of Nature*. Obviously the veneers of rosy gloss fall apart on deeper consideration, but on initial appearance, these are rosy reconstructions indeed.

This consistent emphasis differentiates the zombie genre from its literary precursor, Gothic literature, which moves consistently toward expulsion of the terror or horror that crystallized the need for the representation, often restoring "conventional boundaries" (see Fred Botting 170). It is further differentiated from most other entries into the horror genre which hold out hope for eventual salvation against all odds from state controlled or other forces. Things can go back to normal, most horror films suggest, but no such possibility exists in representations of zombie apocalypse. Romero's Night of the Living Dead, leaves the viewer with the distinct sense that though the uprising has been put down, a return to normalcy will never be possible.

Murphy (Keith Allan, wearing headphones) in *Z Nation* uses his ambiguous half-human, half-zombie status to control zombie hordes.

Dead Snow offers another ideal example; its zombie Nazis (the aforementioned *draugr*) appear settled and ready to abandon the long pursuit of the vacationing Norwegian campers who have disturbed their ill-gotten treasure horde. The final scene, in which the lone survivor has nearly escaped, features instead the Nazi commander bursting through the car window. There is no hope for a return to normalcy in the vast majority of zombie films (and those that offer such hope, we suggest in "Curing the Apocalypse," offer a retreat to pre-apocalyptic ideological conditions that will inevitably reproduce the apocalypse). Even those that end well, such as *Shaun of the Dead,* still feature zombies, even if they can only play video games. There is a fundamental recognition in the zombie film genre that the world has become forever apocalyptic: expulsion is unreasonable.

The End to Come

The future of the zombie apocalypse masquerades as a temporal future while nevertheless reflecting the conditions of our present existence as real-world viewers. We hope that some discrete temporal break exists between the present and a world in which the apocalypse is, in fact, possible; in other words, we yearn for a sort of epochal firewall between ourselves and the end of our world. Yet the horror of zombie films rests on absence of this clear firewall, and plays with the idea of interconnected time to evoke the terror of the uncanny. Yet characters and films still look forward, and there are many ends to the end of a zombie apocalypse. Sometimes the zombies starve, sometimes they succumb to head-shots, sometimes they rot, and sometimes they continue perpetually.

Starvation, for instance, is a common future presented amongst zombie representations. At the close of *28 Days Later,* for example, we see zombies crawling around the streets, shells of their former ravenous selves, clearly starving. *iZombie* picks up this possibility, its zombies transitioning from more-or-less humans who enjoy a side of brains to rotting, ravaged monsters when they hold the side. Even in the film version of *Pride and Prejudice and Zombies* (2016), which features zombies that don't completely transition until they eat human brains, zombies must eat some kind of animal brains to continue to exist as animated creatures.

Returning to *28 Days,* its zombies are, we must recall, the result of the human-created Rage virus. There are two particularly compelling ways to interpret the insatiable need to consume human flesh as brining about the end of the end. First, and perhaps most directly, authors like Matheson and the team responsible for *28 Days Later* are wryly pointing out that humanity has the capacity to eat itself, and zombies are the incarnation of this tendency. Second, as has widely been suggested, the zombie drive to consume flesh is analogous to our own compulsion to *consume* pretty much anything without actually being sated. Romero took his shots at this point in *Dawn of the Dead* echoed, ironically enough, in the mass-marketed first person shooter video game *Dead Rising* (2006). In Romero's *Dawn*, zombies trash their way through a shopping mall, epitomizing our own need to shop. As Arthur Miller wrote via Solomon in *The Price*, "Today you're unhappy? Can't figure it out? What is the salvation? Go shopping" (41). The consumptive drive of the zombie even finds analogue in our dietary habits. As Denise Cook points out, "We eat junk food, yet we do not satiate our nutritional needs. Thus, we eat more and more, mindlessly eating until we die" (55). Compulsive zombie flesh eating mirrors our own consumptive compulsions that are, perhaps, too taboo to engage outside the zombie frame and which threaten to be the end of us. So, even as we eat ourselves to death, we must wonder whether zombies might do the same.

And yet, the question of the end of the zombie does not find its answer solely in the head shot or the starvation flic. Does death ever come? Do they ever just become totally stagnant? Or are they still just barely alive? This becomes a teleological question for humanity. If zombies reflect our own ends, as we argue, they ultimately bear out our consideration of our own future. What will happen to us? This question is left frequently unsettled in zombie films, perhaps with the obvious reason that we can't with any certainty look forward in our own history (though we certainly try). While we address efforts toward the cure in Chapter 6, we must also wonder about the worlds of the films that are not interested in possible cures and about films in which the cure fails (as it almost always does).

We don't simply imagine the possibility of eternal continuation, but perhaps in inhabiting the eternal present of the filmic moment, held outside of time as the fictional narrative present, we create a sort of memorial that lasts outside the ravages of time. It's hard to say whether viewers find, like G.M. Hopkins, a model of time beating level, or the endless expression of Wordsworth's "still sad music of humanity," or perhaps like Keats' Ode on a Grecian Urn:

> we are teased out of thought
> as doth eternity: Cold Pastoral!
> When old age shall this generation waste,
> Thou shalt remain, in midst of other woe
> Than ours...

It is worth noting that we live in a profoundly existential cultural moment that seeks a fullness of existence as against a perceived plague. After all, "you only live once," as the saying goes. This period of interest in apocalypse is populated by anthems declaring the importance of living in the moment. Katy Perry looks forward only to this "Friday Night," Rihanna claims that we are young right now in the aptly named "Right Now," Fun serenades the generation in "We Are Young," and Ke$ha tellingly sings "Die Young," which advocates experiencing life fully because of the perceived imminence of death. Even the classic comic hero Wolverine, the one who cannot die, is finally going to be killed. This cultural moment is seen as already exceptional, as devoid of future. We live in a diseased time.

Diseased temporality, as Elissa Marder writes, describes the move into the "'fictive' temporality of literature" (5) from the reality of the world around; the move works in two ways. Marder argues that the retreat to the page provides for the writer "an antidote to the corrosive temporality of lived life" and "a way of counteracting the failure of life to provide an experience of temporal continuity" (5). The zombie film provides just such a retreat for viewers now, just such a counteraction that hopes against all apparent odds to restore some continuity to the fragmentary and dislocated existence that has been the hallmark of literature—and perhaps existence at large—since Romanticism.

Diseased Temporality: Twilight

To understand this simultaneously forward and backward looking temporal relationship, particularly as it is imagined in this time of infinite present, we turn to theory surrounding evening or twilight. Twilight is the period of the day that is itself situated neither in the past nor the future, neither night nor day. We live, perhaps, in a time of diseased temporality, in the twilight moment of the pre-apocalypse, which has become possible but has not in effect occurred. In *Dead Time* Elissa Marder

Columbus (Jessie Eisenberg, with gun) and Tallahassee (Woody Harrelson) pursue Twinkies in *Zombieland*.

exposes a poetics of diseased temporality that may fruitfully be set up alongside David Collings' poetics of cultural dismemberment exposed in *Wordsworthian Errancies*. In both critical texts, there is emphasis placed on the moment of cultural production and loss through rereading.

First, Marder argues that the poet Baudelaire attempts to "deny loss, escape reality, and stop time" (8). These are precisely the efforts at work in zombie apocalyptic representations: apocalyptic nostalgia adopts visual signs that deny loss, escape reality, and stop time. Watching zombie films with an eye for what is lost and what is mourned, the viewer cannot help identify in the post-apocalyptic filmic world of *Zombieland*, for example, the last vestige of the world as it was, and perhaps the thing that might redeem it from its wasted state: the Twinkie. The Twinkie becomes, in *Zombieland*, the sign of post-apocalyptic hope for human nature even as it figures loss throughout the film. Characters and viewers alike hope to deny the loss of the world by suggesting that this representative delicacy might postdate the apocalypse. Escaping reality is the vital gesture in both the creation of and the viewing of apocalyptic representations. We put a zombie mask on our real fears so that we don't have to face them directly (as we discuss in Chapters 4 and 5). Stopping time is more complex. We seek, always, to resist the coming of the apocalypse that will end the world as we know it even as we imagine its advent into a filmic version of our real world. Thus simulation and archive become exemplary tools with which to consider apocalypse, as we address in Chapter 8. Nevertheless, these processes rarely occur in time in a linear fashion.

Marder writes in *Dead Time* of the possibility of preproducing pain, anticipating its coming, in order to inoculate oneself against it (89). This is, in effect, what we do with apocalyptic worlds: we imagine the darkest possibility conceivable to come in order to ward off the pain when it, or something like it, arrives. And yet, apocalyptic nostalgia adds the register of imagining the pain to come that looks back on the world before the pain, the world as it is imagined to be now, in all its rose-tinted glory. Our engagement with the apocalypse, and specifically with apocalyptic nostalgia, is a looking forward to looking back; as with the creation of a scrapbook, we are excited to look back on the present moment as that which is no longer but which we might remember fondly. The effect of this look valorizes the present even as it inoculates against a bleak future. The sense of shifting time implicit in this back and forth look sets a condition of atemporality, broken time, that is hardly present in the present moment. This conditional relationship to the present (what would or might come) could be called the "as if"—looking to the present as if through the lens of occurred apocalypse. The Twinkie, then, or medical school (in *iZombie*), or the teaching of English (in *Fear the Walking Dead*) become significant. Our everyday actions matter and are invested with meaning if they might postdate the having-come apocalypse and if they might represent the world that was better than it is in the imagined conditional future.

That apocalyptic visions might be born from apathetic and bored satisfaction with the present world seems unlikely, therefore, despite the expert proponents of this apparent possibility (Stephen King, for example, among them).[1] To suggest that apocalyptic iterations have become extraordinarily popular just now because all is well seems to be artificially optimistic. Since 9/11, arguably the period of explosive growth of popular apocalyptic iterations (see Christopher Zealand, for example), our fears of the collapse of the world as we know it have become pressing. It is certainly true that in order to collapse, the world must be collapsible, and therefore have something worth saving. This ought not to suggest, however, that the world as we know it is functioning normally or in a sustainable fashion as we fret over the possibilities of its toppling. The temporal moment is necessarily trembling and tenuous. We hear the clicking of the roller coaster as it prepares for its first careening fall. Increasing awareness of catastrophic climate change, terrorist organizations bent on destruction of Western ideology (maintaining their own apocalyptic worldviews, no less), physical acts of terror, and the like threaten us. The likelihood of economic distress in which, despite the current period of relatively high employment, an increasingly disastrous wealth inequality means that many are underemployed or failing to achieve even the scantest vision of the American dream all point toward a state imagining the world around it failing. The recent advent of the concept of the Anthropocene is no coincidence. We are, therefore, taking our subconscious for a roll in the grass of the very real and present threats that suspend the possibility of living consistently within all of the threats to reality.

Our cultural moment, which seems fixated alternately on the hope of constant progress toward the newest invention of some imagined technological breakthrough (that, in fairness, has been marching along at a shocking pace through Apple, *et al.*), and the throwback every Thursday, continues to shiver. Vacillating between past and future, ever unstable, we have created the zombie, a creature that is forever both future and past, to represent ourselves in this temporality. Human past and future is figured in the zombie face.

The inevitability of the grave registers on the zombie countenance even as its distinct human features recall what it once was. Its very instability calls to attention the insecure boundaries of the human in time. We effectively disremember with the zombie figure. Into a future that is uncertain, we populate a figure that no longer occupies the role of human, imagining the effect of cataclysm on our world, signifying the erasure of self and society. The zombie is effectively a cultural distortion, a disfigurement of culture, in all its constitutive terms and practices, and must be read as such. It is no accident that this language echoes Collings' in *Wordsworthian Errancies*. The understanding that the poet, William Wordsworth, is trying to "write a culture that survives in the form of its own destruction" (3), is perhaps even more overtly applicable to the zombie apocalyptic project at large than Wordsworth's Gothic leanings. Zombie temporality is precisely always already post-apocalyptic even when it features an apocalypse that is in its earliest stages, as in *Fear the Walking Dead*. That the temporal moment of the iteration (when the film/show/text is set) occurs across the interruption of an apocalyptic event from the present moment (again, that which is understood as apocalypse, which may not be cataclysmic) suggests the possibility that the apocalypse is already in effect—that we perhaps already live in a time of suspension of the constitutive elements of culture ripe for reimagination.

We empathize with T.S. Eliot's attempt to "deny loss, escape reality, and stop time" (Marder 8). Eliot prefigures the zombie story in response to the wartime literary modern concerns in the early twentieth century when he imagines London plagued with walking corpses in "The Wasteland":

> Unreal City,
> Under the brown fog of a winter dawn,
> A crowd flowed over London Bridge, so many,
> I had not thought death had undone so many.
> Sighs, short and infrequent, were exhaled,
> And each man fixed his eyes before his feet.
> Flowed up the hill and down King William Street,
> To where Saint Mary Woolnoth kept the hours
> With a dead sound on the final stroke of nine.
> There I saw one I knew, and stopped him, crying "Stetson!
> You who were with me in the ships at Mylae!
> That corpse you planted last year in your garden,
> Has it begun to sprout? Will it bloom this year?
> Or has the sudden frost disturbed its bed?
> Oh keep the Dog far hence, that's friend to men,
> Or with his nails he'll dig it up again!
> You! hypocrite lecteur!—mon semblable,—mon frère!" [lines 60–76].

We are indeed the hypocrite reader, the friend, the brother. We, too, have inherited Baudelaire's diseased temporality, his dead time as Marder puts it, and Eliot's postwar meditation speaks as incisively now as a hundred years ago; the narrative space in the poem shares a temporality with the zombie present and our own, through memory, ill-bounded by the death and time. *Night of the Living Dead* heroine, Barbra, becomes Eliot's hypocrite reader, friend, sister as she, shell-shocked, repeats "we're going to leave soon." Her haunting future is that of the viewer and her friend, Ben. The perhaps of the future, what might occur, becomes the condition of friendship, the anticipation of the other beyond the possibility of their death. This is the apocalyptic mode of existence, one that is ever engaged in the past and the perhaps, that which was and also always that which might be. The time is marked by the stroke of the clock.

Eliot turns here to concrete imagery—as we have nothing else to use, really, and the turn ends up using the body-holding garden for a dual purpose: as both a concrete place and setting for the poem, but also as sign of the imminence and immanence of eternity, its ever-presence, and its status as "to come." This places Eliot at the limit of time, at the limit of life, at the limit of life and death, at the very limit of mortality, which is also the limit of the human. Eliot uses the garden as a way to deny loss (in this case of life), escape reality (through the fabular, fabulous, the fable), and stop time (so that life can happen in the present). In this way, his apparent refusal to get to the point is a temporal technique of liminality. Time is stopped and we are transfixed. We must read slowly, remember, and reflect. Eliot vindicates the moment of life: the moment of the responsible self that is in time and that may yet live even with a view toward eternity. Perhaps, like us, Eliot hasn't figured out the end of time. The friendly dog digs at memory and future simultaneously.

Jacques Derrida helps us connect the possibility of the future to Eliot's Stetson, the figure outside of time already wearing an American hat in 260 BCE on the shores of the ancient Roman battle. In *The Politics of Friendship*, Derrida engages the perhaps, the linguistic figure for what might come, as the condition of friendship:

> Now, the thought of the "perhaps" perhaps engages the only possible thought of the event—of friendship to come and friendship for the future. For to love friendship, it is not enough to know how to bear the other in mourning; one must love the future. And there is no more just category for the future than that of the "perhaps." Such a thought conjoins friendship, the future, and the *perhaps* to open on to the coming of what comes—that is to say, necessarily in the régime of a possible whose possibilization must prevail over the impossible. For a possible that would only be possible (non-impossible), a possible surely and certainly possible, accessible in advance, would be a poor possible, a futureless possible, a possible already *set aside*, so to speak, life-assured. This would be a programme or a causality, a development, a process without an event [29].

If the condition of friendship is, as Derrida suggests, that we might anticipate the death of the friend, both the zombie and Eliot's Stetson live in light of this reality. The possibility of the future to come, the death of the friend, is that possibility that Eliot relates and the mode of apocalyptic living. That the friend will die, or perhaps live on, is the haunting future. What is to come, Eliot prefigures, is the death of the other and the death of the self that is too terrible to consider and thus must be painted with impossibility, with a figure surviving the thousands of years from Mylae to London, imagining only the death of the other that is not friend. Stetson and the narrator live on. Eliot's prophylactic is incomplete, though. To attempt to make the death of the friend impossible, to attempt to disengage from the dead crowd on the bridge, to attempt to deny apocalypse is a self-consciously hypocritical endeavor.

There is an interesting ongoing discussion surrounding our present state, but more specifically the trajectory of what is to come. Millennials sense the distinct possibility that we are not only living in a twilight state, but further that we have apocalyptic visions as a warning that may possibly act to stave off the coming cataclysm, if only we would pay attention to the signs around us. It's not that we are headed for cataclysm just now, they might say, but it'll come eventually. The idea that humanity exists at the end of time is certainly not new, but the fact that we can study and understand the technical ways in which we might commit societal suicide is new. The possibilities of genetically modified food, pesticides, ozone depletion, global warming, underemployment following the recession, the omnipresent threat of terror, and the recognition that we are vaguely already at war somewhere, all work together to make the generation uneasy. We're not living in leisure, contemplating the perfection of our own existence and fantasizing some kind of interruptive horror; there is the distinct recognition that, as the slogan goes, we had better enjoy the little things for they seem unlikely to last. Life is distinctly transient and ephemeral at times.

The apocalyptic lens, operating according to the premise that the world has forever changed from that which we knew, filters perception through the moment of the advent of the apocalypse. This is not to say that the apocalyptic event has come or that we perceive it as imminent. We are, perhaps, quite comfortable at this moment of relative economic stability, leisure, and comfort. However, we similarly dwell on the imminent advent of Earth-shattering revelation that interrupts our existence and which comes in a form that has been unanticipatable. It is utterly new, it creates that which is utterly new, even if the experience has been imagined to the point of tiring its possibilities. History itself is reshaped according to our vision of apocalypse, and its material experience becomes the anchor for what is to come.

Serialized iterations of apocalypse (such as that which has been slowly developing in *The Walking Dead*) extend the shivers even more thoroughly in complex webs of temporality and nostalgia. The creation of the parallel world, in which characters that we have come to know exist, that itself operates according to an ongoing linear temporal model, creates multiple valences of the experience of time. We long for the world (as if from a post-apocalyptic perspective) in which we live before the apocalypse, and we also paradoxically remember fondly the time before we had come to know the extent of the apocalypse in the filmic (walking) world, a void filled by *Fear the Walking Dead*. *iZombie*, however, acts as if cataclysmic apocalypse is impossible despite the rapidly spreading contagion emanating from its main character, Liv Moore, who cannot engage in reality and enacts continuous nostalgia through carnosarcophagy.[2] "It is becoming acceptable to engage in social taboo; what has been seen as proper to humanity, the avoidance of taboo, has broken and begun to destruct the possibility that there is anything proper to the human. Derrida terms this discussion carnophallogocentrism, a nickname for the problematic conditions disrupting attempts to separate what is proper to the human: sacrifice, masculinity, and speech" (Pielak 112). This process of eating the meat of the human (specifically the brain), tragically creates a living sarcophagus that remembers, quite literally, the dead, and brings them into the present of life, as alive. This preserves the possibility of the carnivorous human, the human willing to eat in order to add to itself, to satisfy the craving to eat other creatures. It preserves the position of human power, even though it is the human eating itself here, the cannibal. It is ultimately taboo to eat the human, and *iZombie*'s lovely zombie protagonist engages the taboo, breaking the bounds of law within the show, encouraging us to do the same, and preserving the state of the human, paradoxically through the zombie. If it is true that tragedy awaits humans who transgress boundaries, carnosarcophagy in the zombie film distorts that possibility. It is perhaps the fundamental record of the boundary transgression that already took place; this, perhaps above all else that Liv experiences, leaves her beyond the boundary of the human (it may, indeed, be the only notable thing, as her pale skin, and other semi-zombie features are hardly distinctly inhuman). What tragedy are we to understand here, then? The end of the human isn't so bad.

The tragedy seems to be falling outside of time into a period of cultural dismemberment in which it is no longer possible to operate in the present world. In each representation characters attempt the inevitably doomed project of predating the apocalypse. It is telling, for example, that in the first few minutes of the first episode of *The Walking Dead*, Rick awakens in the hospital to a stopped clock. The viewer instantly knows that time (and perhaps temporality itself, the ability to operate in a liner time model) has ceased.

Three types of apocalyptic worlds, each with their own characteristic relationships to the clock, appear. Pre-apocalyptic visions feature a moving clock, apparently working as it always has; mid-apocalyptic visions feature the stopped clock on the wall, with the hands frozen at the point of disjuncture, in which nostalgia figures heavily; post-apocalyptic visions feature a new temporality, in which time has already been reconfigured, nevertheless paying deference to the lost world through complex webs of nostalgia and recreation. The viewer's relationship to the temporality of apocalypse focuses the point of the viewer's awe.

Pre-Apocalyptic Visions

Simultaneously characterized by, on the one hand, depictions of normalcy, and on the other, fear of that which might become, pre-apocalyptic visions feature worlds in which physical and ideological structures are substantially intact. The old world is still extant, though it is pressed by the coming of apocalypse. Even in this set of visions, the relationship of the world to the force of regulative law has collapsed. By regulative law here we mean the idea that the world functions as it ought with the understanding that people are governed both by social pressures (Foucauldian disciplinary normativity) and the force of codified law. This is the exceptional apocalyptic state that we have described that situates the possibility of the coming of the apocalypse into the world in which law has already failed to properly operate. Though the time may have seemed impossible, the world rests on the brink.

Fear the Walking Dead offers, in its first season, an exemplary portrayal of a pre-apocalyptic vision. A recent spinoff of *The Walking Dead*, *FtWD* is set in Los Angeles at the very beginning of the same cataclysmic apocalypse shaping the walking world of *TWD*. In its first season, *FtWD* begins with a stoned late-teen, Nick (Frank Dillane), who wakes in a church looking for his missing girlfriend, Gloria (Lexi Johnson). She is, he soon discovers, busy eating the face of another man. With this startling revelation, Nick runs from the church into a street and is hit by a passing car. As the camera pans out, the audience realizes that life is continuing as usual outside the myopic world of the church. This parallels the isolated apocalyptic worlds of *Dead Alive* and *Dead Snow*, for example, in which the world outside that of the protagonist's continues to function uninterrupted. *FtWD*'s Southern California setting remains as vibrant and bustling as ever. As soon as the scene fades back in, Madison Clark (Kim

Dickens), Nick's mother, is getting her family ready for the day, just like on any other school day. She is, as a guidance counselor, an interesting protagonist for the series. In some ways, her role becomes that of guide for the viewer of the show. The episode continues with relatively strange occurrences, but the audience soon begins to wonder if Nick's girlfriend-zombie wasn't actually a hallucination, after all. The pre-apocalyptic vision maintains an ambiguous relationship with reality and its sensory data. Viewers are forced to attempt to read between the lines, to find sense in the gaps between pieces of sensory information.

This relationship further causes the viewer to more explicitly take back the perceived doubt and apply it to our own society, which also seems to be functioning normally, but which very well might be no less suspect than the show featuring the zombie-girlfriend. The world (both that of the show and our own) hasn't yet descended into the chaos that accompanies cataclysmic apocalypse, but the sense that tragedy is to come is inescapable. Nick claims that he's never hallucinated before when confronted by his step dad, Travis (Cliff Curtis). His vision is real, and he's convinced. We tend to believe him, as we've seen it with our own eyes, but early on in the show, that seems only to implicate us in the insanity. Finally, Nick's veracity is proved when Travis, having gone to investigate the church, falls in a pool of blood. Tragedy, perhaps inevitably, infects the world as it appears deceivingly static.

A troubled relationship with the law explicitly figures in the show before the close of the first episode. By its end, police presence is heavily escalated and children have begun to disappear from school. Footage goes viral of apparently dead victims eating their rescuers, thus directly attacking first responders, those responsible, in part, for mediating the power of the law to the populace. The coming apocalypse masquerades as an illness that causes violence, perhaps our real fear. As protesters exercise their freedom of speech, ironically enraged over the expression of law enforcement violence, looting breaks out and vandals mob the streets. Schools and emergency services quickly shut down. Full-fledged riots in the show's second episode threaten to undermine all social order and threaten the lives of Travis and Chris (Lorenzo James Henrie), a father-son pair of protagonists who are stranded downtown, by chance, in a barbershop run by the Salazar family. By the end of the second episode, even though zombies have not become rife, the populace has begun to fall apart, bringing about a slow sort of cataclysm.

Tobias (a wayward youth played by Lincoln Castellanos) and Madison Clark dialogue again in the second episode, acting as a sort of Greek chorus for the audience. Tobias starts: "It's all going to go to hell—and that's what they don't get—when civilization ends, it ends fast." Madison responds: "they're going to contain it." Tobias' witty response feels inevitable: "the same they that's supposed to warn us?" (*FtWD* 1.2). The irony that Tobias, the high school student, gets to guide the guidance counselor is not lost on the audience. It is a characteristic trope of the zombie genre that youth gets to speak power to the adult generation; this appears amusingly in *Scouts Guide to the Zombie Apocalypse*, for example, as well as both versions of *Pride and Prejudice and Zombies*. Government authority, as it is consistently undermined by injustice and inefficacy in this show, offers no real cure. Nor does it offer hope. There is, in the show's representation of the coming of apocalypse, inevitability in its end. Despite the recognition that this show takes place in the already-cataclysmic world of *The Walking Dead*, the viewer is asked to appreciate this spinoff as a flashback to the genesis of the apocalypse.

Viewers of *The Walking Dead* perhaps feel an overwhelming need for an explanation of the genesis of the apocalypse afflicting the common world, but no such cause is made readily available in either show. Rather than exploiting simply its place in time as at the dawn of a cataclysmic apocalypse, *FtWD* takes this elision a step further to revel in its slow coming. As if savoring the moment of the advent of catastrophe, the first six-episode season has barely got the world affected (infected) by its end. Slow pacing adds another dimension to the coming of apocalypse. It's not just pre, mid, and post, but also transitioning into apocalypse (or perhaps from, as in *Night of the Living Dead*), that structures temporality in pre-apocalyptic and mid-apocalyptic filmic worlds. This transitional structure embodies a slow loss of the world as it was known, contributing to a sense of absence that pervades the show.

The show's emptiness is not just about absence from the screen, though it is that, too. Significant characters' absences leave the show distinctly missing. Missing implies not only longing to be near, but also that there is something fundamentally missing *from* a character's or show's very being, and that something is the one in absentia. In an apocalypse, apart from the plot considerations of separation as a narrative device, accompanied by characteristic reunification, character disappearances resonate as profound absence, as embodiments of loss that characterize the already fraught and coming cataclysmic apocalypse. As characters disappear, they are missed and are missing. First, Nick's parents miss him, though the audience is keenly aware of his presence. Alicia (Nick's sister, played by Alycia Debnam-Carey) temporarily loses her boyfriend, Matt (Maestro Harrell), who appears missing until she hunts him down. Nick goes missing again as he is taken to a camp for those posing a danger to the citizens once the town has been locked down by the military. By the third episode, the fact that Travis is missing from the house has become a point of key discussion. Alicia and Nick recall their missing father (who has died before the narrative present of the show) and fear that Travis will similarly fail to return even while they apparently dislike him. Travis goes missing again as he searches for his son in the middle of the second season. By the latter episodes in the first season, the family is living in a military-quarantined town and martial law has been enforced rigorously: normalcy itself is missing. Characters are missing until they're not, in almost every case turning up dead, instead. This missingness, absence, is decidedly not nothing, but represents an out-of-time status in which a character carries on outside of time relative to the other characters on the show and perhaps in, or perhaps out of time for the viewer. This is not simply describing the narrative present. This temporality is an apocalyptic temporality that attempts to come to terms with the loss-of-self characteristic of apocalypse, even non-cataclysmic apocalypse, in that the self has to be reconfigured to act in a new world.

The very nature of reality is in question as the world falls apart during the course of *FtWD*'s first season. This is, perhaps, representative of the cultural cannibalism (recalling Collings' cultural dismemberment here) further characteristic of the apocalyptic genre. Even as zombies eat characters that we have come to appreciate, there is the distinct sense that more is being eaten than their flesh. Attacking first the ideological apparatuses that would shape dominant culture, the world of *FtWD* comes apart in a structured and strategic fashion.

The coming-apart begins with the church in the first episode—that has become a crack house. It then extends into the hospital in which Nick is treated, which somehow degenerates during his stay there from a functioning medical treatment facility to a haven of disorganization that can't keep track of its police-prisoner-patients. The degeneration is quick. This pairing is particularly significant as it represents the transition Foucault documents in "The Social Extension of the Norm" from religion to science, and particularly to the science of medicine as the frontier of human knowledge and the chief place of disciplinary exercise on the body. Thus the enforcement arm of the norm has become itself infected and consequently ineffective, necessitating a second transition toward apocalyptic normativity, toward an institution that might maintain the exercise of discipline on the bodies it engages.

We can only speculate on the shape of this appendage for this particular apocalyptic iteration as it dawns into apocalypse, but we might guess that the group unit forming around the Clark, Manawa, and Salazar families might be the institution, and with the recent departures of both Travis and Daniel Salazar (Ruben Blades) who had been the enforcers, that Madison Clark may well take shape as the group's de facto enforcer. Rick has clearly served in this role, alongside Deanna (until her recent death) in *The Walking Dead*. However, the pairing in *FtWD*, comprised of an English teacher (Travis) and former military enforcer (Daniel) is particularly interesting as representative of normativity. The audience is tempted to vilify Daniel, as an enforcer in his former life, and his final act of arson seems to justify this villainization. Recurring themes of pre-apocalyptic violence, ranging from the school bullying of Tobias to Daniel's state-sponsored torture background, demonstrate applications of force in the show. That the barber might be a butcher is particularly frightening, perhaps most of all when he engages again in torture in order to assist in the gathering of information about the military occupation of the town. Travis, of course, as an English teacher, seems to be far from frightening—holding a position more or less mocked for its innocuousness. As an enforcer of ideology, however, the education discipline is ideally situated. Together, the pair forms the two arms of ideological influence on the characters occupying the pre-apocalyptic world, one engaged in force and the other in education. With Madison Clark in this role, it is unclear how the group will move forward.

There is, throughout the show, an ethical system bent toward survival at any cost and away from virtue. This is nowhere more evident than when Salazar's character teams up with the Clark family to torture Andrew Adams for information about the detainees held at the military compound. However, Madison's feeding of Celia to her caged zombies seems a close second. Contagion runs rampant in the apocalyptic state through zombies, to be sure, but worse through humans responding to the apocalypse. Furthermore, contagion spreads not through the operation of ideological state apparatuses (which have been supplanted, as when Travis becomes a leader rather than a teacher) but through direct transmission—through the figurative bite of the apocalypse. This is the final direct dismemberment of culture, the destruction of the apparatuses of cultural transmission that enable time to function in the normal world. When Tobias expresses his paranoia about the government, the disruption is obvious; in a dialogue with Madison, Tobias argues, "No one is going to college. No one is doing anything they think they are…. They say it's not connected, they say that but I don't believe them. It is. From reports in five states. They don't know if it's a virus or a microbe. They don't know but it's spreading. People are killing" (1.1). Madison responds: "if there's a problem we're going to know about it. The authorities would tell us" (1.1).

Apocalyptic beginnings erupt into the world dismembering social structures and destabilizing the progressive hope of the better, brighter future in favor of threat response. The hope is pervasive that time might be frozen in order to arrest the coming apocalypse, freeing the populace to live in its normative world uncritically. Nostalgia for the unthreatened world is as yet mostly unnecessary, though its germ as an attempt to deny loss and stop time is already extant; shock and immediate threat response are the modes of existence characterizing these apocalyptic worlds.

Mid-Apocalyptic Visions

Mid-apocalyptic visions continue to be characterized by threat response, though the horror has become imminent. The struggle to survive is constant. These films feature sites of physical and ideological struggle and (often rapid) deterioration; the world as it has been known is crashing around the protagonists in these depictions. Clearly many film versions that begin in the pre-apocalyptic phase quickly deteriorate into this temporal category. The apocalypse need not affect the whole world in these visions, though it often does. In *Night of the Living Dead*, the whole world is not explicitly engaged, but there is a national governmental response, for example.

Perhaps more insidiously, several of the most recent representations of zombies maintain the distinct impression that we are already zombies (a point addressed in Chapter 2). This is not just in the sense found in the walking world (that we're all infected) but in the *Shaun of the Dead* sense: that we go about our routines in an always already zombie fashion. *Shaun of the Dead*, *iZombie*, and *Fear the Walking Dead* each feature characters who recognize that their post-zombie lives are not in substance different than their pre-zombie lives (Shaun, Liv, and Nick, respectively). In *Shaun of the Dead* and *FtWD* there are cataclysmic apocalypses, but in *iZombie* there is not; its apocalypse is of the sort in *Dead Alive*, in which zombies can hit the park or a party while others go about their lives apparently unaware of the infection. Nick recognizes this paradox in *Fear the Walking Dead* when he says, "I've been living this for a long time and now everyone is catching up to me." This is the same impetus that motivates the shambling processions pre-apocalypse in *Shaun of the Dead*, and that accounts for the mirrored scenes after the disease has begun its spread. Shaun walks through his everyday routine, past a soccer playing boy, into the market, and so on, failing to notice that the world as he knew it has ended. He fails both because of his own cursory participation in the world and because of the stupefaction of the masses of 20-somethings living alongside him. The movie's clear point, which is so eloquently verbalized by *FtWD*'s drug-addicted Nick, is that we're already zombies. TWD confirms this horrifying possibility early on through Dr. Edwin Jenner (Noah Emmerich) at the CDC.

Thus high functioning, apparently anti-apocalyptic zombies appear to occupy a new plot point on the spectrum of available zombie types. What if the world doesn't end, in fact, when zombies are unleashed on it through the use of a drug (as in *iZombie*)? They continue to serve as a mirror for our deep social fears, they just get to live out the cure in their own representations. That our world might already be apocalyptic is perhaps most strongly portrayed by mid-apocalyptic visions.

Nevertheless, there remains a distinctly world-crashing perspective amongst these films (even when it technically isn't). *iZombie* figures as an exemplary mid-apocalyptic world, therefore. The show's world is one with the power to transform even Major (Robert Buckley), a man recognizable as a typically Captain-America figure, into a drug using zombie hunter apparently capable of murder for hire (a fate that apparently continues to cause conflict). The mid-apocalyptic world is uniquely transformative in effect.

The premise for the show *iZombie* is unique. It knits several tropes together to feature a zombie protagonist named Olivia Moore—who is most often called Liv, with an unmistakable wordplay for live more. A medical resident pre-infection, post-infection Liv works as a medical examiner at a morgue in order to easily access brains, which she needs to eat in order to keep herself from turning into a full-fledged, flesh rotting zombie. Aside from cannibalistic desire, her symptoms are relatively minor: pale skin, white hair, and occasional, temporary fits of rage in which she gains superhuman strength and her eyes turn blood red. Medically, her blood pressure is low, she seems to have less blood overall, and her pulse has slowed. Otherwise, she looks and functions like any other (attractive) human, retains a high-functioning job, and even maintains relationships, if poorly. Many of us would hope to be so lucky.

Perhaps the most interesting element of the premise, however, is that when Liv eats the brains of the corpses at the morgue, she sees flashes from their lives (this part of the premise is clearly shared with *Warm Bodies*), which she creatively uses to solve their murders. In the second episode, Liv eats the brains of an artist and has a revelation: "The passionate mind is selfish. It is so focused on what it desires, reason becomes background noise. Javier's brain made me cross the line that divides what I long for and what I can never have. There were so many nights I could have been with Major, but I stayed home studying. Days I could have spent sucking the marrow out of life, I spent building a resume for a life I'd never have. There were parts of me that were dead even before I became a zombie. So maybe that means it is possible for parts of me to spring to life even now that I'm dead" (*iZombie* 1.2).

The possibility that a zombie might be gutted of the essence of self by eating the brains of others (and thereby taking on elements of their personalities) is very much both a nod to zombie origins—through the possibility that another might control the animate human corpse—and a recognition that zombies now might need to be awakened to the larger possibilities of life; they might be able to retain control of their own actions, deciding which self they ought to pursue. Zombie eating in *iZombie* becomes rather a world-expanding educational device, sucking the marrow out of life, than an insatiate desire to destroy humanity. Liv laments her previous failures to live life to its fullest with Major (who is her ex-fiancé), having chosen, like Prospero in Shakespeare's *The Tempest*, to spend time studying instead of loving. The dead parts of Liv's life need to spring to life, so to speak, so that she might in fact live more. This is precisely the element of the cure portrayed in the film: it might cure society at large of its apathy and misguided failures to marrow-suck. This is clearly true even while another of the show's protagonists, Liv's partner/ boss, Dr. Ravi Chakrabarti (Rahul Kohli) searches diligently for a cure using zombified rats as test subjects. The world of the show could not, therefore, be afflicted with a cataclysmic apocalypse; it must function from the perspective of a personal apocalypse, and the zombie infection rages only to create conflict for the individual characters affected so that they might reform. And while there is also an ostensible traditional cure, the real cure is already in the works within Liv.

The show experiments with several key questions, seeking answers that might help understand the progression of the infection, echoing the scientific method in its methodical pursuits. "What happens if a zombie that is this far gone gets to feed?" for example, is explored in episode 1.3. One of Liv's fellow residents, Marcy, had been trapped in a pit since infection at the same party as Liv. However, while Liv found a near inexhaustible source of accessible human brains and feeds regularly, Marcy remained isolated and completely degenerated, losing the vestiges of her self to the ravages of infection. Liv and Ravi attempt to feed her, hoping for a miraculous reversal from Marcy's far more typical zombie state. But, feeding the former cardiac resident proved ineffective. Unfortunately, she remained a full zombie. Marcy continued as a too-far-gone zombie until Liv was forced to kill her after falling into the pit.

The contrast between the two zombie versions is heightened as Liv is faced with guilt over her momentary transformation into "full-on zombie mode," evident twice over as the elements of control, that are inherent in the humanity that holds back the zombie rage—the Aristotelian self, responsible for control over one's base instincts—is effaced. Liv feels so guilty for the brutal ending of Marcy that she cannot even allow herself the succor and momentary nepenthe offered in the form of a serial killer's brains. "Marcy was real. She was alive. She was a person. And I killed her. That's the thing about pain, isn't it. Really feeling it doesn't make it stop. It just shows you you're still alive" (1.3). The condition of living, the experience of self experiencing pain, is characteristic of the mid-apocalyptic film. The revelation of self-consciousness as participating in the end of society (even if it's only in the form of a personal apocalypse) marks time as mid-apocalyptic. This often engages apocalyptic nostalgia, wistfulness for a time of ignorance before the realization of the threat of cataclysm.

Apocalyptic nostalgia, perhaps above all else, prevents our own actions occurring between the present and the coming of the apocalypse from having meaning. This nostalgia depicts a site of misrecognition of the present, in that the one engaging in it cannot look around and operate fully in the present moment due to a lingering longing for a time that is already past and that has not been fully assimilated into the present moment. The one experiencing it further fails to recognize the ideological condition structuring the existence that lapsed at the dawn of apocalypse; therefore, apocalyptic nostalgia elides the time between the past reflected moment and the future apocalypse from which we might look back toward the past present. This elision makes meaningless whatever actions might occur during the period and allows instead a wistful look at a time when actions seemed to matter, though they perhaps mattered only insofar as they brought about the present apocalypse. Any wonder that occurs seems to be the wonder of responsibility, the understanding that human action might in some way lead to any outcome other than that of the now-having-occurred apocalypse.

Perhaps it is not immediately clear what misrecognition of the present might mean. This is the sort of willful misrecognition that Žižek documents, in which we look at reality around us and pretend as if it is real though we know in actuality that it's not. In the same way we assign value to money though we know it doesn't have intrinsic value. In apocalyptic representations, we recognize that life is good even if it leads to apocalypse. And worse, we recognize that there is a functioning understanding of law, though in retrospect we recognize that it leads to the conditions of the coming of the apocalypse. We live in a state of exception in which law is suspended, and the wistfulness of apocalyptic nostalgia pretends law operated properly, before. Times were simpler then (i.e., now). The world was ordered and Twinkies were readily accessible. Hard work and study could lead to a medical degree and a satisfying career as a doctor.

If misrecognition of the present (evidenced through apocalyptic nostalgia and perhaps otherwise) is a condition of the mid-apocalyptic temporal status, which is further marked by the intense pursuit of survival as the world is physically, or at least conceptually crashing around the participant, there is nevertheless a sense of moving toward a remaking of self by its conclusion. This new self must respond to the world as it is becoming, and the selves in these crashing worlds are necessarily, therefore, becoming responsible selves through their chosen responses. These "becoming-selves" are necessarily unstable, learning to account for the appetitive and its control, taking account of the horrors of apocalypse.

This is a further characteristic of stopped time, in that the self experiencing the stoppage has fallen quite out of stability and linear progression. The world and the self are simultaneously moving toward post-apocalyptic iterations, having already begun to account for the impossible conditions that have become possible in the world at large. The film worlds of *Scouts Guide to the Zombie Apocalypse, 28 Days Later, Dead Snow, Planet Terror* (2007), and both versions of *Dawn of the Dead* (1978 and 2004) echo these conditions.

Post-Apocalyptic Visions

Perhaps the final version of the zombie temporal model is characterized by a particular form of grave loss and at least one character who has been forced to remake her or himself in response to the already destroyed world. Loss has come, so in order to deny it, the self has to be reimagined. The world as it was known is ended and is in the process of reconfiguration already. *Zombieland*, toward which we must now move, is an exemplary post-apocalyptic film. As Columbus (Jessie Eisenberg) develops his rules, he begins to come alive for the first time, ironically in the already dead world. *World War Z* (the film), *The Walking Dead, Fido,* and *Z Nation* similarly engage the post-apocalyptic world effectively, as do films like *Land of the Dead* and *Warm Bodies*.

A surprisingly significant instance of post-apocalyptic nostalgia occurs in *Zombieland* (2009) when Tallahassee (Woody Harrelson), the Twinkie-loving zombie exterminator, remembers his puppy—who Columbus eventually realizes is a thin veil for his lost son. In a movie otherwise overwhelmed with humor, this moving scene is disruptive, even though the horrific post-apocalyptic world is pervasively characterized by loss already. The depth of the character is revealed through this instance of nostalgia, set against the bizarre fascination with the pre-apocalyptic world that otherwise maintains as its pinnacle the lowly Twinkie. While pursuing the Twinkie with Tallahassee, Columbus waxes philosophical: "It makes you sick. You know, it makes you sad. It makes you … it makes you think if you can go back to the way things were right now, you know. You'd be out in the back yard, you know, trying to catch fireflies. And instead this. Something about a Twinkie reminded him of a time not so long ago. When things were simple and not so fucking psychotic. It was like, if he got a taste of that comforting childhood treat, the world would become innocent again and everything would return to normal" (*Zombieland*). With its jolting, comedic tone, the film takes a representation of life that we all know to be both trivial and symbolic (of consumption, mass marketing, and the nevertheless somehow pure pleasures of childhood) and invests it with apocalyptic significance. The golden pastry comes to stand in for a lost child, and for the world in which the lost child could be alive. Watching zombie films with an eye for what is lost and what is mourned, the viewer cannot help identify in the post-apocalyptic filmic world of *Zombieland* the last vestige of the world as it was, and perhaps the thing that might redeem it from its wasted state. If a Twinkie might survive, so might the human longing that could remake the world. The Twinkie becomes, in *Zombieland*, the sign of post-apocalyptic hope for human nature. It is the embodiment of relative nostalgia, which then figures both the profound loss acting on survivors and the paradoxical hope enacted through memory, unassimilable, of what might yet be.

There is a fundamental contrast in zombie films, and sometimes even within the same zombie film, concerning the post-apocalyptic, imagined perception of pre-apocalyptic life. With this end in mind, the film version of *World War Z* opens with a montage of popular culture images such as the colors of people's socks, the migratory patterns of insects, traffic reports, the weather, traffic stops, talk shows, and myriad other mundane details that somehow knit the fabric of the pre-apocalyptic world that we, too, inhabit. Gradually transitioning to the diseased state in which the apocalypse strikes, the film moves from mundanity to gravity quickly, rapidly transitioning to images of death and violence, particularly involving animals, though never abandoning the impression that the pre-apocalyptic state is somehow trivial. Other zombie films and representations maintain nostalgia for a time when the world was not yet facing an apocalypse. This occurs repeatedly in *The Walking Dead*, for example, when Rick flashes back to time with his family—which was so much more innocent. The contrast, it seems, has to do with the state of the world that the apocalypse interrupts.

In *The Walking Dead*, we find an ideal example of an alternative apocalyptic world operating alongside this one (for some five seasons now). Even as we long to predate the apocalypse (returning us to the present day before the apocalypse) we simultaneously long to return to the time (as in the first season) when everyone wasn't infected with the zombie disease. There was a time when it seemed like a place outside the apocalypse might be found if only Rick's family could be reunited; that time did not necessitate the question:: how many people have you killed. The complex web of nostalgia adds to our investment in the show and its atemporal existence.

It is, with this in mind, no accident that the explicitly post-apocalyptic *Fido* is set in a 1950s style American town. The film begins with a Cold-War style propaganda video ostensibly produced by Zomcon, the company responsible for helping humanity to survive the radioactive space particles that "cause the reanimation of dead bodies." Overtly satirizing race and class relations in America, *Fido* also features a public service announcement short film within a film entitled "A Bright New World." For the postmodern viewer, this represents a rupture in time returning us to when "homeland" was easy to define and when the world operated according to clearly defined (if unfair) social relations; the mini film is shot in black and white and features characters like Mrs. Smith (an everymom character played by Lynn Pendelton) and stereotypical American soldiers erecting steel fences around prototypical towns.

Zomcon is presented as a savior for the zombie infected world, having produced the "domestication collar," reintroducing zombies into society as productive, if exploited, members. Safety buttons are placed throughout the town, and viewers are given the sense that there is a power interested in protecting citizens from the zombie threat. Productivity can continue even after death in this ideally capitalist society. Zomcon operates through a complex system of surveillance and disciplinary ordering, including the collars that control zombies and the propaganda systems that reproduce the conditions of power. Society has been significantly remade. The film within the film pokes fun at this relationship, featuring an elementary classroom, complete with boy scouts (called Zomcon cadets) sitting in the front row, eagerly applauding the corporate propaganda and picking on a boy, Timmy Robinson (K'Sun Ray), who asks, "are zombies dead or alive?" The class is the audience for the film within the film. The film's images are set alongside a soundtrack featuring songs like "99 Pounds of Dynamite" (1950, Buddy Stewart) and "Powder Your Face with Sunshine" (1948). The songs help to connect the fantastic filmic world to that of the viewer.

Nostalgia is, after all, longing for a time when things were simpler. Longing for a time when the problems facing the one engaging the wistful

Fido (Billy Connolly) wearing a Zomcon domestication collar performing manual labor.

recollection were either nonexistent or were able to be managed convincingly. Apocalyptic nostalgia, rather than simply recalling a simpler world, highlights the complexity and untenability of the world in which one currently exists. Thus the film that engages in this double nostalgia, pulling the reader into a time nostalgic for a world before the apocalypse, to watch a world nostalgic for a time before its own apocalypse, exposes the possibilities of relative nostalgia, except that this film isn't nostalgic at all. It highlights, rather than the possibilities of blissfully pleasant nostalgia, gentle melancholy for a world just beyond our reach, the ways in which the world was never really that simple after all and the ways that our own pre-apocalyptic world is plagued by its own host of troubling concerns. The double look back (before the apocalypse, back in time) unsettles the twin possibilities of hope and cure.

While it is conceivable that any particular film or series could exist with more than one of these temporal relationships, one is generally weighted far more heavily and that weight shapes the content of the film and its effect on the audience. Apocalyptic ethics, the experience of nostalgia, and the understanding of the relationship between the characters and the viewers are all at stake and dependent upon the temporalization of the image. The temporal setting of the image is very often intimately connected to the cause of the particular apocalypse depicted. We have explored the range of possibilities inherent in zombie representations with regard to temporal settings, connecting the filmic worlds to our own. It is, therefore, finally, to causes that we must turn next.

Through the distortion of temporality we are not attempting to deny loss that is to come or that even might come, but rather to deny the loss that we've already experienced. We seek to deny its very possibility. Thus the zombie mask, the cover for whatever it is that really frightens us, takes shape to intervene between the world and its present. This is the locus of the apocalyptic and the space into which apocalyptic causes interrupt. These causal interruptions appear as if they fundamentally alter current conditions all the while mirroring them instead. Nevertheless, they offer one means of accessing the fears that we otherwise could perhaps not face. With this we turn to an analysis of apocalyptic causes, moving slowly toward the possibility of their cure, possible only when they can be isolated and understood.

4

Apocalyptic Causes

(by Matt Lewerenz, Chase Pielak
and Alexander H. Cohen)

"Whence, I often asked myself, did the principle of life proceed?"
Victor Frankenstein (*Frankenstein*)

The remaining chapters explore this book's central cause-to-cure analytical arc. First, we explore the causes of the zombie apocalypse and examine their meaning. We then consider the experience of the apocalypse itself, and finally consider the meaning of various cures (or, the attempts to reach a cure, which may be out of reach). This framework, we argue, is useful in exposing encoded meaning in zombie film and literature. Again, we must consider the distinction between cataclysm and apocalypse. An apocalypse marks an ending; it is disruptive, but not always absolutely destructive. Cataclysm, however, entails total destruction. Some, but not all, apocalypses are cataclysmic. As we consider the status of humanity in an epoch during which megaextinction is a technical possibility, it is no surprise that cataclysmic events detailing human extinction have come to dominate the stories that we tell ourselves.[1] Catastrophic global extinction, however, is not the sole fear represented in zombie apocalypses. We consider, too, not just zombies themselves, but their relationship to humans. The zombie narrative is about more than the sheer horror of the horde: it is about the birth of the inhuman, the struggle of the survivors to avert their seemingly inevitable fate, and the race for some sort of cure (or, at least, manageable—if cowardly—detente). After all, a zombie is uninteresting in a vacuum. All it does is wander around and groan and bump into things. But add some terrified humans, a decaying society, and the quest to deliver humanity, and things get much more interesting.

So, within the panoply of zombie apocalypses represented in film and other media, we ask: where does the zombie come from, and why does this matter? The genesis of the transmutation of humanity into something distinctly inhuman merits consideration.

Researchers have noted the importance of the cause of the zombie contagion, several having begun to consider what this might mean. For example, Cory James Rushton and Christopher Moreman argue that "conflicting explanations for the zombie plague are part of the answer to the genre's ability to proliferate and to generate generic 'rules'" (2). Of particular significance, we argue, is Rushton and Moreman's assertion that the cause of the apocalypse leads to the generation of rules. When apocalypse occurs, the world ends as it was previously known; this necessarily includes the cessation and reconfiguration of law. The survivor, who has known nothing but a rule-based existence, demands a return to a world in which rules are still codified in law. But in an apocalyptic world, law cannot work as it did. The nature of the apocalypse determines *how* the rules of the apocalyptic world will vary. This is perhaps most interesting in iterations featuring prisoners, who, paradoxically, lead a particularly rule oriented life before the apocalypse, as in *The Walking Dead*, for example.

In this chapter, then, we explore the birth of disaster. To borrow from comic book parlance, this chapter focuses on the origin stories of zombie apocalypses. We analyze six distinct apocalyptic originations: magical control, metaphysical anxiety, extraterrestrial uncertainty, apparent causelessness, military-scientific overreach, and cultural transgression. These origins are often explicitly displayed and they act as a blueprint for the particular brand of apocalypse depicted. They also implicitly display the cultural concerns played out (consciously or unconsciously) in the creation of each depiction. Finally, the causes we identify are neither exclusive nor evolutionary; there can be, and often is, overlap. As importantly, there is not a distinct periodization for the expression of these causes. Cold-War concerns don't necessarily produce a particular apocalyptic cause any more than millennial fears, for example. They often significantly overlap. This multiplicity of causes defines, in part, the state of apocalypse in which we find ourselves.

Here, we focus primarily on the cause of the apocalypse as told in narratives, but are aware that the question of origin is far more complex. We seek to ask: what is the surface-level, or given explanation for a zombie outbreak in a zombie narrative (i.e., space radiation), and what is the underlying, symbolic tension that is the driving force behind the apocalypse? Zombie narratives are deeply-embedded fictions with age-old roots, stories of sometimes not-quite-fantasy that reflect back to uncomfortable truths about who we are and provide cautionary tales about where we might wind up. The earliest zombie narratives and many later films situate the zombie creature in contexts of race, sex, and control, within an overarching framework that is concerned with what Sartre calls "the problem of the Other." "The Other is the indispensable mediator between myself and me.... By the mere appearance of the Other, I am put in the position of passing judgment on myself as on an object, for it is as an object that I appear to the Other" (*Being and Nothingness* 198). Zombies act as mirrors through which we come to see ourselves.

Magical Control

Magical manipulation, as a source of zombification, capitalizes on fears of control and monstrosity. It is among the earliest commonly expressed sources of the zombie, and one that is closely tied to both expressions of the Gothic and the perceived experience of plantation slaves in the New World. The idea has antecedents that predate the traditional zombie canon; see, for instance, film and literary narratives such as *The Cabinet of Dr. Caligari*, and *Frankenstein* (1816). However, as Dr. Arnold Blumberg notes, as far as zombies go, "for all intents and purposes, [critics] have agreed that it all starts in 1932 with *White Zombie*" (*Doc of the Dead*). Directors of early zombie films like *White Zombie* married a Gothic aesthetic familiar to viewers with a stylized and misinterpreted concept of Haitian spirituality. The films were a "weird fusion of a misunderstood sensationalized folklore with an established and successful cinematic tradition for monsters. The early films are always about black people menacing white women. It's really the enslavement by the former slaves that makes that monster so initially terrifying" (*Doc of the Dead*). Many early zombie films touch on common themes that are also obviously and deeply indebted to their roots in an enslaved culture. Further, issues of power and control dominate. These zombies reflect the fear of uncertain control, and this control is caused by the manipulation of sorcery. Such manipulation, which is often abetted by arcane hand gestures, is analogous to the power of the plantation master.

Revolt of the Zombies (1936) and *King of the Zombies* (1941) likewise draw on this conceptualization of witchcraft to deal with issues of control and possession. *King of the Zombies* is particularly interesting because it moves beyond the plantation analogy while still contending with issues of control. Here, a Nazi spy uses voodoo rituals to transfer the soul of an interrogated prisoner into the body of another person. *King of the Zombies* embodies authority in Nazism, which in 1941 was a symbol of unquestioned domination. In films that feature magical control, there is seldom a wide-spread outbreak or cataclysm; the focus is instead on the relationship between the zombie master and the slaves, and between authority and submission.

There is also certainly a shared affinity between traditionally Gothic literature and zombie apocalyptic representations. Common interests mark both genres: excess, homes under attack, suspense and terror (to say nothing of horror), the superhuman, the paradoxical employment of and disdain for markers of class, and ultimately transgression. It is this interest in taboo and transgression that ultimately gives rise to the zombie genre as much as to the Gothic genre. Cannibalism is among the chief taboos; transgressing both its prohibition and the expectations of death shape the genre. Zombie causes are very much symptomatic and representative of transgression in action. This transgression occurs as the singular manifestation of contagion in these control-oriented films, and finally necessitates a cure—that may or may not arise. Significantly, while magical control may not cause widespread, world-ending cataclysm, it plays with the similar theme that, we argue, provokes all apocalypses: transgression from humanity's natural state.

Metaphysical and Extraterrestrial Anxiety

While early zombie narratives are expressly concerned with the problem of the Other in the contexts of race and gender oppression, they forego a detailed exploration of the apocalypse. These earlier stories take place in microcosmic worlds that experience small-scale disruption indicative of an apocalypse, but seldom, if ever, is society at-large subject to zombie hordes. A thematic shift in zombie literature begins around the post–World War II era, where the problem of the Other is combined with anxiety about the end of the world. It was a scary time for people experiencing the power of combining modern technology with rising nationalism, the experience with Japanese, Italian, and German Fascism, and the ideological tug-of-war between juggernauts during the Cold-War. And within this context of fear, science was continuing to march forward, becoming a significant arm of the state and the Cold-War through the "space race." This, in turn, evoked fears not just of international struggle and Soviet bombs falling from the skies, but also more basic fears of what might lay in galactic *terra incognita*. Into this soup, enter the zombie.

Invasion of the Body Snatchers is one compelling entry here. It does not deal with zombies in the sense of undead humans, but it does incorporate many of the tropes that define both earlier and later zombie narratives, including social upheaval, loss of agency, and a metaphorical analysis of the problem of the Other.[2] In the film, Dr. Miles Bennell (Kevin McCarthy) confronts an alien invasion of soulless clones formed inside large seed pods. As he watches friends, strangers, and those in authority turn into emotionless automata, devoid of humanity, Bennell confronts existential uncertainty plaguing the human. Sartre describes the problem: "being-for-itself must be wholly body and it must be wholly consciousness; it cannot be *united* with a body. Similarly, Being-for-others is wholly body; there are no 'psychic phenomena' there to be united with the body. There is nothing *behind* the body, but the body is wholly 'psychic'" (*Being and Nothingness* 281). Others exist for us, *a priori*, as objects. We are nowhere more readily confronted with the objectivity of the Other than in the human/zombie dichotomy (mirroring the human/alien dichotomy, or even the capitalist/communist split). In facing the zombie, humans face the specter of themselves as biological objects, utterly devoid of the psychic element that allows for identification with each other. Thus, when we see a zombie, we are seeing everything we are, yet we are incapable of seeing it because we can only perceive the zombie Other as an object. An object that is trying to devour us. The protagonists of *Invasion of the Body Snatchers* are confronted with this issue when they discover that those whom they formerly associated with a homogenous psychic/biological entity, having lost their consciousnesses, are now reduced to solely bodies.[3]

Significantly, in *Invasion*, in addition to this individual level of ontological confrontation, the plague with which the film is concerned is also societal. As critic Michael Dodd notes, the film is a multifaceted exploration of American angst in the 1950s. By "simultaneously exploiting the contemporary fear of infiltration by undesirable elements as well as a burgeoning concern over homeland totalitarianism in the wake of Senator

Joseph McCarthy's notorious communist witch hunt, it may be the clearest window into the American psyche that horror cinema has ever provided" ("Safe Scares"). *Invasion* was originally intended to end ambiguously, much like America's uncertain grip on its future, with Miles Bennell frantically flagging down traffic and warning motorists and then the audience directly, "They're here already! You're next! You're next!" However, Allied Artists Picture Corporation, which released the film, insisted on a more upbeat note, so a prologue and epilogue were added to suggest that the government had been notified—although director Don Siegel leaves the efficacy of this intervention ambiguous. Ron Rosenbaum takes a distinctly sociological view of the film, saying it is about "the horror of being in the 'burbs. About neighbors whose lives had so lost their individual distinctiveness that they could be taken over by alien vegetable pods—*and no one would know the difference*. And those evil pods that housed the aliens and stole the souls of the humans: were they not metaphors, embodiments of the Cape Cod pods of Levittown and the like, whose growth and multiplication came from sucking the individuality out of the humans housed in them?" (qtd. in Halberstam 140). While *Invasion of the Body Snatchers* is often categorized as science-fiction, it traffics in many of the same tropes as zombie narratives. In the 1950s, space, the last truly foreign place—the "final frontier," if you will—became the tableau in which Americans acted out the tensions that arose from winning the last global, "moral" war, only to be caught in a game of nuclear brinkmanship with the Soviet Union.

This is reflected in the nostalgia of the recent film, *Fido*, for example. But it finds its paragon in the modern zombie era film, *Night of the Living Dead*, which incorporates allusions to extraterrestrial radiation as the culprit, though it is never made explicit.

Much has already been said about *Night of the Living Dead*; it is widely acknowledged as the forerunner of the modern zombie narrative, establishing many of the central tropes of the genre and serving as a polarizing cultural force and subject of cultural criticism—despite its creator's reluctance to accept the role of innovator and commentator. Romero, as well as the cast and crew, have always insisted that whatever cultural impact the film had and whatever underlying symbolic dynamic critics uncover is purely unintentional. His creatures weren't even initially called "zombies." Romero is careful to clarify: "we didn't have a name for that creature. We called them 'ghouls'" (*Doc of the Dead*). He thought his "ghouls" were something new until he read a review of the film in *Cahiers du Cinema* that called the creatures "zombies," and he had to acknowledge that that is indeed what they were (*Doc of the Dead*).

At one point in the *Night of the Living Dead*, a group of scientists proposes that the plague is the result of strange, high-level radiation that a NASA probe returning from Venus was "carrying" upon re-entry (indicating it was not initially contained in the probe itself), but they are cut off by a general who disagrees that this answer is by no means definitive. One of *NOTLD*'s lasting attributes is that, because the cause of the plague is ambiguous, it can be read in a number of ways. Perhaps the most terrifying possibility is that, rather than being the result of extraterrestrial or man-made radiation, the zombie apocalypse has no cause, or its cause is never to be known. In this respect *NOTLD* represents a new direction for horror films. Not long after Barbra first meets Ben, Barbra, hysterical, asks him, "What's happening?! What's happening?" Perhaps, in a zombie apocalypse, the survivors never know what it was that caused the dead to return to life and feed upon the living, just as, in a nuclear apocalypse, the survivors may never know who fired the first shot or why. Without science to assert a specific cause and a mass media network to broadcast the news, the cause might as well be any of a number of possibilities: scientific error, divine retribution—or no reason at all.

Reading the cause as being the NASA probe/alien radiation situates the film in a quasi- extraterrestrial causal context, yet earlier films gave space a more prominent role in the apocalypse. Italian horror director Mario Bava's *Planet of the Vampires* (1965) deals with themes of extraterrestrial infection and zombieism in the modern sense of zombies as the undead, as does *Plan 9 from Outer Space* (1959) and *Invisible Invaders* (1959).

Space-related causes of zombie outbreaks then fell from prominence until the mid–1980s, when a series of movies including *Night of the Comet* (1984), *Lifeforce* (1985), and *Night of the Creeps* (1986) all incorporated themes of extraterrestrial agency. This outbreak cause, of course, reflects the great era of space events/movies: the *Star Wars* and *Star Trek* franchises, "Star Wars"-the Department of Defense initiative, the *Challenger* disaster, *E.T.*, et al. Looking up, and what might be looking back down, frightened us to death.

NOTLD, despite its modest beginnings, defined many aspects of this particular fright, which is rather that we are empty than that space might be particularly full. The film's zombies are a narrative representation of human isolation embodied as reanimated cannibalistic corpses. The modern zombie narrative, of which *NOTLD* is the forerunner, is the quintessential post-modern existential tale of heroic antiheroism and of creating meaning out of a bleak and meaningless existence.

In the world of the zombie apocalypse, humankind is confronted with its own emptiness. "The being which wants to find a foundation in being is itself the foundation only of its own nothingness," proclaims Jean-Paul Sartre in *Being and Nothingness*. Zombie narratives allow us, to borrow from Thomas Pynchon, to "project a world," envisioning the inevitable end of the world as we know it that will tear apart the fragile fabric of our modern society. Space was one convenient tableau on which to enact this fantasy, being basically a great big Unknown outside of our own little fishbowl.

Causal Uncertainty

Without oversimplifying, causal ambiguity evokes fears of causelessness. Destabilizing uncertainty about the identification of a specific cause, and the ambiguous signification of apocalyptic cues work together to produce a sense of causelessness. We cannot process and assimilate what we do not know. And without understanding cause there is and can be little hope for the possibility of a cure. In *The Walking Dead*, creators have intentionally left the specific cause of the outbreak uncertain. From Rick's earliest hospital-waking memories on the show, there has yet to be a specific revelation. Glen Mazzara, a co-creator, said of the show, "If you define what caused the outbreak, that puts us in the world of science fiction, and this isn't science fiction to me, it's horror" (qtd. in Goldberg). Mazzara's point, that causal uncertainty is horrifying, is reflected in the show's early futile venture to the CDC (in Season 1). The show's particular brand of causelessness has proved to be rigorously inestimable and incurable, allowing the show to continue to operate as an alternate reality that ever more nearly reflects the state of the world in which we live, and which, therefore, allows us to see our own state.[4]

Romero's *Dawn of the Dead* (1978) is a key early example of apocalyptic causelessness. While nominally a sequel to *NOTLD*, the film represents a departure from the approach the director took ten years prior. Aesthetically, the production values are higher, and Romero teamed up with Italian horror auteur Dario Argento for the soundtrack and editing. The cause of the zombie outbreak in *Dawn of the Dead* is even more ambiguous than in *Night*. There are three possibilities: 1. it could be utterly causeless, 2. it could be the result of the same space probe radiation given as a possible cause in *NOTLD*, and 3. it could be divine retribution. No compelling evidence is ever presented to suggest that any explanation presented is more relevant than any other. In *The Return of the Living Dead* (1985), which takes its title and not much else from a novel written by *NOTLD*'s co-author, John Russo, the events of *NOTLD* are attributed to trioxin, which therein is described as a military defoliant (its actual use is as a source of formaldehyde and cooking fuel). Romero himself has never revealed his sociocultural critical intent, if any. The lack of a definitive cause in the narrative prompts a viewer to search into the underlying symbolic economy of the film for causality.

No mention is made in *Dawn of the Dead* of the space probe from Venus. Instead, there is an allusion to the biblical apocalypse. The tagline for the film is "When hell is full, the dead will walk the earth." Actor Ken Foree's character, Peter, says the line towards the end of the movie, as he and two other survivors survey the specter of the dead mulling through the overrun shopping mall (perhaps not unlike the undone dead in T.S. Eliot's unreal city). Peter says his grandfather, a practitioner of voodoo, used to tell him that reassuring homily when he was a child. In the *Dawn of the Dead* reboot (2004), Foree has a cameo as a televangelist, using the same line in the context of preaching doom-and-gloom to a sinful remnant audience. Even so, the possibilities of the divine cause are left unexplored. What does it mean, after all, for hell to be full? The film, then, points more vaguely to the possibility of a fallen world (rather than a specifically divine event) as the cause of apocalypse.[5]

The realization of a fallen world without specific reference to a biblical or theological antecedent places these films firmly in the causeless category. To varying degrees, supernatural zombie films like Sam Raimi's *Evil Dead* series, Lamberto Bava's *Demons* (1985), *Night of the Demons* (1988), *Dellamorte, del'amore* (1994) and, more recently, *(Rec) 2* and Max Brooks' novel *World War Z*, all ask the quintessential zombie narrative questions within the context of a fallen world (some with slightly more religious connotation). In the novel *World War Z*, an old Chinese woman near the source of the contagion claims the plague is the revenge of spirits of the deceased for having their ancient cemetery and resting place flooded during construction of a dam—a detail left out of the film version, which situates itself as more firmly causeless. However, in the novel, it's not clear whether this is folklore surrounding the ruins where the plague originates, or if local customs are accurate.[6]

Regardless of the plague origin in *Dawn of the Dead*, the film is also one of the earliest and most effective uses of the zombie narrative to address capitalist materialism and consumer culture. The apparent causelessness of the infection is closely related to the sense of drift endemic to America. It created the trope, nearly ubiquitous in modern zombie narratives, of the modern consumerist society cannibalizing itself. This is deployed heavily across the spectrum of modern zombie narratives, for purposes of either nostalgia, critique, or both. Examining *Dawn of the Dead* in its historical and philosophical contexts reveals that, at the level of underlying symbolic economy, it is a perfect demonstration of the cause/cure model.

The 1970s were a dynamic period of transformation in American society. As David Frum argues in *How We Got Here*, the 70s were integral in shaping American culture. "They were strange, feverish years, the 1970s. They were a time of unease and despair, punctuated by disaster. The murder of athletes at the 1972 Olympic games. Desert emirates cutting off America's oil. Military humiliation in Indochina … the dollar plunging in value. Marriages collapsing…. A president toppled from office" (xxiii). *Dawn of the Dead* has its finger firmly on the pulse of this malaise, and it effectively reads like the feverish dream of one who has lived through all of this turmoil. The causelessness of the apocalypse reflects the apparent inability to make sense of society. This was the era of Watergate, Vietnam, new drugs, new diseases, and over-the-top glam rock—the Aquarian ethos of the 60s devolving into the jaded coke and disco orgy of the 70s, with selfless peace and love crumbling into a narcissistic, consumerist free-for-all.

It is this consumerist free-for-all, this cannibalizing of both the conservative values of the 50s and the liberally reactive values of the 60s, that *Dawn of the Dead* encapsulates so effectively. Both in terms of aesthetic and cultural values, the film embodies the hyperreal. When the protagonists, fleeing the chaos of the city, first glimpse the suburban shopping mall that will become their refuge and prison, one asks "What the hell is it?" This new method of consumption is unsettling, standing as it does in the midst of a vast, empty, blacktopped parking lot. It is a self-referring sign that rises up from the cultural and geographic landscape without a referent. In *Consumer Society* (1970), French theorist Jean Baudrillard wrote about this new phenomenon of shopping malls, citing them as evidence that Western culture had reached a place where simulacra—simulations—had usurped the things they were supposed to represent; these copies had themselves become reality—*hyper*reality, a reality of unattached signs which signify only themselves—is enacted. Baudrillard succinctly describes the corpulent consumer society that waits, like a fatted calf, for the coming slaughter:

> Our ... malls mimic a newfound nature of prodigious fecundity. Those are our Valleys of Canaan where flows, instead of milk and honey, streams of neon ketchup on plastic—but no matter! There exists an anxious anticipation, not that there may not be enough, but that there is too much, and too much for everyone: by purchasing a portion one in effect appropriates a whole crumbling pyramid of oysters, meats, pears, or canned asparagus ... and this repetitive, metonymic discourse of the consumable, and of commodities is represented, through collective metaphor and as a product of its own surplus, in the image of the *gift*, and of the inexhaustible and spectacular prodigality of the *feast* [33].

For the Marxist Baudrillard, this organization is unsustainable. It will eat itself. *Dawn of the Dead* is the consumerist vehicle (as a consumable piece of media) that channeled this angst and manifested it in clear metaphorical terms: society has pushed itself into strange new territory, where reality is not reality but rather hyperreality, a new orientation that only nods to the old order, but which is in fact based only on itself.

In the new order, politics is an impotent and deceptive exercise in bombast: the story begins in a TV station, as two commentators heatedly argue with one another, not realizing when they are no longer on the air. The nuclear family has fallen apart: several of the main characters relate that they are divorced, a topic that is not even on the radar of *Night of the Living Dead*. And, in *NOTLD*, the protagonists are generally morally neutral, if not classically heroic at times. But in the post–Vietnam, post–Watergate 1970s, heroes are hard to come by. *Dawn of the Dead*'s heroes, as the character Peter makes clear during the initial helicopter escape from the overrun TV station, are "thieves ... bad guys." *Dawn of the Dead*'s protagonists are 1970s consumers, dissolute and adrift. They seek refuge from Others (who are themselves consumers) in that palace of capitalist consumerism, the shopping mall, but instead of a paradise of consumption they find themselves at a smorgasbord where they are the featured dish.

It is no surprise, then, that *Dawn of the Dead* utilizes irony to a greater degree than *NOTLD* and other previous zombie narratives. Irony is the mode of expression ideally suited to a hyperreal society, in which signs expose underlying, antithetical, pragmatic meanings.

The third of Romero's original three *Dead* movies, *Day of the Dead* (1985), can also be situated in a causeless context. While there is a great deal of focus on the scientists' attempts at controlling/curing the disease, little effort is expended to explain its cause. The most significant attempt comes, as it does in *Dawn*, near the end of the film. John (Terry Alexander), soliloquizes about the cause of the plague, and says that perhaps God is responsible for the destruction: "Maybe he didn't want to see us blow ourselves up.... Maybe he figured we were getting too big for our britches trying to figure shit out." This evident theology is certainly more akin to a fallen world view than one that is more than nominally divine.

While the overt cause of the plague is then an indistinct "act of God" (if the insurance industry treats uncontrollable natural forces as such, certainly survivors of a zombie apocalypse would, as well) the film's underlying apocalyptic cause is fairly straightforward: people are not good. In *Day of the Dead*, most of the human characters are despicable. Even the well-intentioned Dr. Logan (Richard Liberty) is dubbed "Dr. Frankenstein" for his gruesome experiments on the undead—his boundaries between acceptable and unacceptable behavior having been erased by the nightmare he has been living. The distortion of apocalyptic ethics is ubiquitous in the genre, with cannibalism, experimentation, brutality, and the generally inhumane becoming the new norm, rewriting normativity in the exceptional state of apocalypse.

The protagonists of *Day of the Dead* are essentially acting out Sartre's play *No Exit*, with zombies. Forced to live together in an environment where the gaze of the other is the true hell, the denizens of the underground bunker grow to see that their human compatriots are the true monsters. Or, at least, that is how each human in the movie objectifies the others. Dr. Logan is a monster because his experiments are gruesome; he is killed by Rhodes (Joe Pilato) after Rhodes discovers Logan has used soldiers' corpses for his experiments recalling poor Private Mailer in *28 Days Later*, the soldier who is kept as an experiment to see how long it takes to starve a zombie to death. Rhodes is a monster because he appears inhumane and cruel. For his part, he considers Sarah (Lori Cardille), McDermott (Jarlath Conroy), and Dr. Logan as weak and as liabilities to

Bub (Sherman Howard), one of the few sympathetic characters from Romero's *Day of the Dead,* **offers a salute. Thanks to Dr. Logan's (Richard Liberty) unconventional treatments, Bub is able to remember pieces of his former life and enjoy some vaguely human pursuits. Significantly, he retains some emotional connection to Dr. Logan, who feeds him flesh. Logan is eventually killed by Captain Henry Rhodes (Joseph Pilato), a military man, and Bub avenges his death using a pistol—but salutes following the shot, acknowledging Rhodes' rank. Bub's sense of honor despite being undead suggests that Bub might just be more honorable than many of the humans that surround him.**

him and his men—their humanity and compassion make them monsters to him. We see here the inextricable interconnection of the Beings of individuals: "I am possessed by the Other; the Other's look fashions my body in its nakedness.... The Other holds a secret—the secret of what I am" (Sartre, *Being and Nothingness* 340).

Below the surface of the explicit (or implicit, or unstated) cause of the outbreak, and the individual ontological implications of zombie narratives, *Day of the Dead,* like all of Romero's zombie movies, also processes the social anxieties of its era. While *Night* focused on race and Vietnam, and *Dawn* focused on consumerism, *Day* is concerned with feminism, and with racial tensions that, despite two decades of the Civil Rights Act, were still acutely present in Reagan's America. In *Day of the Dead,* the white military elites sit atop the social pyramid, followed by the scientists, then John the civilian, African-American helicopter pilot, and, last but not least, the zombies. This system is reinforced through the frequent use of racial epithets. "Spic," "jungle bunny," "yellow bastard"—the white military grunts in *Day of the Dead* are equal-opportunity bigots. When Bub (Sherman Howard), the "nice" zombie who is one of the movie's more sympathetic characters, shoots Rhodes and then proudly salutes, the viewer is forced to confront the uncomfortable truth that the zombie is more human, or honorable, or humane, than his living counterparts. This destabilization of the expectations of the human, of the humane, is fundamental to the state of apocalypse and its suspension and rearticulation of normative social law.

One of the most significant zombie films of the twenty-first century, *Shaun of the Dead*, is an apparently causeless zombie narrative. No explanation is given for the apocalypse that wreaks havoc across Britain in what Romero referred to as his favorite zombie movie other than his own. Lead actor/writer Simon Pegg credits the earlier film *Resident Evil* as being an inspiration for his homage/send-up, though he had already begun to develop zombie narratives before *Resident Evil*'s debut. In the early-2000s, a number of successful films, including *28 Days Later* (2002), *Resident Evil* (2002), and the *Dawn of the Dead* reboot (2004), thrust zombie movies back into prominence, and *Shaun of the Dead* is both one of these influential films as well as a response to earlier narratives. The film's staying power lies in its ability to deftly appropriate elements of the zombie genre in the creation of a *bildungsroman* (a genre we complicate in our next chapter) centered on the film's eponymous antihero. Shaun (Simon Pegg) is an affable, if immature, underemployed young man who is afraid of commitment and anything else that smells of responsibility. That is, until the zombie apocalypse forces him to face his shortcomings and step up to the challenges of the eschaton. Although the film eschewed the more contemporary fast zombies in favor of the classic shambling zombie, *Shaun of the Dead* is forward-looking. For Max Brooks, *Shaun of the Dead* is the "2nd most important zombie movie ever made because of the social commentary. It encapsulates an entire generation of young English people in the very same way Kevin Smith's *Clerks* did for [the 90s]" (*Doc of the Dead*).

Shaun of the Dead adopts for itself Romero's template of causal anxiety, despite the contemporary prevalence of military-scientific causes in films like *Resident Evil* and *28 Days Later*. Nevertheless, the film, with its closing shots of Shaun and his newly-zombified pal Ed (Nick Frost) playing video games, envisions a world of zombie-human cohabitation. It has this in common with another prominent causeless zombie film from the

Shaun of the Dead, which George Romero disclosed liking nearly as much as his own films, shares a causeless anxiety with many other zombie films. No explanation for the zombie apocalypse is given, or even attempted. However, the film is forward looking in that it envisions a world after the apocalypse has occurred in which humans and zombies live together peacefully. In the shot above, a living Shaun (Simon Pegg) and an undead Ed (Nick Frost) play video games together after the dust has settled.

same era, George Romero's own *Land of the Dead* (2005), and particularly with the later entries: *Fido* and *Warm Bodies*.

In *Land of the Dead*, humankind's ugly side is again on display, as sympathetic zombies fight back for their dignity against the mostly repugnant survivors of a city-state holdout ruled by the megalomaniacal Kaufman (Dennis Hopper). The film is also firmly in the apparently causeless category; the apocalypse is *a priori* in this narrative, and no effort is made to explain its cause. What becomes important, then, is what happens in the story, and how the characters develop and treat one another—much as it was in *Shaun of the Dead* and in Romero's earlier *Day of the Dead*. And, as in *Day*, Romero continues his critique that humans are not a particularly decent bunch. However, by the film's end he goes a step further, foreseeing a future of zombie and human coexistence. The film's protagonist, Riley (Simon Baker), refuses to unleash his arsenal of rockets against the zombies that are streaming into the city. "They're just looking for a place to go, same as us" (*Land of the Dead*). With the reconciliation between humans and zombies, Romero shows himself once again to be an innovator, setting the groundwork for what will become one of the more important themes in zombie narratives over the next ten years: coexistence. Before this theme fully matured, however, a number of films emerged from the relative dearth of zombie films during the 1990s which explored the idea of the zombie apocalypse as the result of military-scientific transgression.

Military-Scientific Overreach

The origins of a military-scientific cause for a zombie outbreak lie, at least in terms of the recent past, in a persistent subgenre of zombie narrative, the Nazi-zombie film. Years before *Night of the Living Dead*, filmmakers were drawing on the real-life horrors of the Third Reich to create stories about Nazi horrors and experimentation run amok, and even these seem to reflect the lingering horror over weapons of mass destruction developed during World War I.[7] The horror of experimentation on humans in a period in which there is no legal protection for persons is incredibly frightening. The apocalyptic debacle that was Hitler's Germany provides a fertile landscape for exploring the implications of science without humanity and of a security state in which law is suspended in favor of individual control. *The Frozen Dead* (1966), *Shock Waves* (1977), *Zombie Lake* (1981), *Oasis of the Zombies* (1982), *Outpost* (2007), *Dead Snow, War of the Dead* (2011), *Dead Walkers* (2013), and *Frankenstein's Army* (2013)— all attest to the fact that, if there's one thing that's creepier than a zombie, it's a Nazi zombie. The cause is nearly always the same: Nazis, either through science or the occult, create an army of the living dead to further their maniacal vision of world domination, much to the chagrin and detriment of a group of attractive and unsuspecting victims. While the cause in these films is, of course, Nazi hubris, these films are in actuality one of several variations on a causal theme of human overreach that lies at the heart of numerous zombie narratives (and whose literary antecedent is Mary Shelley's *Frankenstein: or the Modern Prometheus*).

As Shelley's title implies, the idea that humans might transgress by surpassing or attempting to surpass a human limitation is as old as antiquity—the myths of Prometheus and Icarus being two notable examples, and the aforementioned ancient Israelite story of Adam and Eve reaching beyond their boundary to become like God is another. In zombie narratives, the overreach comes in several varieties, most of which have some overlap with one another. These transgressions are typically militaristic-scientific and/or cultural. Border transgressions inevitably expose shivers in the law, instances in which it begins to appear to be suspended. The *Return of the Living Dead* series, for example, is an early, prominent example of military overreach causing the contagion outbreak, and it is also the franchise that gave zombie lore the trope of zombies as brain-eaters.

The Return of the Living Dead (1985) was based, at least eponymously, on a novel by *Night of the Living Dead* co-author John Russo, and as such it was intended as an alternate sequel (further complicating the provenance of the outbreak in *NOTLD*). We are told in *The Return of the Living Dead* that the source of the outbreak in *NOTLD* was a chemical spill—a defoliant called trioxin, developed by the U.S. Army during Vietnam. This recalls the relatively ambiguous chemical spill in *State of Emergency*, the film opening this text, and the ever cheeky *Planet Terror*, which features a zombie-making militarized gas. The spill in *Night of the Living Dead* sets the stage for a similar catastrophe in *The Return of the Living Dead* once a remaining canister of the stuff is unleashed by a couple of hapless medical supply workers in a warehouse located next to a cemetery.

The Return of the Living Dead was a theatrical success that inspired two immediate sequels and countless imitators. As mentioned, it gave the genre the trope of brains as the preferred zombie delicacy, and it is probably the most iconic to overtly tap into the youth culture of the 1980s. In contrast to earlier zombie films, including Romero's *Dead* series, the *Return of the Living Dead* series focuses on young protagonists. The first film features an ensemble group of teenagers who represent various youth subcultures: there is a new wave kid, some punk kids—the meanest of these, "Suicide" (Mark Venturini) is the group's de facto leader and chauffeur—a hip-hop kid, and two "regular" white kids upon whom the film ultimately focuses. It was also one of the first zombie films to include overt slapstick humor, representative of the over-the-top narrative sensibilities of the 1980s—and which returned in films like *Zombieland* and *Planet Terror* (in which Cherry, Rose McGowan, the female protagonist, loses a leg only to have it replaced by a machine gun). To be sure, *Dawn of the Dead* has its share of humor, but it is darkly satirical, while *The Return of the Living Dead* offers up a Confederate zombie who uses a police cruiser's radio to tell HQ to "Send more cops!" The blend of comedy in a military scientific apocalyptic context offers the possibility of an apathetic response, laughing in the face of danger that characterizes many more recent films.

The Return of the Living Dead 3 (1993), unlike the second unexceptional film, remains one of the most notable zombie films of the 1990s. *ROTLD 3* hearkens back to some of the Gothic traditions of the zombie narrative—as do other 80s and 90s films like Stuart Gordon's *Re-Animator* series (1985–2003) and Peter Jackson's *Dead Alive*. Director Brian Yuzna calls *ROTLD 3* "Romeo and Juliet in Hell" (Jay Slater 25). In *ROTLD 3*, one of the first post–Cold War zombie films, the direct cause of zombification is, as it is in previous *ROTLD* films, trioxin. The military is seeking to use trioxin's resuscitative properties to create a super-soldier (see any Nazi zombie film ever). Curt (J. Trevor Edmond) is an average teenager whose father works for the military outfit in charge of the trioxin experiments. Like many teenage boys, he and his father butt heads. Curt decides to run away with his girlfriend, Julie (Mindy Clarke), but a motorcycle accident derails their plans as Julie dies of a broken neck. Here the movie departs from the narrative arc of earlier *ROTLD* films and instead becomes in essence a variation on the story of Orpheus and Eurydice. Curt braves the world of the dead in order to bring Julie back. Their love, flying in the face of death and contravening natural law, can only invoke the wrath of the gods and bring disorder and upheaval, demonstrating the suspension of the bounds of normalcy. The film shares similar Gothic sensibilities with *Dead Alive* (1992), but in *ROTLD 3*—a film that is more romantic-horror than the romantic-horror-comedy sensibilities of *Dead Alive*—the protagonists do not survive.

Julie also presents an interesting character in zombie narratives, one that foreshadows Milla Jovovich's turn as Alice in the *Resident Evil* franchise. While the film is ostensibly about zombies and the power of love in the face of death, Julie is the film's true focus. "Clarke tries to make the most of her after-death angst [but the film is] little more than a twisted catalogue of fetishistic imagery for horror movie aficionados keen to have a female zombie they can actually find attractive" (Blumberg 314). *Zombies and Sexuality* makes much of the attractive female zombie; clearly fantasy continues to find a home in apocalyptic tragedy.

Nevertheless, the first *Resident Evil* film, in its very opening sequence, bifurcates the role of the Umbrella Corporation, as "9 out of 10 homes contain its products," yet "unknown even to its own employees, its massive profits are generated by: military technology, genetic experimentation, and viral weaponry" (*Resident Evil*). The film locates the ideal associative connection between the military and scientific experimentation, the fantasy of which so often shapes zombie narratives. We implicitly fear a military that controls private sector scientific research, even in films that feature anti-apocalyptic heroes like *Iron Man* (2008).

ROTLD 3 stands at a crossroads of zombie representation, when the familiar trope of government-sponsored causality begins to give way towards a focus on the private sector. Already, the military personnel in *ROTLD 3* are shadowy figures; by the time *ROTLD 4: Necropolis* (2005) is released, the organization responsible is a private corporation, intent on harnessing trioxin's power for their own insidious intent, *à la* the Umbrella Corporation of the *Resident Evil* series. The point is that there is a distinct interest in zombie causality through biological overreach, picked up as a theme in popular culture, which can be independent of or entrenched within military research (as in the work to develop biological weapons, for example).

Military scientific causes continue to matter, as *Scouts Guide to the Zombie Apocalypse* attests with its patient zero referred to as simply D.O.D. The film recalls the experimentation in Will Smith's *I Am Legend* (which emphasizes even more substantially the scientific nature of the cause over that of Matheson's antecedent novel and Heston's intermediate film, *The Omega Man*). *I Am Legend* offers this cause: "Take something designed by nature and reprogram it to make it work for the body rather than against it … in this case the measles virus, which has been engineered at a genetic level to be helpful rather than harmful." The altered virus is a cure for cancer that turns out to cause a zombie disease. *Feed* makes further use of this possibility, with its cures for the common cold and cancer that combine to cause a zombie disease. These texts reiterate Mary Shelley's warning, extended from Victor Frankenstein to his friend Walton (a representative of the listener interpellated into the story): "I will not lead you on, unguarded and ardent as I then was, to your destruction and infallible misery. Learn from me, if not by my precepts, at least by my example, how dangerous is the acquirement of knowledge, and how much happier that man is who believes his native town to be the world, than he who aspires to become greater than his nature will allow" (31). Dr. Frankenstein's is a scientific overreach, in which he discerns the principle of life and learns how to bestow it. The figure that he creates, however, though sensitive like a human, is certainly not human. It is a creature pillaged from the depths of the grave and reanimated to be something less. Shelley, through Frankenstein, encourages readers to be satisfied in the goodness of human nature, to abandon the scientific pursuits that would reveal the secrets of life.

Cultural Transgression

In a similar vein to stepping beyond the roles traditionally ascribed to safe science or the judicious use of power, sometimes zombie apocalypses are initiated by deviation from social norms. In these cases, the basic goodness of human nature is heavily critiqued. Take, for instance, *Dead Alive* (1992): a romance-horror-comedy that relies on Gothic aesthetic and narrative elements such as the supernatural, facing death for love, and a heightened sense of emotion combined with a suppressing tension manifested in the abhorrent use of a lawnmower. Jackson's cinematography and soundtrack add to this exaggerated approach. To heighten the dramatic stakes, there is a strong Oedipal dynamic between the protagonist, Lionel, and his Mum—a classic Freudian love triangle between him, his mother, and his would-be girlfriend, Paquita (Diana Penalver). And it all is the result of a zombie plague outbreak caused by a blatantly cultural transgression, a reach beyond the bounds of cultural expectations that is seen as a violation.

The zombie contagion enters the setting—a 1950s New Zealand society—when a zoologist collects a Rat-Monkey from "Skull Island" (a fictitious place west of Sumatra, incidentally also the home of King Kong), threatening natives with his automatic weapon as they attempt to stop the spread of contagion. Significantly, it is suggested that the contagious monkey arose through the breeding of African slaves and native animals. While the contagion in *Dead Alive* clearly fits the symptoms of an infectious disease (including bursting puss pockets, hemorrhaging, etc.), the subtext is clear and common: this is a disease created directly by humans who have ignored social, cultural, or ethical boundaries in the pursuit of some corrupt purpose. In this case, the catalyst for sparking apocalypse is the impulse to collect that seeks to bring the world under control by gathering one of every creature (or other item) and displaying them safely in the zoo. Many zombie films punish those who reach beyond the capacities of the human. Yet the punishment, rather than punishing transgressive individuals, instead destroys the function of law.

In films such as this, the cause for punishment extends out from individual relationships to breaches of cultural boundaries: the vengeful dead attack those who personally wronged them, or those who broadly transgress a societal norm. In *ROTLD 5 Rave to the Grave* (2005), a new club drug, Z, is responsible for turning the hedonistic youth who consume it into undead, day-glo cannibals (who, in true *ROTLD* fashion, are annihilated by the U.S. military). In *Contracted* (2013), a young woman is date-raped by a man who has had sex with a corpse, and, after suffering a slow and gruesome decomposition, she becomes patient zero in a zombie outbreak. In *Antisocial* (2014), a mind-controlling code is embedded within a social networking app that turns its users into bloodthirsty zombies.

In the earlier revenge narratives, the transgression of the protagonists typically results in a supernatural cause for the resuscitation/contagion, but in each of these later "transgression" films, the cause of the contagion is itself also the cause for the underlying social tension—the explicit and implicit symbolic economies are united. Twenty-first-century Western society is grappling with a number of issues overtly and implicitly reflected in these texts. We are confronting a failed drug war that has seen the use and acceptance of old drugs like marijuana increase as well as the appearance of new drugs like "bath salts" that allegedly turned users into flesh-eating "zombies" (inspiring the 2013 comedy *Bath Salt Zombies*). Alexandra Petri's insightful article, "Zombie Apocalypse: Are Bath Salts to Blame?" expertly identifies the human and human culture as the central problem that we attempt to veneer by suggesting that drugs might sufficiently alter the "real" human to enable apocalyptic behavior. Further, we have not come to full terms with the implications and etiquette of social networking. We are grappling with problems of sexual consent in schools and in the workplace, and with gender and marriage equality. All of these issues are bubbling just beneath the surface of our cultural consciousness, and, increasingly, zombie narratives are being utilized as a means to process these anxieties.

Zombie narratives often reflect society grappling with postmodern cultural pluralism, including non-heteronormative and heterogeneous racial orientations and representations. It is a reframing of the issue of coexistence with the Other, along a continuum of antagonism, from most-antagonistic films like *Zombieland* (2009) to not only peaceful coexistence but sexual intermingling, as in: *Fido, George: A Zombie Intervention* (2009), *Warm Bodies, The Returned* (2013), and *Life After Beth* (2014). These films all depict a fluid line between human and zombie worlds, where characters interact across traditional boundaries and work towards a peaceful resolution of their difference and the reestablishment of social homeostasis. A cultural interest in tolerance has extended toward our zombie kin, and the causes of apocalypse now very often reflect failure to

observe this norm. We have begun to extensively treat apocalyptic iterations as if they are real possibilities, perhaps owing to a combination of
recent threats like mad cow disease and Ebola, and the Žižekian paradox
that we know what we're watching is fake, but we respond as if it were
real, in part because it is real, in that it is a representation of our real conditions of existence.[8]

Whence, then, the causes of undeath? First, the cause of the zombie
contagion itself physically manifests in films proceeding from conceptual
disease surrounding magical control, metaphysical anxiety, extraterrestrial
uncertainty, causal uncertainty or causelessness, military-scientific overreach, and cultural transgression. These categories of zombie causes
describe the genesis of the particular disease, but more significantly, they
offer clues as to the disturbance in the creating culture that raises its dead
as a self-reflection.

The secondary aspect of the cause, that it infects culture to become
apocalyptic, i.e., both revelatory of the problematic that demands attention
and that brings about at least the simulacrum of an end of the world as
we know it, is equally of interest. That we might produce visions of apocalypse indicates a fundamental disturbance that is indicative of a broader
underlying concern: we are living in a state of apocalypse. Seething fear
concerning the loss of self and agency that plagues culture, particularly
in light of the suspension of a system of normative cultural and judicial
law, catalyzes the development of apocalypses within this system. Our
fears ultimately transform disease agents into incurable and massive infec-
tions that destroy social order and the possibility of living together (perhaps of life altogether within our current capitalist, military-scientific,
and juridico-illimited system), ultimately increasing the fundamental
value of a pickaxe as a survival tool. Or perhaps zombie representations
simply document the suspension or dissolution already taking place. As
Sartre observes, "Nothingness lies coiled in the heart of Being—like a
worm…. Man is the being through whom nothingness comes into the
world" (*Being and Nothingness* 22–24). While we may not be able to answer
Shelley's question, "Whence does the principle of life proceed?" we can
certainly address an equally pressing question, "Whence undeath?"—a
meaningful projection of our own drives and fears manifested in zombie
film.

5

Apocalyptic Living
(by Chase Pielak and Fanny Ramirez)

"We're going to have a decision to make..."—Hershel (*The Walking Dead*)

Thus far, we have focused largely on zombies themselves: their role in society, their historical credentials, their taxonomy, and even their origin stories. We have considered zombies so closely because they help us understand what it means to be human. Questions of being dominate zombie texts and film; considering questions of zombie being leads us to consider the nature of our own being, which is ever shaped by and shaping the everyday society in which we live. As zombie apocalyptic representations explore the possibilities of an end of the world as we know it, they shed light on our current state. In this chapter, we shift our focus of analysis somewhat, from the zombie to the *abhuman* and the effects on the human of living in an apocalyptic state. The figure for such a subject, one that exists in an ambiguously apocalyptic state, is the abhuman. "The abhuman subject is a not-quite-human subject, characterized by its morphic variability, continually in danger of becoming not-itself, becoming other" (Hurley 3–4). Descending from Gothic literature, the instability of the abhuman in apocalyptic literature becomes dangerously close to defining not only the zombie body but that of the supposedly human characters as well. Significantly, humans living in an apocalyptic state are similarly in flux, themselves morphic.

To explain: humans within an apocalypse develop in light of that apocalypse. It reflects our fears, corporate and individual, and threatens, inevitably, the possibility of becoming zombie.[1] The apocalypse demands response; if there is no response, the human will cease to be. Further, zombies mirror the humans they pursue; or, put another way, they force humans to mirror them if those humans want to survive. This is, perhaps most fundamentally, the question of the zombie. The ontological question of the posthuman, what humanity might be in the face of the apocalypse, seems to have an answer that is the same as ever: perhaps we have always been posthuman. We are after ourselves, following ourselves, always already approaching ourselves and our species. The apocalypse throws into sharp relief the fact that we live in consideration of our own end.[2]

For Jacques Derrida and Emmanuel Levinas it is the apprehension of death that distinguishes humans from other creatures and establishes irreplaceable singularity. While it may be true that animals can apprehend their own death (and the death of a friend, perhaps), the zombie, that is already ostensibly dead, cannot apprehend its own end; it has ceased to be human. It is inhuman. It cannot sacrifice (itself). This creature is the salve to our wounded status as hierarchically human that has been inaccessible through the closest interactions with animals—the inability to self-sacrifice removes the veneer of closeness to be able to say that even thus, wearing clothes, sleeping in beds, drinking alcohol, and eating filet mignon, Orwell's pigs are not really human; the zombie, though it was once, is now distinctly not human—and therefore unlike my pet dog, who would, without hesitation, sacrifice herself for me. But even among zombies, the rules are not set in stone. For example, R in *Warm Bodies* and Liv in *iZombie* are capable of self-sacrifice and are quite irreplaceably singular. As zombie signification changes, so must the signifier. We increasingly demand of our mirror zombies that they expose our human capacity, precisely because we are focused on our own abhumanity, our own shifting conception of self that has become significantly indistinct.

So how can we consider being human as differentiated from zombie being? How can we say what we are now? This chapter analyzes Carl Grimes, a character growing up in a world in which zombification has become not only a possibility but a certainty. Indeed, this twist on the traditional zombie infection is one of the central innovations of AMC's *The Walking Dead* (*TWD*). Everyone in the world of *TWD* is already infected by the zombie contagion, as viewers finally discover at the end of the second season of the wildly popular show (II.13).[3]

Upon death, the inhabitants of this alternate, walking world will all become zombies as we know them. Returning to Kevin Boon's zombie definition is appropriate for *TWD*'s zombies, which share a common trait: "the original self has been altered in a way that guts its essence" (7). This characteristic is, in fact, precisely what *TWD* calls into question. The show plays with the possibility of becoming zombie, paradoxically in a world in which everyone already is. But the inhabitants of the walking world maintain the essence of their humanity, their agency, the ability to make decisions and a sense of responsibility.

This turning drama foregrounds another drama of agency: that of a young boy coming of age who still seems poised to become the show's hero. Living in light of the reality that the survivors of the walking apocalypse have already become zombies (even if they haven't technically turned yet), in the presence of and in constant confrontation with death as the end of the self, changes the coming of age story, the *Bildungsroman*, into the *Bildungstod*, the story of coming of age into a dead world. What is really at work in the coming of age story is "the integration of a particular 'I' into the general subjectivity of a community, and thus, finally, into the universal subjectivity of humanity" (Redfield 38). Coming of age is about becoming human in community. But in a world in which humanity has already become something other than human, characters must gradually learn to become zombie subjects who nevertheless maintain their essential humanity. The threat of zombie potential is not the simple end of self upon death. Rather the threat is that the self, or some version of the self, will come back ready to destroy the community, to separate the community from its general subjectivity (and life!) and thus humanity itself. The stakes are high for the characters and, by extension, for viewers.

Viewers experience the show from the vantage point of a world in which really actually becoming zombie seems impossible, even though we are inundated with fictional representations of just that. As spectators we engage in a weekly fantasy for an hour before turning back to the "real world" and assuming our daily routines, conspicuously free of zombie attacks. But are we ever really fully removed from the ubiquity of the zombie phenomena? Peter Dendle writes of a "consistently collapsed binary between us and them" occurring in recent representations of zombies in popular culture from movies to Facebook ("And the Dead" 162). Zombie walks, in which people dress up as zombies and shamble *en masse*, are increasingly popular as Sarah Juliet Lauro notes in "Playing Dead: Zombies Invade Performance Art … and Your Neighborhood." Post-apocalyptic zombie videogames such as Telltale Games' *The Walking Dead* adventure game, which won more than 90 "Game of the Year" awards in 2012, and myriads of other games since, continuously rank among the

Over the course *The Walking Dead,* we watch Carl Grimes (Chandler Riggs) grow up as a unique case study in the implications of growing up in an apocalyptic world.

best-selling and highest ranking games. Even police officers are resorting to zombified explanations of criminal acts, as when a man attacked and ate part of another man's face, which Alexandra Petri identifies as seemingly inhuman in her *Washington Post* article "Zombie Apocalypse: Are Bath Salts to Blame?"

The boundary between the walking world and our own is distinctly crumbling. This collapse is twofold between audience and visually portrayed zombie, as much as between the living human and the undead. Inasmuch as zombies always start from this shifting boundary distinction (as ambiguously both human and dead), *TWD* further disrupts the boundary between us and them as its humans are already zombie and yet nevertheless struggle to retain their humanity. Carl Grimes, Rick and Lori's son, specifically mirrors us living in a walking world. He becomes human or zombie or both in a posthuman world. As his character grows up during the seasons of the show, *TWD* participates in a self-construction project that involves the viewer as much as the character.

We, too, have to learn how to live in this walking world that stands in remarkably for our own as we follow the show's progression. It is the present world that has imagined this show into existence, making possible its far-fetched visions for the end of the world. Furthermore, rather than its genre's typical interest in mirroring larger social fears, *TWD's* emphasis on taboo and transgression of normative social expectations leads us to recognize in the *Bildung* project for young Carl a mirror for the viewer who is growing up walking alongside the show's character. *The Walking Dead* demonstrates its transgressions in another set of instances in which normative and legal boundaries have collapsed. To this end, we watch a massacre in a church, the takeover of a hospital by a maniac, the care for a zombie child by the Governor, cannibals, ravaging thieves, and even Morgan's distinctly counter-cultural transformation reshape the walking world over *TWD*'s six seasons.

Carl Grimes is an obvious figure for coming of age in this new reality, one that is by all accounts totally inappropriate for children. Carl's entry into the walking world transitions him from an almost invisible character, constantly lost by his parents (the joke amongst fans signifying his persistent absence had been, "Where's Carl?") to one capable of violence and agency, and specifically of decision making. He confronts the post-apocalyptic world of *The Walking Dead* in every episode, but during the third season this confrontation takes on a new meaning when he is forced to shoot his own mother. Depicting parricide, Oedipal taboo, Carl's action makes explicit that he is working to build himself along the lines perceived as required to grow up into this terrifying and disturbing world. This taboo, following Stefan Horlacher's definition of the term, offers the chance to witness the negotiation of the "values and beliefs" as well as the "borders and power structures" of the post-apocalyptic world of *TWD* (13), and, in turn, our own—the culture that envisioned this possibility. It is in the act of watching a tween boy learn to make decisions in a walking world that we confront our own walking image, the visage of ourselves growing up into a world encountering apocalypse.

Our image in this walking world takes shape as we watch a character developing identity rather than simply fearing its loss. Identity formation in a posthuman world demands engagement with taboo and transgression reconfigured in light of apocalypse. Zombies, of course, engage the taboo of eating human flesh, exemplifying transgressive eating and transforming ordinary human consumption into its appalling cannibalistic cousin. The show explores human eating extensively with the Terminus crew in Season 5. The look on Bob's (Lawrence Gilliard, Jr.) anguished face leaves the viewer disgusted as the Terminus crew eat his leg in front of him, taunting him, "you taste much better than we thought you would." The joy is short lived, though, as Gareth (Andrew West) and company discover that he is "tainted meat." In this apocalypse, for this group, human identity has shifted to that of eaten animal. It's a reality that we are thus forced to imagine—and one in which Carl must live.

The eating of human flesh is not what we expect of those who have not yet become fully zombie; nor is the shooting of one's mother. The remaining human identity, the essence of the self, ought to suitably discipline human characters in line with communal expectations. This is our process. Julia Kristeva's dizzying process of self-creation in light of horror, named abjection, offers a critical lens through which we can read Lori's death. Kristeva could be speaking for Carl when she writes, "'I' am in the process of becoming an other at the expense of my own death. During that course in which 'I' become, I give birth to myself amid the violence of sobs" (2). Carl, by killing his mother, effectively births himself into the walking world.

Reflecting on Carl's character as he grows up walking forces us to consider what makes us human, why we engage in horror (and specifically zombie horror—involving both death and murder), and why fans find Carl such a distasteful character. It also prompts us to plumb the depths of the fears that frame our response to this wildly popular show. There are three story arcs that significantly shape Carl's development as a survivor and influence the audience's reception of his character. Each arc marks a new step in Carl's maturation process and situates the reader in closer parallel with the character, transitioning Carl from overt object to realizing his own agency to finally taking part in the life of the community in the walking world. In many ways, we use Carl as a stand-in for all of humanity, which must contemplate its existence and development in the light of real and imagined apocalypses.

Arc 1: Where's Carl?

This arc begins immediately in the show's first episode. Before we learn much of Rick's character, before we can even process the extent of the apocalypse, we discover that Rick is a father.[4] Carl, his son, is notably absent and an object to be sought during the first several episodes. This resonates with zombie tradition that plagues the family apparatus as a key representative of social order hampered in a post-apocalyptic world. It further echoes Gothic literature as a space in which the family becomes rather a site of domestic disturbance than safety or tranquility. As we witness Rick struggle to find his wife and son, Carl is both a non-entity and everything. Rick identifies the quest for his family as the entirety of his existence, effectively eliding their selves in exchange for the quest itself: "All I am anymore is a man looking for his wife and son. Anybody that gets in the way of that is gonna lose" (*TWD* I.2). Carl's arc shapes the show and its characters immediately.

While Rick was separated from his family and the quest ensued, Shane (Jon Bernthal), Rick's former partner and friend, took over his role in the family both as surrogate father to Carl and as husband to Lori. During this period there was still a sense that normalcy might return, and the audience perhaps believed that if only the family might be reunited, normalcy must surely be on its way. As the family camped in the wilderness with a group of survivors, it seemed still that it might be possible. Then, in the third episode of the show, "Tell It to the Frogs," the family was finally reunited; for a brief time, it seemed as if, even in this crazy world, normalcy had returned.

Almost immediately, however, Rick accepted the de facto mantle of leadership for the group of survivors and was forced to return to the inner city to rescue Merle (Michael Rooker), another group member, whom he had handcuffed to a roof. The family was again fractured, and the viewer's gaze was diverted from the boy in the background to Rick, the action hero, pursuing a last semblance of pre-apocalyptic ethics in the walking world. Nevertheless, Rick's motivation throughout this arc continues to center around Carl who offered a glimmer of hope for survival in the walking world. When, at the end of the season, the group was presented with the opportunity for quick, painless destruction at the CDC, the hope bound in Carl and the drive to maintain his life demanded that the characters continue to live.

In the meantime, viewers recognized that Shane, who stepped in as surrogate father in Rick's absence, continued to share the burden for Carl's education. In effect, Carl briefly had two fathers during the awkward episodes at the end of the first season. This parenting in triplicate helped to inculcate the boy into social expectations, including an apparent demand for worth and agency/autonomy. This excess of parents set Carl up for a perhaps premature adoption of autonomy, opening the next arc.

Arc 2: Carl Lives

The next arc corresponds with the start of Season 2. Carl, finally allowed some autonomy, accompanies his father through the woods as they search for young Sophia (Madison Lintz), who fled the group during a zombie encounter. Appropriately against the backdrop of a churchyard, the group collectively decides to divide to search more effectively. As they part, Carl demands to be included, "I'm going with you. You need people, right, to cover as much ground as possible…" Carl makes an unknowing gesture here, including himself among the group of people, assigning himself the agency necessary to qualify as a full-fledged person. Rick reluctantly agrees to let him come along, "always within our sight, no exceptions" (II.1).

It is worth noting that this conversation takes place alongside a subplot in which Andrea (Laurie Holden) accuses Dale (Jeffrey DeMunn) of taking away her agency by confiscating her pistol when she intends to commit suicide at the CDC. The effect of this juxtaposition, of Andrea losing the means to make decisions while Carl accidentally gains responsibility as a group member, foregrounds human agency and the ability to make decisions that underlies agency.[5] It is also worth noting that Rick reaches his inclusive decision only because another of the children in the group has gone missing and is seen as incapable of surviving on her own. The loss of a group member, while expected, is all the more potent when the lost member is a child who ought to have been protected. The viewer is in effect herself searching alongside the party, demanding to be included alongside Carl, for the sake of spectacle as much as an earnest desire to help the one lost.

As Carl's group of three searches along the river, Carl experiences a moment of wonder at nature. The group comes upon a buck in a forest clearing, and Carl approaches with the smile of discovery. The animal is aware of his presence and stares at him, apparently distracted by his impossibly close presence, only to fall with the boy at the sound of the gunshot that fells them together. While approaching the deer, Carl is accidentally wounded by a member of another group who had been hunting, Otis (Pruitt Taylor Vince).[6] When Otis says, "I never saw him 'til he was on the ground" (II.2) his response to some extent echoes that of the viewer. Carl didn't matter until he was suddenly seen: ready to be visible. It is through his untimely injury, significantly at the hands of another human even during the zombie apocalypse, that the viewer begins to realize his importance as a figure reflecting our own state in this world. He mirrors our pervasive fear of loss of agency and loss of self even as he attempts to come to terms with the trace of beauty retained in the walking world that is so very similar to our own.

Carl's life-threatening wound forces the group into a state of emergency and drives the plot of the show as the group unites with Hershel Greene's (Scott Wilson) family. Interestingly, zombies have virtually disappeared from the beginning of Episode 2, allowing a focus on Carl's drama, but with another significant effect. The viewer is effectively forced to concentrate on saving Carl. As he clings to life, the tenuous hold causes us to reflect upon our own place in this walking world. For Peter Dendle, the zombie figure is situated ideally as a mirror for life ("And the Dead Shall Inherit the Earth" 159). This Lacanian mirroring doubles the viewer. The walking world is, always already, a reflection of our own, in which our fears concerning the lack of agency, the tenuous nature of social norms and expectations, and ultimately the possibility of death, have been realized.

And so it happens that, by the third episode, after surgery has been performed to save young Carl, Rick and Lori have time to reflect on their programmed responses toward life[7]; they discuss—in an aside that incorporates the viewer as a third member of the conversation—whether or not it would have been better to let their boy die. This feels odd for the viewer, who has begun to identify with Carl. That he might be better off dead suggests the possibility that we might also be better off dead. This engages the viewer in the thinly-veiled real-world ethical questions that underlie the show: if we lose the possibility of a stable system of meaning, if we are forced to operate in a world in which we lose agency and responsibility (to others and to ourselves), is it worth continuing to struggle for existence? Is it worth continuing to exist in a state of apocalypse? Put another way, is abhuman existence worthwhile?

Rick's response to the failed grasp for a cure at the CDC comes back to haunt the viewer here; he affirmed life and offered an exhortation to life together and self sacrifice for the other: "there's just a few of us now, so we've got to stick together, fight for each other, be willing to lay down our lives for each other if it comes to that. It's the only chance we've got" (II.1), ultimately suggesting a basis for meaning. This is the new normal established in the walking world and one of the rules to which Carl must be bound in order to come of age. Viewers realize here that we must also come of age in this world. We must be willing to give of ourselves, to give the gift of death, in this world. Jacques Derrida reasons in *The Gift of Death*: "Responsibility demands irreplaceable singularity. Yet only death or rather the apprehension of death can give this irreplaceability, and it is only on the basis of it that one can speak of a responsible subject, of the soul as conscience of self, of myself, etc. We have thus deduced the possibility of a mortal's accession to responsibility through the experience of his irreplaceability, that which an approaching death or the approach of death gives him" (51). One's irreplaceable singularity, the individuality of self, invested by virtue of life (and made evident only by death), is both the key to responsibility and inherently to be preserved at all cost. Sacrifice for life, for the life of the other, can only be possible in light of the anticipation of one's own finitude and that of the other, and this is what the walking world makes plain. Living with this premise in mind paradoxically doesn't cheapen the value of life but instead makes it more potent.

As we engage death, we value the content of life, even as we anticipate our own death and that of the other, with whom we have built community. This affirmation to live remembers the end of the other, the inevitable turn from human to zombie that marks the new end for the characters in *TWD*. The affirmation to live, then, is all the more potent because the characters exist in a world in which they have already died; the characters are already undead, infected with the seed of immortality that will nevertheless absent them from all that constitutes the self that they know. They cling to life, thereby resisting both death and imminent undeath. The life-death trajectory is interrupted (perhaps indefinitely), resulting in a necessarily new set of relations to each other, but which nevertheless foregrounds the need to sacrifice to retain irreplaceability in the face of pervasive death. Thus when Rick and Lori consider whether or not this is a "world for children anymore" the conclusion that "well, we have a child. Carl is here in this world now" becomes all important (II.3).

The reader must wonder alongside Lori about Carl, and inevitably ask the same questions of our own world: "Why do we want Carl to live in this world? To have this life? So he can see more people torn apart in front of him? So that he can be hungry and scared for however long he has before he…. So he can run and run and run and even if he survives he ends up—he ends up just another animal who doesn't know anything except survival?" (*TWD* II.3). Survival is clearly not enough, in *TWD* or in our own walking world. But the show doesn't allow the questions to stand indefinitely. When Carl wakes following the successful surgery, he tells his mother about the deer that he has just seen: "you should have seen it.... The deer. It was so pretty mom. It was so close. I've never been..." (II.3). The boy's gloss over his medical emergency, in favor of childhood wonder, focuses the viewer's attention on the reason for living, effectively answering his mother's uncertainties. After this brief respite, Carl suffers a seizure. Rick again decides to give his own blood, this time against the explicit warning that he "might go into cardiac arrest" (II.3).

The conclusion that life must be preserved, while feeling distinctly foregone, explicitly demands that the viewer accept a new form of life. Here, the anticipation of loss of self increases the value of the time that we have in which to be ourselves. So, Rick's answer to Lori's earlier question: "Why is it better for Carl to live even in this world? He talked about the deer, Lori. He talked about the deer" is both dead-on and dead wrong (II.3). Carl is, shortly, irreplaceably singular; he is a human being, and has come to be despite the prevailing presence of the absence of self. He has come of age into a walking world, in which he will apparently inevitably become zombie, but he is not yet. We are fundamentally hopeful creatures, particularly when considering the possibilities (of coming success, joy, etc.) inherent in the future before children. When this hope is violated, when the life of a child is ended prematurely, we are horrified. The act of letting Carl die would perhaps be one of the most transgressive acts possible for parents in any world, even in one in which the future seems so bleak. Hershel demands a choice, and Rick demands it of Lori, who decides to make the choice to operate. This very impulse resonates across literature that explores what it means to be human; it is precisely what prompts Victor Frankenstein to erupt, in his bleakest moment, with the clinging hope that characterizes humanity even in the face of abjection: "How mutable are our feelings, and how strange is that clinging love we have of life even in the excess of misery!" (Mary Shelley 119).

At the same time, Carl's near-death scene furthers the shift in viewers' identification from almost exclusively with Rick to a growing affinity with Carl, who is during this period utterly helpless to bring about much of anything, let alone hope in a zombie-afflicted world.[8] This near-death experience changes Carl's attitude towards the world. He suddenly becomes more aware of his own mortality and that of those in his community.

When he finally recovers from his nearly fatal injury, Carl again begins to participate more fully in the life of the group. He grows bolder and is determined to help in the continuing search for Sophia. After he is discovered to have stolen a pistol from the group's RV, he pleads his case: "I'm not gonna play with it, mom. It's not a toy. I'm sorry I disappointed you, but I want to look for Sophia and I want to defend our camp. I can't do that without a gun" (II.6). Carl surely speaks honestly when he argues that he will not play with the weapon, but he has already been deceitful in his attempts to cover up the theft. The ability to deceive (or at least to selectively reveal) is a critical skill and one indicative of agency. In an atmosphere of fierce competition for scarce resources and constant threat from hostile neighbors, it is incumbent upon the one intending to survive to deceive liberally. At any rate, Rick and Lori relent after much deliberation about the state of the world and Carl's relative readiness for the responsibility of handling the weapon, and he is allowed to attend shooting practice with the group.

This begins his somewhat more autonomous operation in the walking world, as he is now about to defend the group and accompany the adults on patrol as they search for Sophia. Holding a weapon is a key point of membership in the group, and weapons are distributed as surrogates for potency, and thereby agency, repeatedly throughout the show, perhaps most notably to Andrea. In Episode II.3, for example, Dale hands Andrea back her weapon that he's been holding to divest her of the power to take her own life, acknowledging her regained right to agency.

The ability to hold a weapon, to hold life and death in one's hands, marks the beginning of a key turn for the show, though Carl has yet to appreciate the possibilities inherent in his newfound potency. The show takes a marked turn toward communal development both as they work to reform a new family structure while living at Hershel's farm, and as they consider the appropriate structure for rules governing entrance into and maintenance of the community. During this period, unfortunately, Carl frees a walker who later attacks and kills Dale (II.11). This event is immediately preceded by the capture of a youth, Randall (Michael Zegen), from a rival group, and a discussion amongst the group members about the relative ethics of putting their prisoner to death. This early scene is echoed in later episodes both during stays at the prison and through the Morgan subplot while the group rebuilds another family structure in Alexandria.

In arguing with Rick that the prisoner should not be put to death, Dale makes the connection for the viewers: "You think about your son. The message that you're giving him. Shoot first think later. I'm asking for one day to talk to everybody. You can give me that. Think about Carl" (II.11). Rick relents, but the discussion is what matters; the group is up in arms about the new rules, about the possibility of "keeping humanity" in light of this walking world. Killing an unarmed prisoner is certainly taboo in this world as well as that of the show. And yet, the group is threatened by anyone who can lead hostile rivals to the camp. Shane is worried that everyone is going to "pussy out" and relent, to let the youth live. This question of what it means to be human and to play by the rules establishes community commonly bound together. The presumption of law has already deteriorated and the group is fracturing around the prisoner precisely because his presence foregrounds the absence of law and the need to rewrite the rules. "If we do this, [Dale says], we're saying there's no hope, rule of law is dead, there is no civilization" (II.11).

Dale's final exhortation before storming out, "please, let's just do what is right," turns the group toward finding another way than execution, but he never witnesses the move; on leaving he says, "this group is broken" (II.11). This break has been evidenced most clearly, perhaps, when Carl enters the execution scene and says to his father, brandishing his weapon at the kneeling prisoner, "Do it, dad, do it" (II.11). This is the final straw before the prisoner's attempted release. Rick is horrified that his son "wanted to watch" (II.11). The viewer feels that perhaps Carl is headed toward becoming blood thirsty rather than a functioning member of the community; perhaps Shane's role as surrogate father has been more influential than Rick's leadership. It is at this point that Dale meets the walker freed by Carl and is overcome. The guilt over causing another character's death (and apparently imagining Dale as a stand-in for his father), and over his own inability to pull the trigger to kill the walker, causes Carl to reflect much more significantly on his own ability to shoot a walker—and more generally on the value of life and community in the post-apocalyptic world.

Arc 3: Life Together

It was this development and corresponding reflection that ultimately allowed Carl to grow up in the walking world. The culminating act, which began his final and present developmental arc, specifically allowing him to become a fully participative subject, was the scene in which he shot his mother to prevent her from turning. A few episodes into the third season of *TWD*, Lori's long pregnancy had finally reached its conclusion. As she prepared to deliver the baby within the assumed safe confines of the prison, zombies attacked, forcing everyone to take cover and trapping Carl with his mother and Maggie away from the rest of the group. During a heart-wrenching goodbye scene, Carl's mother reminded the viewer of the young hero's incredible perseverance and indirectly asked him to make the right choice, the humane decision of ending her life to prevent zombification from happening: "You are gonna beat this world. I know you will. You are smart, and you are strong, and you are so brave, and I love you…. You gotta do what's right, baby. You promise me, you'll always do what's right" (III.4). Shortly thereafter, Lori became unresponsive and had an emergency C-section (in a profoundly unsterile environment). After having delivered the baby, Maggie turned around to get ready to leave the boiler room. Her behavior seemed to indicate that Lori was beyond saving and the survival of the baby became the priority. This is when Carl stepped in and stated "We can't just leave her here. She'll turn…. She's my mom" (III.4).

Lori appeared doomed, even though Hershel could conceivably have been within reach and it is not out of the question that she could have survived (we had watched Carl survive a seemingly fatal wound, after all, though Carl himself did not get to witness his own miracle cure). Nevertheless, Carl made the decision to end her life with Maggie's pistol rather than risk the possibility that she might turn and finally, fully become zombie. So, recognizing that she was at least likely to die, and critically before her eyes opened again, Carl determined to take a preemptive shot. Shooting his mother was no simple response out of terror. It was no preprogrammed response, but a decided action, explicitly not out of fear as a reaction, but a decision.

This depiction interestingly reverses that in George Romero's *Night of the Living Dead* which iconically features a little zombie girl, Karen, preparing to eat her mother after murdering her with a trowel (see Zani and Meaux 103). Whether the audience identifies with the heroic leader, Ben (who is ostensibly mistaken for a zombie at the end of the film and shot by a militia), the catatonic Barbra (who is carried off and presumably eaten), Tom or Judy (who are burned alive), or the isolationist Harry (Karl

Hardman) and family (who are finally ended by Karen), no character with whom we might identify is allowed to survive the advent of apocalypse.

This contrasts sharply with *The Walking Dead*, which, as a serialized show, must incorporate characters with whom the audience can identify and engage to keep viewers involved with the show. However, there is a further and more subtle need for a Carl in the walking world. We cannot accept the premise that there could be no identifiable survivor in a walking world as it seems more and more to reflect our real conditions of existence. Carl's act of shooting Lori, though shocking and disturbing, is a sign of his humanity in this apocalyptic and cruel world, and the act marks the culminating point of his coming of age journey even as it recognizes the inherent possibility of living in a walking world in a way that was not really possible to imagine when Romero began his franchise.

It is the turn of an ultimately transgressive act, the engagement with exemplary taboo, and not his engagement with emotion that causes Carl to finally become a part of the walking world, to enter into community fully and completely, to mirror our own entry in the walking world. Through the final disintegration of social expectations that had held the world together before the apocalypse, and the establishment of new social norms governing the expectations for life together (i.e., that one will sacrifice for the life of the community), Carl enters the community as a participating member and allows us to finally grow up walking alongside him.

The audience cannot help but to question logically and emotionally the decision-making process involved in shooting one's own mother. For Kristeva, the mother is "the object that guarantees my being as subject" (32) and "the border of my condition as a living being" (2). In ending his mother's life, Carl distances himself from her parental control and puts on the mantle of subjective agency; he becomes fully human through this decision act. It takes a few episodes before the extent of his actions truly sink in. For a while, Carl is in a surreal state; two episodes after the event, as the reality of his decision sets in, he confesses to Daryl, "I shot my mom. She was out, hadn't turned yet. I ended it. It was real" (III.6). In this arc the community itself coalesces around a new set of social values, a new set of walking rules, to allow its new hero to participate in community with those who would be dead.

It has been said that the zombie genre is intrinsically about depersonalization.[9] Yet it seems that *The Walking Dead* is in many ways about the personalization of those we once knew as zombies. Carl becomes human and we become human alongside him, in part because of the gift of death (the willingness to sacrifice life for the other and the pressing apprehension of the death of the other) and in part because of engagement with taboo as a reformulation of or toward the purpose of reformulating communal rules which occurs in light of the zombie apocalypse. This ongoing shaping, this desire to come of age, is, furthermore, why we watch *The Walking Dead* and shows that are like it. We want and need to become ourselves. It is the walking world that allows us to do so. So, the answer to the question "Where's Carl?" has been staring us in the face all along: Carl is right here, every time we look in the mirror.

The shifting of identity implicit in the walking world finds its answer in instability, even as it attempts stability through interaction with transgression. This is one means by which the show attempts a possible cure for the apocalyptic state: it rewrites the rules for life repeatedly, even though there may or may not ever be a proper cure. The act of rewriting, of becoming self in an apocalyptic world, serves as all the cure needed. Nevertheless, the search for a cure—actual and metaphoric—continues to drive the show and its apocalyptic ilk.

6

Curing the Apocalypse

I think we are in rats' alley
Where the dead men lost their bones.
—T. S. Eliot

A vital subset of zombie films and texts fixate on the possibility of curing the zombie apocalypse, and many more contain elements of the cure. These cures often take one of three shapes. A cure may directly reverse the effects of the zombie contagion on either the infected or uninfected. It may act as a prophylactic to keep the uninfected (or less infected) from developing the full range of symptoms. Or, a cure may they recreate society in a way in which both human and zombie plague can coexist— in other words, curing the world rather than the contagion itself.

In each manifestation, the apocalypse takes place in a state of exception in which the world, under a sovereign agent, operates outside governmental and social law. Yet despite the apparent efforts to subvert catastrophe, the cure for the zombie contagion requires reproducing— and thus affirming—the pre-apocalyptic power systems in the absence of law that led to the state of exception. The cure brings humanity full circle: it reproduces the ideological conditions that created and spread the zombie contagion in the first place. Considering the cure to the zombie apocalypse, no matter what form it takes, demonstrates how the state of exception has become the rule, which explains, in part, our horrified fascination with representations of the zombie apocalypse, particularly when focused on the cure.[1] Here, as we have throughout this book, we hone in on exemplary representations of apocalyptic cures as pursued in *Fido*, *World War Z*, *I Am Legend*, *The Omega Man*, *Warm Bodies*, and AMC's *The Walking Dead*. Taken together, these cures flesh out the shape and practices for curing the apocalypse. These representations can then be used as a guide to consider the myriad other cure shapes that appear.

The creator of a world populated with zombies has complete control in shaping this world. However, this presents a problem. This world is necessarily shaped from real events which furnish the raw materials of imagination; the cure manifests in this infected world which reflects our own in order to fix it. Zombies in this world paradoxically take away the possibility of knowability and this is precisely what makes them so dangerous and so terrifying, necessitating the fix. We can know them entirely; there is fundamentally no possibility for them to surprise us since they have lost the essence of self; they can exist only as a product of our overlaying our own consciousness on them. We cannot accept the demise of the other as such, the possibility of the other, that maintains an unknowability outside of the self. This is the essence of life, perhaps, that it can operate outside the confines of the observer. Zombies exist without any real alterity—they are coextensive with the ends of the self and they do not go beyond the self. They are other only in the sense that they are not "me." This terrifying possibility causes the need for a cure; we cannot allow this position to persist. In many ways this is the inevitable response to the abhuman as raised in the last chapter.

The State of Exception and Reproduction of the Apocalypse

The key element of the state of exception is that it exists outside the force of law. Law is not absent, but rather empty (Agamben 48). It lacks power, reach, and force, and the world exists outside its boundaries. This is anomie. The pure violence of apocalypse films "neither makes nor preserves" law (60). Apocalyptic violence represents both human desire and the inability to assimilate the world as we find it.

When a cataclysmic apocalypse begins, humans typically embrace taboo and engage in murder, looting, theft, riot, rape, and exploitation.[2] Centuries of private property laws collapse, the notion of ownership degenerates into whatever one can defend, and traditional ideas of morality decay, though bands of humans may still adhere to certain moral codes; Daryl (Norman Reedus) poignantly engages this in *The Walking Dead* Season 4 Episode 15 when Daryl and Len (Marcus Hester) fight over a rabbit and the need to "claim" property. In the episode argument over the half rabbit necessitates death. Hobbes' "state of nature" is enacted and it becomes a state of war (see Section xiii). For those infected, this state of exception is even more intense. Zombies entirely transcend the bounds of governmental and moral laws: they cannot show restraint. They are infected with taboo compulsions to kill and consume flesh; they are no longer alive and therefore unable to resist inhuman impulses.[3] This exceptional state is characterized by both the living and undead reaching beyond their potential. In transcending these boundaries, human and zombie alike reach beyond the borders of written and natural law to become what is sovereign, above the law.

A zombie apocalypse, cataclysmic or not, is catastrophic because the human is conflated with the sovereign; a cure, by its very nature, must untangle this confusion. The cure, then, is the cure for the boundlessness that blends the self and the other while producing subjects not subject to the law. Therein lies the horror of zombie films: for humans, it is the powerlessness over the circumstances that surround them. For the undead, it is powerlessness to change the new reality of their existence. A cure seems so hopeful because it resolves this powerlessness and fixes the state of exception. Paradoxically, however, the search for the cure is doomed to fail because it necessarily takes place within the same system that brought about the apocalypse in the first place. The corrupted human is both the impetus for the apocalypse and a bankrupt savior for its redemption. In other words, survivors who retain their humanity seek to cure the apocalypse through a reification of the processes of humanity.[4] If, for instance, science causes the apocalypse, it is science to which survivors turn for a cure. The cure is therefore an Althusserian nightmare of inescapable ideological reproduction.

The search for a zombie cure, then, is a thinly veiled search for a cure for the state of exception in which we find ourselves, which is caused by some overreach beyond our natural state. We pursue the cure in zombie representations through the use of subjects that no longer function as subjects because they have reached beyond predetermined boundaries, become exceptional, and in so doing have lost self-control. And as apocalyptic survivors chase salvation through science, bureaucratic management, or government control, they do so with some positivist faith in the triumph of human knowledge, which is destined to fail since they are not pursuing the cure for our overreach beyond conditions of existence. Even when the cure represents triumph of the possibility of the human, reaffirming love, hope, family, or order, it only reinscribes an ideological system that reproduces the conditions of the beginning of the disease.

Considering the state of exception and the cure, then, helps us understand both the extent and importance of the apocalypse. The apocalyptic representations we address, beginning with AMC's *The Walking Dead*, share the premise that there is a cure for the apocalypse, and this possibility is, at least to some extent, achieved. These share a myopic focus on transcendent individuals who remake present power structures and live in this state of exception. The survivors rely upon the unstated understanding that the conditions that created the apocalypse—whether embodied in human relations or a traditional government—will deliver them to its cure. Yet such solutions only recreate the conditions that enabled the apocalypse in the first place, even when they succeed in providing what appears to be a cure. And when cures do succeed, they must rely upon forces different than those that brought about the apocalypse in the first place.

The Walking Cure

Rick, primary protagonist of *The Walking Dead* and the *de facto* leader of one band of survivors, is a sheriff's deputy, an embodiment of the state authority that has collapsed before the zombie hordes. Rick seeks to protect a group of survivors by clinging to the trappings of state authority that surrounded his former station, in effect seeking to cure the apocalypse by remaking society. First, he colludes with Hershel to create an idyllic new society amid Hershel's sprawling farm, and later fortifies his society of survivors within the confines of a prison, before most recently appropriating the fortified town of Alexandria. In each case, the survivors struggle to create order and rudimentary government that is often tribal in nature, relying on norms rather than institutions but nevertheless capable of structuring interpersonal relations and creating predictability in behavior; in each case, Rick emerges as the key leader. Yet these new governments fail because this assumption of power is inevitably an overreach of authority. Rick's rise to power in the farm society ends with conflict between himself and a jealous Shane, ultimately arousing nearby zombies and forcing the survivors to retreat. And by stubbornly anchoring himself to the prison, Rick incites the ire of the Governor, who eventually penetrates the prison walls as an archetypical human conqueror; the war destroys this second government by attracting the zombie horde and eliminating natural defenses. Alexandria is somewhat more complicated, as it is already governed and its apparent demise comes not from zombies but from other humans, but the principle is the same. Rick is thrust into leadership as something more than a man; he becomes the decision-maker, a center of society, and a key player in remaking social order. But this rebuilding and centralization of power only recreates the governmental conditions that, apparently, enabled the apocalypse to occur in the first place—these social/societal cures do not cure humanity's overreach and thus they do not deliver humanity from the jaws of doom.

The Governor's iteration of the cure works in a similar fashion, with one crucial point of departure. Whereas Rick was an embodiment of state authority, the Governor was a clerical employee, exemplifying bureaucratic management rather than coercive power. But he too is destined to reinscribe the conditions that created the apocalypse as he searches for a cure. After all, it was not authority alone that sparked the apocalypse; clearly, there were bureaucratic failures at some level as the contagion spread.[5] Nevertheless, the Governor adopts the moniker and methods of the pre-apocalyptic state in extremis. He fortifies his own encampment in Woodbury, creates his own heavily armed military/police force that reports to him as sovereign, engages in wholesale slaughter of all possible threats, and covertly inserts himself into every decision in the life of the group he leads. It is hard to see how the Hilltop will prove any different. Even after the Governor's first group is disbanded or murdered (many of them at his hands) at the end of Season 3, he coalesces a new group during Season 4 and leads yet another brutal attack on the prison that finally ends his life even as it destroys the prison. That this second group has been convinced to attack the innocents in the prison is a clear extension of the state of exception at work in the walking world. The Governor's answer to the walking world repeats consuming-violence.

The Walking Dead also repeatedly engages the possibility of a biological cure. In episode "TS-19," Rick's first group of survivors arrives at the CDC to find one remaining man. Dr. Jenner (Noah Emmerich) explains, "Well, when things got bad, a lot of people just left. Went off to be with their families. And when things got worse, when the military cordon got overrun, the rest bolted.... Many could not face walking out the door. They 'opted out.' There was a rash of suicides. That was a bad time" (*TWD* Season 1). When asked why he stayed, Jenner responds, "I just kept working, hoping to do some good." He has, by the time the group arrives, decided instead to end his own life with the building, which is set to self-destruct, and does so imminently. Jenner, drowning in hopelessness, is barely convinced to let the survivors out of the CDC before it explodes. The survivors had hoped that the science, doctors, and the bureaucratic arm of the state would offer them a cure for the disease, but this hope proved to be bankrupt; this catastrophe effectively ended the pursuit of the medical cure in the show. Worse still, the search for the supposed cure nearly killed the remaining survivors. In seeking to tame the contagion and exert their sovereignty, the group both failed to find salvation and nearly stumbled into its own demise. Of course this process is echoed when Eugene Porter (Josh McDermitt) promises a cure if he is only safely transported to Washington, D.C. Again, hope for the cure proves unnecessarily risky and bankrupt when Eugene is revealed as a sham.

The Legendary Cure

In the relatively recent film *I Am Legend* (2007), Colonel Robert Neville (Will Smith), a doctor, searches for a cure for the infected Hemocyte/zombies. At the film's start, Neville clearly regards zombies as subhuman—subjects to be cured or eliminated. He summarizes the conditions of the infected world in the film: "There were 6 billion people on Earth when the infection hit. KV had a 90 percent kill rate. That's 5.4 billion people. Dead. Crashed and bled out. Dead. Less than 1 percent immunity. Left 12 million healthy people like you, me, and Ethan. The other 588 million turned into your dark seekers. Then they got hungry. And they killed and fed on everybody. Everybody. Every single person that you or I have ever known is dead. Dead."

Neville heartbreakingly asserts that everyone else in the world is dead. His repetitions of "dead" and "everyone" highlight his perceived dichotomy between human and inhuman, a line that is, in reality, much more blurred than his traumatized mind believes. Nevertheless, these beliefs zealously motivate his relentless pursuit of a cure. And he is relentless; there is nothing left for him except for the cure.

Neville's rank and actions suggest that he is, or believes himself to be, both a doctor and an agent of government authority. He is an embodiment of the forces that created the plague, which mutated during clinical trials to cure cancer. In other words, the zombie hordes were created by

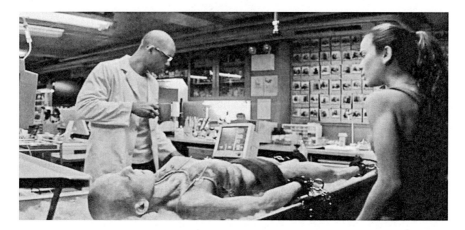

In *I Am Legend*, Colonel Robert Neville (Will Smith) works constantly to find a cure for the zombie infection. His methods are typical of the very conditions that created the plague in the first place: the scientific method, experimentation, and the use of conventional laboratory tools.

botched medical science.[6] Thus the cure-plague proves to be an overreach of our domain as humans and an appropriation of the sovereign—as Neville explains to Anna (Alice Braga), another miraculous survivor, "God didn't do this, Anna. We did."

Despite this sideways clarity, Neville's attempts to cure the plague utilize our traditional understanding of science: scientific method, positivist note-taking, experimentation, and labwork. Like the survivors in *The Walking Dead*, Neville is struggling to cure the plague using the very tools and conditions that created it. Blithe to his own miraculous immunity to the disease, he is caught in the human trap of being unable to recognize his exceptional nature and therefore doomed to repeat the same mistakes. Just as the act of curing diseases proves to be an appropriation of the sovereign, Neville's own insistence on "curing" the zombies proves to be an overreach of his own authority and his ultimate demise: a microcosmic recreation of the disaster itself and a restatement of the fundamental problem that dooms humanity when occupying a state of exception. Neville, like humanity, overreaches. And like humanity, he pays the price.

At the close of the film, he does find a cure (derived from his own sacrificed blood) that appears to work on a test subject but must sacrifice himself to ensure that Anna and her son Ethan (Charlie Tahan) can carry this cure to safety. Anna's closing monologue (and indeed her ability to deliver it) suggests that the cure does succeed: "Dr. Robert Neville dedicated his life to the discovery of a cure and the restoration of humanity. On September 9, 2012, at approximately 8:49 p.m., he discovered that cure. And at age 52, he gave his life to defend it. We are his legacy. This is his legend. Light of the darkness." Neville essentially undertakes to give the gift of death, his own, for the sake of those who evidently need the cure. This is an example of an agent of government reaching beyond the individual human in order to benefit the collective good, attempting to cure the overreach of human potential through another overreach of human potential.

Furthermore, we might note that the cure succeeds due to Neville's miraculous nature (his incredible immunity) and not science at all: the cure was the product of *legend*, not *science*. Anna feels compelled to attribute salvation to some exceptional force. The cure is born from different conditions than those that created the disease: something inherent to Neville himself, the act of sacrifice, the building of a legend, and the creation of a legacy. Nevertheless, the cure is only made possible through experimentation on the dark seekers, which are revealed to be more-or-less human.

Neville's final test subject, the one that is returned to near-human conditions, is the object of a rescue mission organized by the zombie leader, certainly a human-like decision and process. Neville's experimentation, therefore, has been taking the lives of a new kind of citizen deemed less worthy of life. His scientific method repeats the exceptionally lawless state through which the United States government made possible the colonization of the American West and numerous other colonial possessions. Neville finds a miraculous cure through the processes of science because he operates in an exceptional state and forces those around him to engage as well. He becomes the force beyond control to which the world must submit. He is more than a man; he is beyond the laws of man. He is legend.

Despite Neville's self-sacrifice and apparent sovereignty, the film implies that the dissemination of the cure will require further recreating of traditional power structures. It is not clear who controls the survivors' colony at the end of the film, though Anna is met with armed guards who open a substantial protective gate. One can only imagine the continued legal morass that will characterize the rollout of the cure. And of course the newly cured people will need a government to step into the power vacuum. Yet we do not know the nature of the armed men or the society beyond the gates. Might another Governor await? The film is silent on such darker points, but it is virtually impossible to imagine that the state of exception might end despite the existence of the cure as humanity's overreach continues into law and government.

While Anna's arrival at the safe survivor's colony and Neville's sacrifice are wonderful fodder for a movie-going audience that despises disappointment, the alternate ending is particularly interesting. In it, Neville actually realizes that the zombies have *evolved* rather than *devolved* and voluntarily decides to remove the cure from the infected test subject and returns her to the dark seekers. In return, the dark seekers reluctantly allow Neville to keep his life. If Neville symbolizes humanity's last hope amid this state of exception, this resolution suggests that survival is as simple as ceasing to play god. In this ending, Neville recognizes that he has sought to cure something that ought not to be cured—he surrenders, terminating his participation in the state of exception and disavowing his claim to legend, and in return is permitted to persist.

The Omega Cure

The Omega Man (1971) features an earlier incarnation of Neville (Charlton Heston) who even more explicitly reaches beyond the ends of human potential in his attempts to save humanity. The premise is familiar. Here, the state of exception is sparked by science: the zombie apocalypse sprouts from biological warfare between China and the United States. Humanity's overreach, exemplified by mastery over biological agents, is again its downfall. The plague transforms human beings into pseudo-zombies tortured by light who are figuratively dead but nevertheless able to speak, think, and organize; their society is crude but permeated with ideology and ritual. Most notably, they despise and repudiate science, the very force that brought about their transformation. In Los Angeles, these creatures are organized into a collective known as "The Family."

Neville is a doctor and Army Colonel,[7] an embodiment of the *ancien régime* and implicit agent of the now-defunct national authority, who spends his days hunting The Family and his nights holed-up on the top floor of a heavily-fortified apartment building. His existence is a constant state of war with The Family: each views the other as disease to be purified.

Robert Neville (Charlton Heston) lies dead in a water-fountain, his speargun having failed him. Note the religious imagery and similarity to depictions of Christ.

Yet despite his apparent charge, he recognizes that he exists in a world beyond the law, as he ironically comments in the film's opening line, "There's never a cop around when you need one."

Like the other protagonists in search-for-the-cure-films, Neville searches for a cure using the ideological devices that created the apocalypse in the first place. He acquires immunity himself through experimentation, and later manages to cure Richie (Eric Laneuville), who has been infected but who has not fully become a member of The Family. Richie returns to Matthias (Anthony Zerbe), The Family's leader, and advocates utilizing the cure to revert society back to its old form. Richie states, "he's got a serum for what's wrong with you.... Everybody could be normal again." In effect, Richie is arguing for using science to terminate the state of exception.

But Matthias rejects this cure. He refutes the idea that the previous world—the one that Neville and Richie regard as normal—was better than the apocalyptic one. Matthias executes Richie, and later explains to Neville: "none of it was real. It was illusion. Your art, your science: it was all a nightmare, and now it is done, finished." Matthias directly rejects the notion that the ideological conditions that created the apocalypse could be used to help its offspring. The inevitable failure of science to cure the apocalypse is symbolized in Neville's final struggle with The Family, wherein his mechanical speargun jams and he is impaled by a single, hand-held wooden projectile.

In the film's epilogue, Neville does manage to transfer the cure to a small band of survivors, giving hope for the old world. However, his resting position, spear-pierced in a water-fountain, takes the shape of a crucifixion with mingled blood and water around him reminiscent of that from Christ's side. In order to finally impart the cure, he does not reinscribe the ideological conditions that brought about the state of exception but becomes something else—a savior—which is only possible because he sacrifices himself. He becomes the culmination of government and science, a piece of mythology, beyond the scope of positivist science, beyond the scope of human government and exception. A legend.

The Economic Cure

Fido (2006) offers an entirely different notion of the cure that nevertheless adheres to the state of exception propagated in other cure representations. In this comedic film, there is a return to mid-century America, with a key post-apocalyptic difference: space radiation has reanimated dead bodies. Cities operate as fortified safe zones amidst an otherwise infested world, thanks to Zomcon, the massive company responsible for the manufacture and maintenance of collars that control the walking dead and the perimeter fence. Zomcon is literally presented as a "savior." Capitalism seems to be responsible for this particular state of exception, and the controlled zombies return to society to perform productive roles (ranging from landscapers to house servants to girlfriends). Zomcon helps people "become productive members of society even after [death]" and upholds the stated goals of safety and containment until a full-scale breach of the "wild zone" demands a full-scale violent response.

Quickly regaining control, Zomcon evidently overlooks the relationship shared between Fido (Billy Connolly) and the aptly named and newly single—thanks to the death of her husband—Mrs. Robinson (Carrie-Anne Moss) who evidently share a child. At least within the world of the film, and until his death, Zomcon's chief security officer, Mr. Bottoms (Henry Czerny), has ultimate power. He is responsible for the life and death of the citizens in the town and decides when citizens get to stay in the town apparently at whim. Strangely, Fido, the titular zombie, a servant to Timmy Robinson (Kesun Loder) and family, retains enough humanity to choose who to eat—even when his collar fails to control him. The cure in this film, therefore, returns zombies to productivity even while not altering their condition, and returns society to stasis outside the performance of the law. It is effectively an economic cure for death in an exceptional world.

The Warm Cure

In *Warm Bodies* (2012), another zombie retains vestiges of humanity while seeking a cure that is, ultimately, successful. The film begins with a character recognizable as a zombie, R, who criticizes himself: "What am I doing with my life?... I should stand up straighter. People would respect me more if I stood up straighter. What's wrong with me? I just want to connect. Why can't I connect with people? Oh, right. It's because I'm dead." While angst is certainly not unusual for a late teen, this simple gesture destabilizes the traditional zombie understanding: a shuffling shell pur-

In *Warm Bodies*, Julie (Teresa Palmer) and R (Nicholas Hoult) struggle to achieve a tender, loving relationship despite him being a zombie and eating human brains. Unlike many other zombie films, *Warm Bodies* allows for the possibility of friendship and even love between zombies, and much of the film's narrative is centered on the struggle to retain humanity even while flesh decomposes. This idea is highlighted by R's eloquent internalized monologues, which contrast sharply to his brief, monosyllabic ability to speak.

A zombie bonie from *Warm Bodies*. These creatures have lost all traces of humanity save their shape.

suing one desire, eating flesh, gutted of the essence of the self. R specifically retains self, as evidenced through self-consciousness. It is this that enables us to watch the movie as told through the lens of a zombie protagonist.[8] The zombie disease evidently preserves R rather than destroying him. When he dies he does not end. Instead, his self continues in partially zombified form. The cure in this film takes the shape of self-fulfillment, of a restoration of hope for the human and, by extension, the human held within the zombie.

R lives with hundreds of other zombies in an airport. Over time, the films' zombies eventually lose hope and become "bonies," more traditional zombies. R has a love interest in the film named Jules. Her father (John Malkovich), who is essentially old man Capulet, leads the surviving humans. He has produced and leads through a hierarchical governmental structure in which he has authority over the extent of the law and is essentially outside the law. Jules says of her father (Colonel Grigio): "Dad's idea of saving humanity is to build a really big concrete box, put everyone in it, and then wait at the door with guns until we grow old and die." The fantasy that these conditions are caused by the zombie apocalypse rather than preexisting the apocalypse is a part of the film's subtext that never emerges. Perhaps it cannot. Yet the technology of enclosure, such a common theme amongst these films, is the technology of control that enables the state of exception to occur. In the name of safety and protection from the zombie outside, survivors are walled in and power becomes absolute—and absolutely outside the exercise of law.

The film's version of the cure is the retention and the return of memories brought on through love. When R dreams, Jules says, "I think someday someone's going to figure out this whole thing and exhume the world … to revive." This is both the human fantasy and that of the semi-zombie (called a corpse in the movie) in *Warm Bodies*. When, at the end of the film, R sacrifices himself to save Jules' life, he has again finally become human. This is an interesting twist on Derrida's idea of the gift of death, the means of human responsibility and life itself. R dives out a door with Jules on top of him intending to cushion her fall. Falling into a pool, they surprisingly manage to survive together. On resurfacing, R is quickly shot by Jules' father, despite his recovery. Even while Jules' moving exhortation that "we can fix all this" documents the hope of the cure, the blood gushing out of R's gunshot wound paradoxically proves his return to life. R comments, of his exemplary return to life, "the rest of us, well, we kind of learned how to live again. For a while it seemed that a lot of us forgot what that meant." The remaining bonies are quickly dispatched by the collective forces of the humans and corpses.

While the cause of the zombie apocalypse is never explicitly stated in the film, the distinction between the humans, corpses, and bonies highlights its crucial element: humanity is defined by the ability to connect with and love others. Colonel Grigio's cure—to box everyone up with guns at the doors—fails because it refuses to embrace human relationships. Instead, the cure for the apocalypse—the force that brings corpses back to life—takes place outside the bounds of the forces that enforce the apocalypse. The film, for this reason, transcends the state of exception endemic to most other zombie films and arrives at a cure, we hope, albeit one in which life together means the eradication of the inhuman bonies and a reentry into a pre-apocalyptic status quo governed, evidently, by the kinder, softer Colonel Grigio.

Rats' Alley

The cure for the state of exception, then, is a human victory. Turning toward the most militant of recent zombie films, Margo Collins and Elson

Bond argue that Brooks' *World War Z* is framed with human victory pre-supposed: "unlike the bleak endings of many of its predecessors, ultimate human victory is never in doubt here" (188). While perhaps not all of the predecessors are as bleak as Collins and Bond would make them out, unfortunately, even the rare victory frequently turns out to be bankrupt because of an ideological reinscription into the pre-apocalyptic state of exception of choice in the given film. Indeed, framing the zombie apocalypse as a war implies the possibility of victory, or perhaps even the inevitability of its own end, of a post-war world in which the threat has been mitigated. Each of the films we have considered relies on a survivor's narrative; the story is necessarily told by one who has survived the apocalypse. This is the working of the hope for the cure at its finest: that the status quo of human existence might continue, despite the fact that it established the conditions for apocalypse, and despite the fact that it exists from out of (or only within) a society already living in a state of exception, a society that desperately needs a cure and which cannot exist outside the cure.

It's a key point that the cure is not necessarily for the benefit of the zombies. We are the zombies who matter; we are figured by them, even when the representation features a non-zombie protagonist. While many cures are sought, at least initially, to save the masses of those who have become infected, the intent seems instead to sustain or to reproduce the conditions and ideals of humanity that have been explicitly attacked by the zombie apocalypse. Rather than seeking to bring about the reversal of the state of exception, this pursuit instead perpetuates its conditions of possibility. The hope for a cure is inevitably the hope for a return to the static normative order and power relationships that needed (perhaps wanted?) the disruption of an apocalypse, an end of the world as it was known.

Iterations of cures in zombie apocalyptic films are some of the few places through which the states of exception underlying virtually all zombie films are laid bare. These states surface through survivors' methodological pursuits. The suspension of normal life, existing beyond the law, haunts these films. The cure is about the proliferation of the human race, at its basest, but also something else; perhaps it is involved in a redemption of what we mean when we say "the human" when it goes beyond the recreation of the status quo: when the cure is a real cure. We cannot allow ourselves to live perpetually in a state of exception because it removes the expression of human agency. So, we fantasize. We fantasize worlds that are worse than our own (the standard zombie movie with no real cure but generally with some hope) so we can say—at least we're not that bad; we think our world is really ok, after all, even when the result of the apocalyptic world represents only the base continuation of life within the system of the state of exception or within the systems which allowed it to become possible in the first place. We also fantasize a means of cure so that we can imagine a world in which the state of exception can really end, so that there might be real hope for the future of humanity outside a state of exception in which there is no law and in which people participate only as subjects.

T.S. Eliot's epigraph from "The Wasteland" is perhaps the ideal place to begin and end a discussion of a state of exception. The notoriously obscure poem responds to modern disillusionment following World War I and the resultant reconfiguration of the understanding of the possibilities of the human as against massive world war. The world has lost its stability, and citizens wander zombie-like through the streets unsure how the world will ever find a cure. It is an exceptional state indeed when dead bones rise. Perhaps Eliot has in mind Ezekiel 37:10 in which the prophet watches as "breath came into them, and they came to life and stood on their feet, an exceedingly great army" (NASB). That the dead might rise to reproduce the conditions of war is the most horrifying thought of all. We, too, are in rats' alley, Eliot's horrifying embodiment of the place in which the human has become destabilized and the world as we knew it is no more.

The cure for the apocalypse, pursued more or less directly, in and out of this subset of films, represents a false end to the trajectory of the state of apocalypse. The cure is, very much like the zombie itself, a mask for the real conditions of existence obscured within the representation. It is our own situation that we hope to cure. Might we find any hope, then? How might we extend beyond the zombie representation to cure our own world? We offer one possibility, the archive, in the next chapter.

7

Archiving the Apocalypse

"I have an habitual feeling of my real life having passed, and that I am leading a posthumous existence."—John Keats

Short of the possibility of a proper cure, might there be a way to transcend the exceptional apocalyptic state in which we find ourselves? We begin to gesture toward a possible response in this chapter, again, as perhaps must be the case, with a younger generation in mind. And while this is written as a case study with a classroom in mind, it ought as well to inspire discussion amongst the rest of us.

French philosopher Jacques Derrida posits that humans exist in a "twilight state," a time between daylight and night, between tomorrow and today (Jacques Derrida and Elizabeth Rudinesco ix). For Derrida, understanding humanity demanded simultaneous consideration of two factors that mirror the bifurcation between day and night—whatever altogether precedes the twilight and that which follows it. First, we must consider the time in which we live. And, second, we must contemplate the time to come (Jacques Derrida and Elizabeth Rudinesco ix). One needs look no further than the *Divergent, Hunger Games*, and of course *Twilight* series, as well as the plentiful iterations of the zombie apocalypse in film and literature, to observe an unprecedented interest in this, our twilight state. In these works, we are asked to consider what might become of humanity should certain biological, social, political, or ecological forces teeter out of control. In this endeavor, Derrida's conceptualization of humanity existing within the context of twilight is illuminating, and marks the point of departure for discussing apocalyptic film and literature. In analyzing how literature and film conceptualize the end of the world, what might be to come, we must think about where, or who, we are in the present. Second, we must consider our actions and decisions in the present twilight, as these actions will either illumine or hasten the coming darkness.

This chapter highlights the exploration of twilight through an archival project, which began as a final assignment in a General Education Capstone class focused on apocalyptic literature and film. In the project, students created an archive of humanity in the days following a simulated outbreak of a zombie infection, leading to a simulated cataclysmic apocalypse. We argue that this is a valuable exercise because the archive is a tool that forces us to think about the connectivity between past and present, which is, perhaps, an answer to the frightening shadow of threatening apocalypse.

Stories of the apocalypse focus our attention on both past and present; they are necessarily revelatory as a genre, revealing the state of the contemporary culture through their narrative while exploring the potential for the end of the world as we know it. Raymond Brown focuses on this idea in his discussion of the biblical apocalyptic, a literary genre with its nominal exemplar in *The Book of Revelation* (also known by the transliteration of its Greek name, *The Apocalypse*). Brown asserts that apocalypse reveals some form of transformation "from this world to a world or era to come…. The vision of the supernatural world or of the future helps to interpret present circumstances on earth, which are almost always tragic" (775). Brown's focus parallels that of Derrida's twilight here. The revelatory nature of biblical apocalyptic literature is characteristic of apocalyptic literature in broad form: a human is engaged in a transitional vision of the future that reveals deep social fears about the consequences of our current conditions of existence. Apocalyptic narrative structure, then, takes shape as revelation: a human observer witnesses a transformation from present circumstances to some generally tragic future, exposing social fears that bring about tragic outcomes.

Perhaps deepest among these fears is that the future might be foregone, that we lack agency, and that, consequently, our own actions may be irrelevant. By this logic, humans may be conceptualized as existing in two states, again mirroring Derrida: what they are, and what they *may* become. In order to become something other than the inevitable consequence of what we are, humans must maintain some freedom to decide, to act to bring about a surprising outcome in light of what might come that we "cannot foresee, predetermine, prognosticate. This can be called freedom…" (Derrida, *For What Tomorrow…* 53). In evoking the possibility of *the to come*, Derrida conjures a night—a future that does not yet exist—and thereby grounds human responsibility in the present (and, perhaps, too, grounds the possibility of the human itself). It is the uncertainty of Derrida's night that exposes the possibility of the human by allowing meaningful human decision making. The future is not foreordained; real decisions have real consequences. We speak, here, of agency and individual responsibility.

Whether Derrida's day leads inevitably towards a given night is a crucially important concept to consider, not only for society, but particularly for our students, for whom the future looms large and questions of agency predominate. Do they get to make meaningful decisions? Can they control outcomes? Are they relevant members of society? Yet forcing confrontation of these issues in an academic context can be a difficult proposition. One helpful gateway is utilizing the totems of popular culture surrounding them as a gateway to thinking about both ourselves and the future. And, when contemplating the apocalypse, the zombie is a particularly powerful totem.

This is not a novel idea. As many in the academic community have noted, we are plagued by hordes of zombies as never before, in part because these creatures forcibly confront us with questions of apocalypse. Looking at the apocalypse through the lens of the zombie aids in confronting what we mean when we call ourselves human. What is to come? What is possible and what is not yet possible? And what are we, in light of the possible and not yet possible futures that we must necessarily, eventually, confront? Forcing confrontation with these frightening questions is vital. After all, if the one purpose of education is to ensure that the future is somehow better than the past—or, at the very least, that we are aptly equipped to continue existing as a species as the world around us grows more complex—we must be able to simultaneously reflect upon our actions in the present as well as their consequences for the future.

For guidance in helping confront these concerns, we turn to German philosopher Walter Benjamin, who wrote primarily from the tumult that saturated Europe between the two World Wars. He emphasizes the importance of the present as a moment from which one acts; in other words, Benjamin offers us another rendition of twilight. Benjamin regards agency as requiring an unstable present from which to operate, one which is spawned from a universe of potential past actions and that is not a point on a foregone continuum. Benjamin reminds us that the connectivity between Derrida's night and day is crucial, and it is, significantly, bidirectional. Just as our actions in the past and present shape the future, our actions in the present and the eventual future will shape our vision of the past. Derrida's twilight—the moment in which we live and operate—is made real as we kaleidoscopically observe and thereby shape the past, which, in turn, recursively reshapes the present and whatever is to come through a single human lens. Only in this environment can our actions be significant.

Benjamin calls this concept historical materialism, and those who practice it historical materialists: "a historical materialist cannot do without the notion of a present which is not a transition, but in which time stands still and has come to a stop.... Historical materialism supplies a unique experience with the past" (262). This unique experience is just that: unique, singular, and crafted by a human preserving something of her or his self. Such an experience is exemplified through the act of archiving: of taking material from the present, whether written work or other tangible artifacts, to explicitly provoke linkages between past, present, and, in time, the future. The student of the apocalypse, then, might, through archive, construct a bridge between past, present, and future—or between day, twilight, and night—to preserve a unique essence not only of the moment of the archiving and the time before for after, but also of that individual's irreplaceable singularity. The decision to archive a time and the choices made in that process are inherently and definitively human. And they are personal decisions, too: they cannot be substituted or replaced by another being; they are central to the self. Margaret Atwood writes that "human beings hope they can stick their souls into someone else, some new version of themselves, and live on forever. As a species we're doomed by hope, then? You could call it hope. That, or desperation" (120). Through the choices inherent in archiving, we hope to preserve the human; choices make the present real and connect it to the past in light of a future which is not foregone.

Derrida and Benjamin may be obscure figures to some of us, but the fundamental premise from which they operate is not. In fact, given the ever-expanding importance of social media as an archive of one's life, these themes are familiar, seemingly intuitively grasped by hundreds of millions of social media users, as long as one does not mention historical materialism or French philosophy. This is not just a colloquial sense of shared understanding amongst a generation glued to Facebook and Instagram; contemporary scholars have explored how digital media contributes to the sense of the self by linking past, future, and present. The recent academic interest in digital humanities is exemplified by this same focus: our temporal moment is set against the now overwhelming digital archive of the past that threatens to infinitesimally define and codify us through big data, diminishing our uniqueness by a process of making the future as simple as targeted ads and nebulous progress.

Among the key digital humanities scholars theorizing this paradox, Willard McCarty, for example, demonstrates a continuous anxiety plaguing the digital humanities for the last half century specifically concerning the loss of the uniqueness of the self. Advances in animal studies and computing have destabilized anthropocentric certainty around human borders, and "we have been becoming what we make and making what we become" (26). Whether an artificial intelligence or a zoo display, it is the creative process that fleshes out the boundaries of the human. Ironically, it is our very iterability that creates our uniqueness. We make ourselves. Archiving is such a process; the creation of any archive demonstrates a unique self that by its nature creates and preserves the fingerprint of the creator. Derrida, Benjamin, and digital humanities converge in the hand of the historical materialist, the archivist. The archivist is a representation of the unique creator of self.

Recent representations of apocalypse often feature a version of this archival technique, with which millennials engage via popular culture. This appears through the frequent use of carefully edited found footage, generally portrayed as the testimony of survivors. For example, the text of *World War Z* is essentially found footage, very much like *The Blair Witch Project*. It is told through the stories of the living—*WWZ*, as a book, is an archival memorial for what happened, historically necessary—a definitive history. It seems that the new spinoff of *The Walking Dead, Fear the Walking Dead*, begins from this archival perspective. Similarly, *REC* is a Spanish zombie film that tells the story of demonic possession through the eye of a camera, and is presented as an archive to the viewer. Further, George Romero's *Diary of the Dead* tells the story of a zombie infestation through the eyes of a news reviewer. This technique is not limited to zombie films; it abounds in apocalyptic representations of all sorts. *Cloverfield*, for example, tells of the end of New York City through the cameras carried by the protagonists. The vantage is also used frequently in non-apocalyptic horror, through films like *Paranormal Activity*, which utilizes stationary cameras placed by the main characters to tell its horrid story.

In teaching about the idea of apocalypse and the weighty considerations of human nature that come with it, then, the archive can be a powerful and accessible pedagogical tool to engage. It allows for a simulation of the apocalypse in a way that zombie walks or role-playing exercises, when conducted in a vacuum, do not. Simulating the apocalypse via archiving is about more than theater: it is about representing the human in day, twilight, and night all at once. In doing so, it enables the agent to have a voice.

How better for students to come to terms with the possibilities of a silent (post-apocalyptic) humanity than through writing as if there could be no verbal explanation? The archive, as it is imagined, postdates the human and perhaps the possibilities of language. They need to archive the image. Conveniently, millennials are already archivists: they work this into their Tumblr accounts without even thinking about it. The creation of the pastiche, the 1980s collage, has become the Tumblr feed with collected bits of humanity and quotes and images that demonstrate the inner monologue of a generation that will largely fail to read the novels from which they quote. Yet they have figured out their own essence through the collage. The Tumblr account is an archive and an act of self-creation. It weaves together in decoupage disparate elements that illustrate both the fingerprints of the archivists as well as the original writers and photographers to those who care to look. Remarkably, despite the absence of a human to directly explain its contents, such a mosaic can record something of the human. It becomes a sort of cure that speaks from the post-apocalyptic silence.

If we can get students (and perhaps the rest of the world, as well) to recognize the archival gesture implicit in the creation of their Tumblr feeds or their Facebook walls, and to then consciously create an archival project that records the essence of humanity alongside the essence of a responsible self, we offer them a worthwhile pedagogical exercise that engages past, present, and future. Maurice Blanchot, whose soaring work influenced Derrida, seems to support this idea when he notes the permanence of literature as a sort of unintentional archive—a silent refuge that turns "us away from ourselves" even while it preserves the essence of humanity (219–220). To Blanchot, literature fills an essential gap in translating Derrida's night to day; it is vital because living in a silent twilight, unable to interpret the literary language that besets us, is perhaps the most frightening apocalypse of all. This life allows for no connectivity between past and present and, in essence, the loss of essential elements of our humanity. This is equally frightening to teachers, of course. Nevertheless, there is some remedy to this silence in goading our students to engage the archive, which requires finding self and fixing it within the world. This fixity, or at least the illusion of fixity, creates the sense of temporal location and situates the self as irreplaceably singular alongside others. The archive is a remedy to a mute twilight, as it gives voice to the silent gulf existing between what was and what is and what may be. Our students simply need the vocabulary to access this gulf. Apocalypse provides this vocabulary.

Altogether, then, we approach the possibility of cataclysmic apocalypse, in which the world as we know it ends, through a combination of these theoretical perspectives. Derrida guides us to consider the time in which we live as inextricably linked to that which is to come. His perspective makes possible that what is to come may be a surprise because the freedom of twilight imbues humanity with meaningful choices, responsibility, and free will. Brown leaves us recognizing that tragic outcomes are revealed through the human narrative of the present predictions of the future. Benjamin situates the figure of the archivist as the one who might expose where we are now in light of what is to come, both preserving and creating a self that might resist the destruction programmed into our social fears leading to our possible ends. Digital humanities codifies the idea that we are what we make, setting up the model for the archive. Blanchot enables us to embrace and resist the horror of a silent world.

With this framework in place, then, we turn to game studies for a means of enacting an archive into a class so that students can engage these theories practically as they consider both prevailing social fears and the consequent response-ability that makes us human. In the sections below, we apply this theory to the specific course and assignments in which students participate in the act of archiving, then close with a discussion of the experience, learning, and directions for future versions of this assignment.

The Course

The General Education Capstone is an intensive writing course intended to coalesce the transdisciplinary emphases that students have learned through their general education courses and tie these together with their disciplinary specialty as they approach graduation. It takes into consideration ethical, critical, conceptual, and analytical dimensions of human thought, as well as the state of human society and its historical and future trajectories as students write a capstone paper and, in this case, participate in an extended simulation.

This particular course, entitled Film, Literature, and Apocalypse, explores the stories we tell about the ends of the human and the ends of humanity. Students focus primarily on zombie apocalyptic films and other representations of apocalypse in classic and more recent literature. They consider the causes that we imagine will end our species, the impact of ideology, apocalyptic ethics, what might be meant by the posthuman, the possibilities of cures and resistance, what it means to be human, and how to affect meaningful change in a complex world.

Over the span of the semester, students read five novels and watch five films. Literature and films are presented in thematically-tied units and discussed extensively. This discussion is organized around questions about why we imagine the end of our world, the causes that we suspect might end us, the ideas that shape our creation of apocalyptic worlds, how we live in these worlds, what all this says about our species, and what we might do about it. Through discussion, reading, and reflection, students examine the complexities of the world that surrounds us, analyze the social contexts that produce artistic work, and explore our ability to respond. The pursuit of these goals is facilitated by three interrelated parts of the course: intense and deliberative classroom discussion, a detailed research paper about an important problem facing humanity, and the archival simulation. A final exam tests students' holistic understanding of the material.

The course is divided into six units wherein students spend significant time considering the questions noted above. Each unit articulates the influence of these questions on particular iterations of apocalypse and encourages students to work backward from these ideas to consider the ways that apocalypse influences the telling of our stories. William Flesch theorizes that we seek comeuppance in the stories that we tell—that we seek to uphold ideological order through positive and negative reinforcement in the stories that we tell about ourselves—and it is advantageous to consider apocalypses along these lines, for what they tell us about ourselves and why we tell them as we do. Therefore, students consider first what constitutes apocalypse, then identify the ramifications of possible alternate causes. Turning next to ideology and survival, they explore the possibilities of how our ideas about the world reproduce conditions of existence in apocalyptic iterations. Naturally, the next questions that arise concern how to behave in relation to these conditions, so we turn to considerations of apocalyptic ethics. These ideas begin to move toward the end of the human, toward the posthuman, which is addressed next. Finally, the possibilities of cures and resistance might offer some hope to the world, which students attempt to archive as the final project for the class.

The reading list for the course is developed to illustrate different possible apocalypses and to suggest possibilities for that which might survive the apocalypse; each of these texts fits into a unit indicated above, though the effect is cumulative, so that *Pride and Prejudice and Zombies* is as relevant at the end of the course as Aira's *Miracle Cures*. The texts are: Seth Grahame Smith's *Pride and Prejudice and Zombies*, George Orwell's *1984*, Stephen King's *Cell: A Novel*, Margaret Atwood's *Oryx and Crake*, and Cesar Aira's *The Miracle Cures of Dr. Aira*.

The film viewing list is designed to expose students to a broad range of zombie representations that seem to each represent different versions of the fears that we read in apocalyptic creations. Further, these films are paired, in order, with textual representations of apocalypses, offering notable possibilities for contrast. The films are: *Zombieland, Night of the Living Dead, Fido, Warm Bodies,* and *I Am Legend.*

Near the end of the class, students are given the following assignment, which brings together the elements of previous units in order to explore the possibility of human resistance and cure.

The Simulation

On the final Monday of class, you will awaken in the town of Grand Lake, Colorado, following a cataclysmic apocalypse. The world is beset by zombies. You have one week of fictive time to preserve or destroy the most important parts of humanity before you drift into oblivion. You are either a human or a zombie, and you are divided into guilds. For humans, guilds are groups of survivors who have banded together for self-defense. For zombies, guilds represent a small squad of shambling monsters. This particular incarnation of the zombie permits you to retain some element of feral intellect, so that you are not stuck blindly stumbling into walls all week.

If humans, your mission is to build an archive of items that preserve the essential elements of humanity. If zombies, your mission is to designate items to destroy that would prevent the preservation of these essential elements of humanity. The world is going to end on the day of the final, except for your archives, unless the zombies manage to destroy them first. Sorry, survivors, you do not get to outlive the apocalypse. Your archive must speak from the silence for itself.

Whether human or zombie, your guild must act as if it is the only remaining sentient group and must act accordingly. Neither human guilds nor zombie guilds meet each other in the course of the game; in other words, while you are all inhabiting Grand Lake, you will not run into each other. If it helps, think of yourself as living in one possible present of Grand Lake, while other teams live in others. Further, Grand Lake is too secluded to draw either additional humans or zombies during the week that you are playing the game. However, you are competing to collect archival objects. If humans, you collect an object by turning in a summary of the means of acquiring the object, along with a description of why the item is important to preserving the essence of humanity (see below). If a different human collects your archival object first, they get it and you don't, so timing is vital. If a zombie, you destroy an object by turning in an acquisition summary of the object, along with why destroying it would prevent the preservation the essence humanity. If a zombie destroys a resource or archival item, no human can use it. In addition, the objects that you choose are constricted by the bounds of reality. You don't get to invent a pilot, nor do you get to magically develop wings; don't hope for a genie; unless you can creatively procure it, the Mona Lisa is, therefore, caput. The internet does not work, and cell phones cannot make calls (probably they went the way of *Cell: A Novel*, but who knows). Time progresses as it does now, and you have only as many hours as mathematically possible in order to accomplish objectives (hint: prioritize). In the event that two guilds decide to archive or destroy the same item, the following rules apply: once a zombie team has destroyed an item, it cannot be archived by humans. Once a human team has archived it, it cannot be archived by another guild. The guild (human or zombie) that reaches the item in the simulation first gets to archive or destroy it.

The projects must showcase your ideas, and you will, in fact, present these, as if posthumously. You will not be graded on artistic ability, but you will be graded on creativity, as well as the apparent answers to our course questions about what it means to be human, how you can resist, what it takes to survive, and the relative completeness and polished professionalism of the archive you create. Each archive or destructive entry needs to include an image, a cost assessment (with time and resources considered), and, most importantly, a rationale that explains why your archival object contributes to saving the human as you know it. Further, each entry must be justified and cited based on its presence in a course text or film. Each guild member, whether human or zombie, is responsible for three entries; each guild needs to work together to craft or destroy the archive. Each rationale should be approximately 250 words. Each of you will join a guild of five players, with one single-minded goal: create or destroy an archive that preserves whatever you think is most essential about humanity should some pocket of survivors manage to repopulate Earth. Somehow, you must collect each of the objects that you wish to archive. The final product could look like a Tumblr feed, a scrapbook, a Prezi, or some other creative format to showcase your ideas. The future generation will, perhaps, wonder why you have chosen the particular object (what does it uniquely preserve of humanity?), so you will need to tell them. As post-apocalyptic humans will surely wonder, you will need to explain how your guild will recover or destroy the item for archiving. These descriptions should be thorough and creative.

Each object chosen by the guild should fit within one of these categories that help shape what we mean when we say human: art (visual, auditory, performance); economy; faith; gender; language; literature (comedy, tragedy, poetry, fiction, etc.); monument; power relations; relationships; and science.

The guild that most effectively archives or destroys what is central to humanity before it is wiped out (as determined by me and a distinguished panel of faculty experts) will be awarded bonus points. Success is achieved when the key elements of humanity are preserved or destroyed. When the assignment is turned in, it will automatically be preserved for the next generation in my office, the one place that zombies cannot invade; there is, therefore, no need to provide stipulations for the defense of your archive. Each guild member must account for the time that they spend, though the guild should work together to prioritize and accomplish whatever archival projects are deemed essential by the guild. Each archival objective that your guild captures/destroys should be accounted for in terms of time as well as resources required to accomplish the objective.

So, for example, if you think it's worthwhile to collect seeds, you'd better plan to collect native flora only, or to account for the time and gas and vehicle it takes to get to the nearest seed bank.

The Twist

In order to keep the project interesting, several days after the presentation of the assignment, students are given a twist that involves faculty members. Faculty were invited to dialogue with roving bands of survivors and zombies about what they might personally archive. The conversation began with a letter sent to all faculty inviting them to dialogue with roving student groups about what they would choose to archive. Students were required to incorporate one of the faculty suggestions into their archival projects, and to claim the suggestion publicly. This has the effect of steering the conversation, ideally, toward thoughtful representations of the human, often as conceived through the disciplinary lenses of the selected faculty members. Further, this opens the conversation to the campus and engages even those who aren't in the class toward considering these important questions.

Analysis

From the first, students took on the project as if their very lives depended on it. Perhaps those enrolled in this upper division course are already keenly aware that the world as they know it is tenuous and ephemeral, in part because of the looming prospect of leaving college and entering the world-at-large. Students all indicated that they spent more time on this project than they would have spent studying for a written final, and it forced a particularly relevant discussion of the elements of humanity that uniquely engage their chosen disciplines. We discuss one of these reactions below. Another student was so deeply affected that she shared that she had been having nightmares about the course content. Going into the primary education teaching profession with her special education certificate, she was especially impacted by the possibility of facing a world that seems out of control for the powerless/voiceless and encouraged to intervene to reinvent the current educational apocalypse.

This was the subject matter of her term paper, which suggested a teaching methodology focusing on identifying abilities and developing them for differently abled students. One notable roadblock to success was that several zombie students got banned from Google search for periods of time due to a Google algorithm intended to prevent terrorism.

One biology major addressed the question of the central aspects of humanity through more than genetics; the student argued that language and affection are central to being human, and that we engage both through storytelling. Interestingly, the student also chose to archive medical journals, with the stated hope of preserving the scientific method and the desire to share information. The journals seemed to frame the counterpart to using language to tell stories for the student, as they use language in an apparently representational fashion. This student was able to consider the question of what is central to the human animal from beyond the genetic perspective, and to understand a key difference in the way that language shapes our experiences together.

Other students engaged questions that they found to be central to defining the human experience in community. Suddenly the uncertainty of the future, a key anxiety of this generation, becomes more manageable. The assignment demonstrated that there is a means to resist the uncertainty of what may come through the preservation of a record of a meaningful self and relationships, specifically in light of the possibility of apocalypse. Students chose different representations to record, answering several of the same questions with markedly different answers. For example, one group archived sex, while another, concerned with the possibilities of personal and public safety, chose to archive weaponry (ranging from bows to firearms). In a few cases, groups chose to take a trip to an already extant archive, allowing professionals to perform part of the work of archiving for them, trusting that, for example, the National Archive housed the keys to the human condition.

It is particularly notable that this "Facebook Generation" understands accuracy as a function of temporality. Because the internet has been so central to their being, they recognize that information grows out of date and what was once accurate is no longer, and yet remains in existence, accessible to their observation. The world is, as the pre–Socratic Greek philosopher Heraclitus said, in flux (B12). The digital world in which our students reside certainly is, too. Through flashbacks, throwback Thursday posts, status updates that are woefully obsolete yet remain extant, and even through the inevitable announcements of relationship updates that are two or three iterations out of date, this generation is ever faced with a world in flux that is not as it was, and that nevertheless retains vestiges of the past that no longer apply except through a complicated process of nostalgia and memorialization. Perhaps no better metaphor for this exists than Facebook's "Timehop" feature. The Facebook Generation exists in perpetual twilight, understanding that the world is, in many ways, always ending yet also beginning; they are similarly faced with longing for a permanent record of the changes being made, perhaps the result of positioning in perpetual twilight.[1] There is genuine terror, here, as this exercise demonstrates. The archive doesn't have to be accurate—perhaps, cannot be, as context always changes—yet students are always already engaged in the process of archiving what is temporary and tenuous but that nevertheless stands as a memorial of what was. Thus, with the procedural connection already in place, students take to the process of archive uniquely and diligently. It is a form of communication, perhaps even a genre, that is wrapped in the cultural ethos.

The archive, therefore, transitions effectively toward the idea of personal apocalypse, that the end of the world as we know it might not necessarily result in the cataclysmic destruction of all life on earth, but rather that it might end a particular world, time, twilight, or context. And each world may be vast and expansive, bounded only by the rules of perception, and leading to an infinite number of possible nights. As Stephen King writes in *The Gunslinger*, in which a hardened Clint Eastwood–type wanders the ruined countryside after a nameless apocalypse brought about by the man in black, "there are worlds other than these" (264). Of course there exists the possibility that no cataclysmic apocalypse will overtake us anytime soon; even so, there is the possibility that the conditions of existence under which we operate at the moment might end. Will the next connectivity technology replace the internet and social media, for example, radically altering our relationships and means of existing together? Perhaps. This sort of minor apocalypse might just as well upend the world as we know it. Apocalyptic literature and film allows the examination of the ends of cultural conditions that may or may not necessarily end the possibility of life. It is simply life as we know it that ends in an apocalypse. And if it is possible to have a personal apocalypse, each student then may engage their own fears and own possible outcomes through the lens in a philosophically meaningful way.

Moving Beyond the Classroom

The possibility of the archive that might survive apocalypse raises the question: what, after all, can be archived that preserves the human? And there is a further question that matters here: should we be preserving the current state of the human or should we be preserving that forward looking hope for what the human might become? In other words, would it make sense to preserve the human hope for the human future or the human as it exists now? These questions make a potentially significant difference for what objects could be archived. For example, ought we to archive the vestiges of war, like Picasso's "Guernica," for example, or some image of human hope for peace, such as the United Nations?

There is an interesting possibility that any attempt to cure an apocalypse will necessarily result in a reproduction of the ideological conditions leading up to the apocalypse. Thus archive must, in its very creation of a snapshot of self, so to speak, archive a self already inculcated in ideology. If shaping ideology remains invisible, the archive will in its very existence preserve a record of ideology as much as self. This critique certainly needs to be considered, but the very first step toward a cure from the problematic ideology structuring our existence is the exposure of that very ideology, which might through this process become, finally, visible. The archive, then, is, if not the last step of a cure, the necessary first step toward shining a light on the prevalence and function of the disease in order to begin diagnosis.

The archival simulation ultimately demands deep consideration of what we should save in order to preserve whatever it is that makes us human, using a frame of reference or perhaps form of communication with which we are already familiar. Millennials are already faced with the dynamic of a changing world that seems far beyond their control, yet facing the possibility of apocalypse allows them to engage their voices in memorializing what matters to them. While answering course questions demands engagement with literature and film, the archival simulation became a personal exercise in defining the significant elements of human life as it is experienced both individually and socially. Finding one's voice in light of the apocalypse through the archive is a distinct possible means of resistance that demands both specific engagement with questions of human constitution and with the broader cultural themes and fears that shape the human in this temporally isolated (or even isolocated) moment.

Conclusion: Yes, but in a Zombie Apocalypse...

"We're coming to get you, Barbara."—*Johnny* (Night of the Living Dead)

The horror of the multiplicity of apocalyptic causes is palpable; any could potentially bring about a zombie apocalypse; any could end life as we know it. Building on this idea, the first facet of our argument is that zombie apocalyptic representations allow us to safely imagine the possibilities of exactly this sort of end. The end may not necessarily be cataclysmic, but entails an end of the order of the world as it currently exists, specifically through the suspension of normative and judicial law. The second facet, significantly, is that we believe that we already exist in a world that is no longer as we knew it. We are living in a state of apocalypse already. With these facets in mind, we undertake in this chapter to explore the experiences of those using the zombie apocalyptic genre to imagine an end of the world and what it might be like to live in such a time. Then we move toward understanding our own already exceptional state. To close our analysis, we examine this principle where we believe it matters most: as a phenomena experienced among our students). They are the next generation, after all, and our hope for their success in future (potentially world-ending) challenges is one reason why we bother studying the world.

One cannot understand the fascination with the zombie apocalypse, and, ultimately, its importance to the future of our own, everyday society, without considering one of the primary audiences responsible for the ravenous consumption of the recent deluge of books, films, and video games. Here, we speak of our students, their younger siblings, and the twenty-somethings that we've taken to calling "Millennials." Even at the ripe old age of 30-something, we admit that we did not grow up with zombies. In fact, the early objects of our terror were borne of different cultural fears and artistic style. We were aware of zombies, but the zombie revolution had not yet occurred. We still shudder when we think of *Poltergeist* (1982) and Jason Vorhees from *Friday the Thirteenth* (1980). In deference to Wes Craven, we will never allow our children to store their retainers near a light socket. The blighted images of a *Terminator* (1984) laden future still haunt our nights, and when Sarah Connor imagines the thermonuclear blast leveling Los Angeles, we connect with her, emotionally, viscerally. We are the product of our times.

We grew up in a society that was always at the brink of destruction, at least in our minds. We knew that when we huddled under desks for a fire drill, we weren't really hiding from a fire—after all, why would you cower beneath furniture while the inferno closed in on you? There has always been the possibility of a biological or chemical attack, for, however unrealistically, Saddam Hussein's Scud missiles seemed poised to strike our very living rooms when the Gulf War began. Thermonuclear holocaust, even if it could not be entirely conceived by our developing minds, always hovered in the wings. We knew that DEFCON mattered, that bomb shelters were proudly marked, and, from our parents, that the USSR was serious business. Considering the abruptness with which the Berlin Wall finally collapsed, and that the Soviets, as it turned out, were sitting atop a rusting society that was beyond maintenance or repair, this hysteria seems almost silly. But it was *real* to us, and it shaped us, for better or worse.

So what, then, of the next generation? The ones who don't remember Cold War era Bond movies filled with eastern European villains bent on blowing up the moon, or sappy teen movies like *WarGames* (1983) that brought the technical possibility of the end of the world into our shag-carpeted living rooms? After all, the zombie must be a horrifically powerful symbol when it is the first monster that you encounter. We cannot relive that horrible moment of discovery because it is beyond us; we cannot *feel* terror as acutely because, let's face it, when you have survived the Cold War, the L.A. Riots, and Y2K and realized that none of them ended it all, you tend to believe that the world continues spinning regardless of the infinitesimal chances that the Large Hadron Collider might create a microscopic black hole that will steadily devour the planet. And while we can intellectually recognize that the zombie is a symbol for dehumanization and reflective of societal fears of contagion, and even feel our hackles rise during *The Walking Dead*, we can't go back and feel that initial terror. We've already been imprinted.

Zombies reflect the societal anxieties of our times; understanding how millennials experience, process, and understand zombies helps us understand the lens through which they view much more important events. More than this, though, like all monsters, zombies are a sort of Moretti-style crooked prophesy, reflecting fears regarding where society *might* go, in some form, at some point down the line. How do young people perceive this? And what are they going to do about it? These are crucially important questions, and ones that should keep us wide awake when we are lying in our beds, dreaming of long-forgotten Terminators. Because if we are going to stave off an apocalypse, we're going to need a lot of energy.

In this chapter, we argue that the zombie is valuable and accessible as a critical tool with which young people are already familiar, which has helped frame their understanding of society, and which, in turn, helps us to understand our place in the world. Significantly, incorporating zombies into learning is not a unidirectional presentation, but rather entails significant dialogue between generations; it can also help educators better comprehend the moods and mores of students, and—using fear as a window into the human condition—open a dialogue that might bridge the gap between generations. Here, we suggest one method. Our point of departure is the basic premise of the zombie apocalypse—that all bets are off—which then leads to an examination of critical questions that might drive both student and instructor towards a better understanding of the human condition.

We are aware, of course, that many instructors have incorporated zombies into their classroom, and here we merely provide a perspective that complements many already discussed in this volume. It is important to note, too, that this is written to future teacher-practitioners and current educators, but should be valuable to anyone seeking perspective about the zombie phenomena, their dialogue with their educators, and their own place in the post–*Terminator* world. We recognize that there is a notable emotional draw created by the representation of zombies and the end of the world in contemporary films, literature, and culture. It is from these sources, after all, that we all gather important impressions about the world, both in our formative years, and in free time outside of academia.

All Bets Are Off

One important premise underlying the exploration of any zombie apocalypse must be that all bets are off. What we mean by this is that whatever social contract holds together the world before the apocalypse has become null. This accounts for the appearance of cannibals at Terminus, for the bad meat in *Scouts Guide to the Zombie Apocalypse* and *Cooties*, and even for the dissolution of classical literature, as in *Pride and Prejudice and Zombies*. Expectations fall apart when we imagine the end of the world as we know it and the task of survival becomes paramount. While clearly the new world demands a new order, its shape is negotiable. Exploring the uncomfortable feeling of survival outside the boundaries of human society compels us to consider the responsibility resulting from our choices; it is this very responsibility that, in fact, makes us human. Considering apocalypse also underscores the crucial link between the ability to influence events in a meaningful way and the feeling of being human, as well as the possibility of denying this ability to others.[1] Finally, it exposes the mask obscuring larger social fears that our subconscious sublimates when we populate our nightmares with zombies, and invites the removal of the mask. These are all questions that loom large for both students and educators, even if they do not initially realize it.

In order to survive in the context of apocalypse, humans must consider and often shed many of their subjectively-constructed dispositions about what is proper—or, even, what is *human*—and embrace foreign codes of conduct. Prized skills, cultivated over the course of a lifetime, may suddenly become useless; the accountant's ability to create complex macros are entirely unimpressive to the gamboling zombie hordes. White-knuckled survivors must stare into the blank eyes of their former loved ones and desperately ask whether humanity persists so long as the veneer of flesh survives, or if it is acceptable to smash a zombified friend's face with a shovel. And while we have yet to encounter a zombie apocalypse, its antagonists nevertheless persist in frightening us, obscuring fears of more present danger. Zombie threats are inevitably portrayed as overwhelming and overpowering: their shuffling intrusions disrupt and dismember centuries-old social expectations, creating new notions of status and respect. As resources run scarce, social trust plummets, pitting survivors against one another. The relativity of morals and the fragility of life becomes painfully apparent within this state of nature.

After all, our society has been trained to empathize with victims of a zombie apocalypse. Television and film seldom follow the zombie from a first person perspective (though, there are notable exceptions here). Video games more directly force us to actually become a survivor and make awful calculations: Who will live or die? How does one balance the risk associated with acquiring food against the need for sustenance? Can one trust other survivors to play nice in a world without laws? Consider the simplest manifestation here: when a survivor is confronted with a zombie, she or he determines how to respond to the threat. There are really only two options: fight or run, and within these options, a subset of other choices, depending on the attributes of the zombie presently faced. Run up a fire escape or down an alley; fight with a shovel or a pistol? We can all empathize with those facing this scenario, and have been conditioned to discuss it readily.

This bridges, then, to an idea worth exploring: while the human can decide how to treat the zombie, the zombie has no choice but to attack the human (in virtually every representation). That humans decide and zombies don't exposes the nature of human responsibility. Humans try to achieve goals by deciding how to respond, in potentially surprising fashion, always acting under conditions in which outcomes are uncertain. Zombies, on the other hand, mechanically follow a tree of relatively preprogrammed options without considering outcomes (again, this depends on the type of zombie, but is particularly salient in the context of gaming). While both zombies and humans act, only humans decide. These decisions are made with often imperfect calculations toward outcomes that are not foregone. Therefore, human beings are responsible. There are few lessons of greater import that can be discussed in or out of a classroom.

When viewed in the context of humanity struggling to survive a zombie apocalypse, the inhumanity of the zombie hordes heightens the contrast between responsibility and its absence. The hordes march forward as legion, endless and mechanical, while humans must make hard choices including fighting, fleeing, loving, betraying, self-sacrifice, and simply giving up. This further invites an important question: if responsibility is inextricably linked with humanity—that is, if our actions are real, have meaning, and are derived from consideration of the world around us, and we are, therefore, responsible for them—what sorts of decisions are acceptable (morally, ethically, socially, or otherwise), under what conditions, and why? If all bets are off during a zombie apocalypse, what are the limits of acceptable human action in light of human responsibility?[2]

Focusing on these questions encourages us to engage subjectivity, to approach material as individuals in control of and responsible for deciding meaning rather than as zombies. Confronting others with their ability to make decisions amidst the zombie apocalypse can help them understand this important aspect of their humanity. They may begin to appreciate their *voices*—not just their actions, but their expressions of feeling and meaning that accompany their actions—and become determined to use them, particularly when faced with legions of nameless, faceless, mechanical dead. Just as they do when playing video games. We tacitly realize that we have the ability to choose, and must use it. Both zombies and humans can eat brains, but humans choose not to. The power to decide is vital to expressing humanity. We can all connect with this.

Considering the zombie apocalypse can also encourage us to consider another important attribute of humanity: the ability to influence events. In many ways, this is the heart of the traditional zombie survival story: human ingenuity and craftiness facilitates survival. Humans are not powerless, and we can respond to the inhumanity of the zombie hordes by voicing our power. This echoes the "aggressive agency" developed in zombie apocalypse video games, in which players feel the "urge to intervene, to take control" (Irene Chien 64). When we adopt this aggressive agency, though, we also recognize that this agency does not necessarily exist for all living creatures. Zombies force us to consider under what conditions agency can be denied, to whom, and the consequences of such a denial. While this is often approached critically through the apparatus of race and the zombie's Haitian origins, all zombies force powerful questions: under what circumstances could all bets be off? How would this look? To what extent are we responsible to other humans? And the inhuman?

Interesting perspectives, of course, are available in zombie criticism, which can be read, (assigned) and discussed in conjunction with other stories, films, or depiction of apocalypse—cataclysmic or otherwise. Traditionally, "zombie-crit" begins with analyses of the culturally Haitian figure of the voodoo-induced zombie. While zombies, in this conceptualization, are captivated humans rather than the undead, they maintain a sort of continuity with the resurrected corpse figure because of the common questions of agency and responsibility, and particularly the possibility that both might be denied. Chera Kee connects the Haitian zombie and its more recent representations through their similar ability to confront humans with "the very mechanisms that one used for defining the self [which are] slowly eaten away" (22). Amy Fass Emery defines a zombie as a creature that "resembles the person it once was, but its voice and will have been taken away" (328). The fundamental questions of voice and voice denial that unite the Haitian zombie and the recent zombie are made explicit. For Joshua Gunn and Shaun Treat, zombies evidence ideological subjectification as agents of underlying anxiety; the zombie is "speechless, incapable of emotion, slow moving but diligent, and utterly beholden to his or her 'master'" (150); the zombie is a lobotomized subject serving an internal, insatiable lust. Zombies are compelling because they expose threats to human responsibility and influence, real threats, even though the zombies themselves are partially masked by the surreal, fantastic, or ridiculous. This rich literature connects well with contemporary manifestations of zombies, and makes a good insertion into any discussion seeking to use zombies as a window into humanity, choice, reason, and agency.

Another important point easily accessible to all is that zombies invoke traditional human fears—fears that should resonate for both the instructor and the instructed. After all, most classic zombies are helpless before innovation, mechanical in thought, unable to display emotion, devoid of feelings or emotion, and incapable of love or affection.[3] They cannot follow rules, organize, or improve their lot. They are anonymous and nameless. Zombies are, perhaps most obviously, dead. Further, the exceptional case of the zombie apocalypse encourages examination of the conditions necessary for it to occur, which prompts unsettling questions about where our collective humanity might be taking us as society hurtles forward into the future. Knowing that zombies aren't exactly real but treating them as if they were invokes Slavoj Žižek's theory of reality; Žižek suggests that we really inhabit the story that we construct for ourselves, knowing that it is not real but behaving as if it were (32–33). This language enables us to peel back the veil of the zombie apocalypse, to confront the fears structuring reality and to recognize the relationships at work in the reality in which we live. And since all bets are off, we have the freedom to name the threats, to step behind the veil of zombie apocalypse to better understand our own world. Again, the possibilities for dialogue and learning here are vast.

As we consider in discussion the slippery disjunction between human and what we might mean by "inhuman," we can explore questions such as: what does it mean to be responsible for one's actions? What is a monster? How does language work and how does it fail? What does it mean to relate to others, and how does power work on us and others? Are there moral imperatives? And finally, when socially-constructed norms and authority break down, does our humanity persist, change, or simply melt away?

Within this framework, the presence of zombies requires that we consider the nature of agency and responsibility. While these are not new questions, zombies provide important synaptic connectivity to the interests and culture of a younger generation that routinely consumes entertainment populated by the walking dead. Consider, for instance, recent concern surrounding the consumption of bath salts. In an article in *The Washington Post*, Alexandra Petri writes that when we encounter "horrific inhuman crimes," we "file them under zombie ... [because] we absolutely have to blame something" ("Zombie Apocalypse"). The bath salts question is a supposition that a drug concoction believed to be connected to several recent cases of cannibalism caused its users to become zombies and, therefore, to eat people; it foregrounds a criminal denial of responsibility and, consequently, of agency (Petri). This is perhaps not unlike what Liv Moore experiences in *iZombie* with the consumption of "Utopium," the drug responsible for turning-zombie in the series. Can a drug remove or deny human agency? If not, what can? Government? Social norms? Racism? Again, fascinating questions for any generation, with answers equally worth engaging. The answers to these questions govern how we live together, and how we understand the relationships between ourselves, others, and the world around us. Working backward from the premise that all bets are off in a zombie apocalypse, we begin to see that bets appear *on* outside of one, or at least that we might choose to act as if they are. In other words, culpability, voice, and social expectations are powerful attributes of normal human society, and they both make us aware of and shape our humanity.

Of course, it may not be practical at every institution of higher education to host a dedicated course on post-apocalyptic literature, with a special focus on zombies. Fortunately, the important questions above can be injected into a wide variety of discussions that cross disciplinary lines. We offer, below, a few examples of how zombies can be inserted into otherwise living classes in order to push class discussions along this line of inquiry.

Some Modest Proposals

For instance, the question of culpability swiftly arises outside of traditionally apocalyptic literature in such classics as James M. Cain's *Double Indemnity* (1943). Cain's work is about an insurance adjuster, Walter Huff, who murderously schemes his way towards riches. In doing so, he largely follows the conventions of the noir genre, including meeting a woman who serves as the archetypical temptation to commit evil (femme fatale Phyllis Dietrichson). Here, Huff is both hero and murderer. Significantly, as with many works, it can be read through a zombie lens, with special attention given to depictions of zombies in popular culture that parallel more traditional literary analysis. In reading *Double Indemnity* through the zombie lens, Walter Huff adopts the qualities of a zombie. Murder is a responsible action. Huff chose to kill. Huff's attempts to deny responsibility for the act by claiming compulsion seem fantastical. Nevertheless, it is difficult to face the possibility that a murderer could really be responsible for denying life to another. Interestingly, we might also see the novel's first victim, Nirdlinger, as a zombie. After all, the possibility of ending the life of another is much easier when that other is already dead. This seems to echo Cain's choice to leave Nirdlinger without a voice; he is never really allowed to speak in such a way that he becomes a fully human character. He is an exemplary victim. By providing a novel perspective on the noir victim, zombies help provide a lens to explore and classify human understanding of guilt and responsibility.

Another approach to blending literature and zombies might be utilizing Seth Grahame-Smith's *Pride and Prejudice and Zombies*, which overlays zombies onto the nineteenth-century social scene while also engaging topics like historical context, feminism, and irony. Graham-Smith allows Austen's heroine to step outside the bounds of social conventions that weigh on her so heavily in the original text. When the novel's heroine suffers, she is no longer silent. When unmentionables pour in to the opening ball of the novel, Elizabeth Bennet and her sisters engage in the dance with death: "each thrusting a razor-sharp dagger with one hand, the other hand modestly tucked into the small of her back" (14). Elizabeth has become a skilled warrior and the zombie apocalypse demands the need for constant readiness; she must go beyond imagining being an ideal person, and instead act decisively. So, after a perceived insult from the novel's hero, Mr. Darcy, she imagines "that in less than a fortnight she should herself be with [her sister] Jane again, and enabled to contribute to the recovery of her spirits, beginning with the presentation of Darcy's heart and head" (148). Darcy surprisingly reveals his love for Elizabeth only moments later, and her imagination becomes reality: she kicks him in the face. "One of her kicks found its mark, and Darcy was sent into the mantelpiece with such force as to shatter its edge" (151). Elizabeth's battle skills are unmatched, painting in stark contrast her inability to read others (including Darcy), and ultimately herself. We identify both with the omnipresent social pressures governing peer relationships, and the need to act in the face of a zombie apocalypse. The social restraint characterizing Austen's *Pride and Prejudice* has become a call to immediate and decisive action: all bets are off in literature when zombies invade. Again, the zombie lens offers an attractive portal through which to examine power of social convention, the conditions under which it might vaporize, and the potential aftershocks.

The zombie apocalypse can also be meaningfully considered in tandem with political writings. For instance, Marx and Engels' *Communist Manifesto* and Emerson's "Self-Reliance" can be usefully examined through the zombie lens. These push the conversation toward important questions about our place in the world and the aforementioned themes. One valuable reading of Marx and Engels might be that while the equality of communism seems desirable, the inability to embrace the individuality that Emerson so values might well deprive individuals of choice, and thereby fashion them as living zombies.

The fear of becoming a living zombie may also be further reflected and explored through interdisciplinary routes, such as contrasting Stanley Milgram's shock experiments and Ibsen's *An Enemy of the People*. Milgram's work on the power of soft authority in precipitating evil actions and Ibsen's scathing indictments of the power of the media to drive behavior sound distinctly apocalyptic as we have defined it. Such methods, after all, could mark the end of free thought if taken to their logical conclusion (as authors like George Orwell have done). The power of the media, government, and advertisers to frame our understanding of reality fuels a deep suspicion of authority and poses questions about the ramifications of subjugating oneself to societal norms. Again, here, we see the specter of the zombie. Much like the zombie ethos itself, such a discussion is facilitated by the historical soup in which young people have been steeped. The catastrophic global experience of millennials' lives has not been World

War II, Vietnam, or the threat of nuclear war, but rather 9/11, which activates important questions about whether government can be trusted to protect its citizens, and the conditions under which individuals might be reduced to automatons willing to destroy themselves in order to destroy others and thereby fulfill higher political goals.[4] To be fair, the same questions could be posed regarding Hitler's rise to power, the tactics of the South Vietnamese regime, or the threat of mutually assured destruction. Viewed in this light, zombies are far from revolutionary; they are, rather, just a particularly efficacious tool through which we may engage old, but important, questions.

The zombie, as a construct, also injects life into discussions of the changing nature of technology and, in particular, digital media—another concept with which students are ready and eager to engage because it is very much part of who they are. We live in a globally interconnected world, and the interactive nature of technology like Twitter, Facebook, and Instagram suggests that we all have some role—if vaguely understood and disembodied—in shaping this society. And while we may not always know *how* to change outcomes, we *are* frightened of succumbing to the tidal forces of mass media and authority, and being reduced to either bodiless souls that cannot act or cogs in a machine that cannot consider our role.[5] We do *not* want to be zombies, and we know it.

Considering the world as one bifurcated between the living and the zombified, then, forces us to respond to social problems and the itinerant responsibilities facing the millennials' digitized generation. Zombies frighten not only because they are monsters, but because they might make us monsters, or, even more terrifyingly, because we might already *be* monsters. This provokes an intense desire to resist the pressures of automation.

Considering responsibility in a zombie apocalypse scaffolds discussion and exploration of what our other human responsibilities are: to ourselves and also to each other. Zombies frighteningly infect a world in which all bets are off, helping us to identify the bets themselves, the moments when we are constrained and must choose to respond, according to socially preprogrammed norms or outside of expectations. Each of these activities: reading great literature, classical and infected, considering national governments, and unmasking the possibilities of power—allowed and unbidden—demonstrates the way that the zombie lens forces issues of responsibility, voice, and societal fears.

Chapter Notes

Introduction

1. Unless otherwise specified, all references to *The Walking Dead* refer to the AMC television show.

2. Kyle William Bishop offers an excellent critique of the *draugr* in *How Zombies Conquered Popular Culture*, 148ff.

3. Ron Broglio calls this "reading surfaces" and it describes the practice of making meaning from a pre or non-linguistic creature's body; see Broglio's "Thinking with Animals."

4. Normative law is extensively treated by Foucault in *Discipline and Punish*. We mean, simply, that form of unwritten law that controls our behavior apart from the legal requirements of society. For example, that we must not murder would be an example of juridical law, but that we not end up on someone's worst dressed list would be an example of normative law, and the way that it works on us (through shame).

5. Among the excellent scholarship dealing with specific causal concerns as metaphoric outcomes, race and religion find frequent representation. The work of Kim Paffenroth (*Gospel of the Living Dead*) and Chera Kee, as well as the forthcoming book by Dawn Keetley on the Haitian origins of the zombie, explore these categories effectively.

6. From the first, in George Romero's classic *Night of the Living Dead* (1968), taxidermied animal heads confront the film's protagonist, Barbra (Judith O'Dea), from the walls of her house of refuge, invoking just as much fear as the zombies waiting outside. In the recent *Scouts Guide to the Zombie Apocalypse* (2015), a zombie deer attacks the scout leader in the forest just outside his camp. Later in the movie, an entire herd of cats in an elderly woman's house becomes zombified and attacks the protagonists. Ving Rhames' *2012: Zombie Apocalypse* (2011) features a host of creature zombies. *Z Nation* (2014–), *Feed* (2010), and *I Am Legend* (2007), each populated with notable zombie animals, round out the herd.

Chapter 1

1. We incorporate the complexities of Jacques Derrida's work on the linguistic name, "the animal," which, attempting to call up images of amoeba, foxes, and humans, necessarily fails. See *The Animal That Therefore I Am* and *The Beast and the Sovereign* for more on the failure of the definite article as it applies to animals. See Chapter 2 of this text for more discussion of the disparities broadly incorporated into the linguistic term "the zombie."

2. Perhaps this accounts for some of the physically rotting uses of the drug cocktails bath salts and Krokodil.

3. Emory University's Zombethics.com takes a lively philosophical and neurobiological approach to the undead.

Chapter 2

1. Deborah Christie and Sarah Juliet Lauro's *Better Off Dead* features several essays on the Haitian origins of the zombie.

2. Matheson's creatures in the novel version of *I Am Legend* clearly become more like zombies in later film versions, but even in the novel they share some affinity through moments of self-lack.

3. In fairness, Mira Grant also suggests that the Kellis-Amberlee virus keeps the corpse animate and motile largely for the purpose of spreading infection, which would be a process counterserved by extreme decomposition.

4. Walter Benjamin holds that an original image is effectively irreplaceably singular, despite the potential that it might be copied. Roland Barthes' punctum is a compelling point in an image that disrupts the whole.

5. See Henry Krips' thorough explanation of the interaction of these philosophic expressions of the gaze in *Fetish: An Erotics of Culture* 9–10.

6. *Hamlet* IV.2.

7. See Denise Gigante's *Taste* and Marc Redfield's *Phantom Formations: Aesthetic Ideology and the Blidungsroman*.

8. While "zombie aesthetic" has been used critically, often to mean a sensibility associated with a particular group, as when Yari Lanci calls on the term to explore its hopeless capitalist economic implications, the term is ripe for critical aesthetic appropriation.

9. This transformation is inexplicably elided from the film adaptation of the novel. Its social concerns are very often replaced by massive action sequences instead of the interpersonal conflicts detailing socially decorous behavior.

10. In only a few representations is the head-shot insufficient to dispatch a zombie. *Dead Alive* offers a notable example as its zombie nurse (Nurse McTavish, Brenda Kendall) does not die when Lionel throws a metal hummingbird sculpture and pierces her skull with it. (She has already been mostly beheaded at this point.) The film seems inconsistent about what constitutes the necessary trauma to end the life of its zombies. Several hoodlums appear to have been killed through various martial arts moves, but the hoodlum leader, Void (Jed Brophy), is not dispatched until pureed by a lawnmower. Another zombie literally operates as a pile of human guts moving around the screen, complete with a farting sphincter operating as a mouth. The inconsistency seems to stem from the need of Lionel (Timothy Balme), the film's protagonist, to grow as a character before the zombie contagion can end. In many ways, it is his own personal zombie apocalypse, as he attempts to stop the spread of contagion by continuing tranquilization of the zombies into submission.

11. See "Inside the Head of the Walking Dead" by E. Paul Zehr and Stephanie Norman for a thorough neurobiological discussion of the zombie brain.

Chapter 3

1. Stephen King posits in "Why We Crave Horror Movies" that we do in order to take our bored and conforming subconsciouses out for a roll in the grass.

2. See Chase Pielak's *Memorializing Animals During the Romantic Period* for more on carnosarcophagy.

Chapter 4

1. Megaextinction is a defining term of the Anthropocene era, an environmental/geologic term that defines the historical period beginning when humans and human processes began to substantially alter Earth's ecosystem.

2. Contemporaneous films such as *Invisible Invaders* and *Plan 9 From Outer Space* do involve reanimated human corpses.

3. This particular form of metaphysical anxiety continues to plague zombie representations, regardless of cause. For example, in *This Year's Class Picture*, Mrs. Giess cannot decide about the relative humanity of her students. Likewise, in *Fear the Walking Dead* there is considerable discussion between Celia and Nick and the rest of the survivors regarding whether or not the zombies stored in Celia's wine cellar are, in fact, human or not; Madison Clark refuses to see them as capable of being Other. This anxiety haunts the second season.

4. Perhaps this is akin to the biblical fall of humanity; in *Genesis* 3:7, the very first effect of the fall is for Adam and Eve to realize their nakedness, their fundamental human form: "Then the eyes of both of them were opened, and they knew that they were naked; and they sewed fig leaves together and made themselves loin coverings" (*NASB*).

5. In this context, the fall is no more biblical *Genesis* than it is Machiavellian.

6. *(Rec)2* (2009) incorporates a unique origin story with elements of both theology/spirituality and science. On the small screen, *American Horror Story* (2011–) conjured zombies in Season 3 (2014), Episodes 4 and 5, when Marie Laveau (Angela Bassett) used a voodoo spell to summon an army of the undead to attack her enemies

7. Wilfred Owen's World War I poem, "Dulce et Decorum Est," takes on a new pallor in the zombie era:

> In all my dreams, before my helpless sight,
> He plunges at me, guttering, choking, drowning.
> If in some smothering dreams you too could pace
> Behind the wagon that we flung him in,
> And watch the white eyes writhing in his face,
> His hanging face, like a devil's sick of sin [lines 15–20].

8. See *The Sublime Object of Ideology* 32–33.

Chapter 5

1. By becoming zombie, we mean the kind of becoming identified by Deleuze and Guattari as becoming animal in *A Thousand Plateaus*, as well as the direct threat of contagion engaged through the threat of a zombie apocalypse.

2. Perhaps it is only in light of posthumanity that we can claim humanity.

3. Rick reveals to the rest of the group and the audience: "at the CDC Jenner told me, whatever it is, we all carry it. We're all infected" (Season II, Episode 13).

4. From its very first episode, *TWD* places the relationship between parent and child in the foreground. We first learn that Rick is a father in the first episode of the show. In a flashback discussion with Shane, Rick mentions Carl and indicates that Lori made a hurtful comment in front of the boy. Again, the parent/child relationship is engaged when Rick meets the first zombie in the show, a little girl who picks up a teddy bear. She initially shambles on in front of Rick, who only sees her back. When he calls to her, she turns around and we see, along with Rick, that she is a zombie; half of her face has rotted off making the revelation as grotesque as possible. Viewers' sympathy for a little girl alone in the walking world comes back to bite them. Finally, we meet another father-son pair, Morgan Jones and his son Duane (Adrian Kali Turner), as Rick is subdued

with a shovel by the latter. Morgan is an exemplary father, taking all precautions to care for his son, even while desperately seeking to maintain his humanity by taking compassion on a stranger. Taken together, these images of the parent child relationship foreshadow the importance of the *Bildung* motif in the series, and begin to create a parallel alignment between the viewer and both the father and the son.

5. Agency here depends on the ability to make complex decisions between options that are not foregone. The ability to make this sort of decision, in light of the ultimate possibility of one's own death, for Derrida and others, offers a basis for human agency and responsibility. See Jacques Derrida, *The Gift of Death* 51.

6. It is worth noting that the bullet wounding Carl passes through the deer; the initial wounding is entirely accidental. Interestingly, heroism in this walking world betrays a willingness to betray others in a Machiavellian nightmare: Shane kills Otis in II.3 so that he can escape with the medical supplies necessary to save young Carl. Shane makes the decision to shoot Otis and leave him to distract the walkers.

7. Hershel alerts the viewer to the preprogrammed nature of the collective response when he tells Rick and Lori that "if they don't get back soon, we're going to have a decision to make ... whether to operate on your boy without a respirator" (II.3).

8. It is telling that AMC released a game called "Which Character Are You?" that asked viewers to answer questions to identify which character from *TWD* most closely mirrored their personality. The metaphor is not to be overlooked; readers do not identify with which character they "most closely identify"; they identify which character they "are." The game asks, "Are you a survivor?... Or a Casualty?" Rick is portrayed as the most decisive and interesting character with whom to identify; Carl is not even represented as a possible choice for a character to become at this point. The game fails to realize that viewers are themselves coming of age again in a walking world.

9. Sarah Juliet Lauro follows Peter Dendle's use and understanding of the term in her "Zombie (R)evolution" (232).

Chapter 6

1. Giorgio Agamben lays out the conditions necessary for a state of exception in his book of the same name. He argues that the western world is engaged in one such state now (57–58).

2. Some examples from among the many are: *The Walking Dead* (The Governor's character engages in most of these), *Land of the Dead* features an exemplary bad sovereign in Kaufman, and *28 Days Later* (2002) features a nasty combination of human vices.

3. R in *Warm Bodies* (2013), for example, ecstatically eats Perry's (Dave Franco) brain. It is worth noting that even though we project these taboo desires onto the apocalyptic other (the self that has lost its essence), zombies (rather than ourselves), we recognize that we are really engaging in the taboos by paying to watch them occur. Further, we strengthen the ideology that shapes normative values by resisting, by pretending that only a zombie might do such a thing in a state of exception (zombies didn't invent cannibalism, after all, humans did).

4. Interestingly, zombies who retain some vestige of humanity tend to do the same thing: they reproduce the structures inherent in human societies, just deader.

5. We know from the pilot, for instance, that the military was attempting to evacuate hospitals at some point during Rick's unconsciousness, but failed to do so. This is a problem of organization and planning.

6. Since the vast majority of medical research aimed at curing significant human ills is funded by the government in some form or other (through NIH, for example), it seems no great stretch to suppose that the government has had a hand in the creation of

this zombie plague, strengthening the representation of Neville as salvific government agent against the plague of government.

7. Colonel Neville's self-proclaimed specialty is "trying to find treatments for diseases that hadn't existed until other doctors invented them."

8. This move is perhaps best made in the B movie, *Ahhh! Zombies (Wasting Away)* (2007). Viewers are surprised to find in the film that the protagonists, who themselves appear to be fixated on a cure, are, in fact, zombies. The film posits the same sort of state of exception that we have identified elsewhere; the zombies in the film resist the power of the corrupt Colonel South (Richard Riehle), imagining themselves as super soldiers led by PFC Steele (Colby French) until they finally manage to establish a space for themselves, "a zombie society where everyone is equal separate from the intolerance of the outside world."

Chapter 7

1. Katherine Schutte deserves credit for this idea. The cause of this longing, beyond dis-ease, warrants further consideration.

Conclusion

1. In his late work, *The History of Sexuality*, Volume 3, Michel Foucualt has come to understand agency in terms of subjectivity; he writes, "The task of testing oneself, examining oneself, monitoring oneself in a series of clearly defined exercises, makes the question of truth—the truth concerning what one is, what one does, and what one is capable of doing—central to the formation of the ethical subject" (68). This understanding of the connection between complex subjectivity and agency underlies this project.

2. Jacques Derrida writes in *The Gift of Death*, "responsibility demands irreplaceable singularity. Yet only death or rather the apprehension of death can give this irreplacability, and it is only on the basis of it that one can speak of a responsible subject, of the soul as conscience of self, of myself, etc." (51). The responsibility evidenced through the gift and the agency realized through responsibility in light of the possibility of death is the foundation of response-ability.

3. Incidentally, these features are not isolated to the zombie figure. For example, Mary Shelley seems to fantasize that Victor Frankenstein displays these characteristics, while his monster, who much more closely resembles an animated corpse, is quite the opposite.

4. This is often reflected in an intense fascination with conspiracy theory, invoking representations of the Illuminati, massive terror plots, and other systematizing ideas as attempts to make sense of an apparently hostile world.

5. Thoreau's account of this problem reads: "The mass of men serve the state thus, not as men mainly, but as machines, with their bodies. They are the standing army, and the militia, jailers, constables, posse comitatus, etc. In most cases there is no free exercise whatever of the judgment or of the moral sense; but they put themselves on a level with wood and earth and stones; and wooden men can perhaps be manufactured that will serve the purpose as well. Such command no more respect than men of straw or a lump of dirt. They have the same sort of worth only as horses and dogs. Yet such as these even are commonly esteemed good citizens" ("On The Duty of Civil Disobedience").

Works Cited

Ackermann, Hans, and Jeanine Gauthier. "The Ways and Nature of the Zombie." *The Journal of American Folklore* 104.414 (1996): 466–494. Print.

Agamben, Giorgio. *The State of Exception.* Trans. Kevin Attell. Chicago: University of Chicago Press, 2005. Print.

Aira, Cesar. *The Miracle Cures of Dr. Aira.* New York: New Directions, 2012. Print.

Althusser, Louis. *Lenin and Philosophy and Other Essays.* 1971. Trans. Ben Brewster. New York: Monthly Review Press, 2001. Print.

Antisocial. Dir. Cody Calahan. Anchor Bay Entertainment, 2014. DVD.

Aquilina, Carmelo, and Julian C. Hughes. "*The Return of the Living Dead*: Agency Lost and Found?" *Dementia: Mind, Meaning, and the Person.* Ed. Julian C. Hughes, Stephen J. Louw, and Steven Sabat. Oxford: Oxford University Press, 2011. 50–61. Print

Atwood, Margaret. *Oryx and Crake.* New York: Anchor Books, 2004. Print.

Auerbach, Nina. *Our Vampires, Ourselves.* Chicago: University of Chicago, 1995. Print.

Baird, Jeanie. "7 Reasons Grand Lake, Colorado Is the Perfect Town for Surviving the Zombie Apocalypse." 15 Feb. 2015. Buzzfeed. 26 June 2015. Web.

Bath Salt Zombies. Dir. Dustin Mills. Dustin Mills Productions. 2013. DVD.

Baudrillard, Jean. *Selected Writings.* Stanford: Stanford University Press, 2001. Print.

Behuniak, Susan M. "The Living Dead? The Construction of People with Alzheimer's Disease as Zombies." *Ageing and Society* 31.01 (2011): 70–92. Web.

Benjamin, Walter. *Illuminations.* Ed. Hannah Arendt. Trans. Harry Zohn. New York: Schocken Books, 1969. Print.

Birch-Bayley, Nicole. "Terror in Horror Genres: The Global Media and the Millennial Zombie." *Journal of Popular Culture* 45.6 (2012): 1137–1151. Print.

Bishop, Kyle William. *American Zombie Gothic: The Rise and Fall (and Rise) of the Walking Dead in Popular Culture.* Jefferson, NC: McFarland, 2010. Print.

_____. *How Zombies Conquered Popular Culture.* Jefferson, NC: McFarland, 2015. Print.

The Blair Witch Project. Dirs. Daniel Myrick and Eduardo Sanchez. Haxan Films, 1999. DVD.

Blanchot, Maurice. *The Book to Come.* Trans. Charlotte Mandell. Stanford: Stanford University Press, 2003. Print.

Blanton, Robert G. "Zombies and International Relations: A Simple Guide for Bringing the Undead into Your Classroom." *International Studies Perspectives* 14.1 (2013): 1–13. Web.

Blumberg, Arnold. *Zombiemania: 80 Movies to Die For.* London: Telos Publishing, 2006. Print.

Boluk, Stephanie, and Wylie Lenz, eds. *Generation Zombie.* Jefferson, NC: McFarland, 2011. Print.

_____. "Infection, Media, and Capitalism: From Early Modern Plagues to Postmodern Zombies." *Journal for Early Modern Cultural Studies* 10.2 (2010): 126–147. Web.

Boon, Kevin. "And the Dead Shall Rise." In *Better Off Dead*. Ed. Deborah Christie and Sarah Juliet Lauro. New York: Fordham University Press, 2011. 5–8. Print.

_____. "The Zombie as Other: Mortality and the Monstrous in the Post-Nuclear Age." In *Better Off Dead*. Ed. Deborah Christie and Sarah Juliet Lauro. New York: Fordham University Press, 2011. 50–61. Print.

Broglio, Ron. "Thinking With Animals." *Animals and the Human Imagination*. Ed. Aaron Gross and Anne Vallely. New York: Columbia University Press, 2012. 238–58. Print.

Bronte, Emily. *Wuthering Heights*. New York: Norton, 2002. Print.

Brooks, Max. *World War Z*. New York: Random House, 2006. Print.

Brown, Raymond. *An Introduction to the New Testament*. New York: Doubleday, 1997. Print.

Canavan, Gerry. "Fighting a War You've Already Lost: Zombies and Zombies in Firefly/Serenity and Dollhouse." *Science Fiction Film & Television* 4.2 (2011): 173–203. Web.

Chien, Irene. "Playing Undead." *Film Quarterly* 61.2 (2007): 64–65. Print.

Christie, Deborah, and Sarah Juliet Lauro. *Better Off Dead: The Evolution of the Zombie as Post-Human*. New York: Fordham University Press, 2011. Print.

Codorow, Adam. "Death and Taxes and Zombies." *Iowa Law Review* 98.3 (2013): 1207–31. Print.

Cohen, Alexander, and Chase Pielak. "Archiving the Apocalypse." *Midwest Quarterly* 57, no. 3 (2016), 241–275. Print.

Cohen, Donna, and Carl Eisdorfer. *The Loss of Self: A Family Resource for the Care of Alzheimer's Disease and Related Disorders*. New York: Norton, 1986. Print.

Collins, Margo, and Elson Bond. "Off the Page and Into Your Brains." In *Better Off Dead*. Ed. Deborah Christie and Sarah Juliet Lauro. New York: Fordham University Press, 2011. 116–135. Print.

Comoroff, Jean, and John Comaroff. "Alien-Nation: Zombies, Immigrants, and Millennial Capitalism." *South Atlantic Quarterly* 101.4 (2002): 779–805. Print.

Contracted. Dir. Eric England. BoulderLight Pictures. 2013. DVD.

Cook, Denise. "The Cultural Life of the Living Dead." *Contexts* 12.4 (2013): 54–56. Print.

Cooney, Eleanor. *Death in Slow Motion: A Memoir of a Daughter, Her Mother, and the Beast Called Alzheimer's*. New York: Perennial, 2004. Print.

Cooties. Dirs. John Milott and Cary Murnion. SpectreVision. 2015. DVD.

Corzani, Jack. "West Indian Mythology and Its Literary Illustrations." *Research in African Literatures* 25.2 (1994): 131–139. Print.

Davidson, Ann. *A Curious Kind of Widow: Loving a Man with Advanced Alzheimer's*. McKinleyville, CA: Fithian, 2006. Print.

Dawn of the Dead. Dir. George Romero. United Film Distribution Company, 1979. DVD.

Dawn of the Dead. Dir. Zack Snyder. Universal Pictures, 2004. DVD.

Day of the Dead. Dir. George Romero. United Film Distribution Company, 1985. DVD.

De Vise, Daniel. "Exploring the Undead: University of Baltimore to Offer English Class on Zombies." *The Washington Post*. 10 Sept. 2010. Web.

Dead Alive. (Braindead.) Dir. Peter Jackson. LionsGate, 1992. DVD.

Dead Rising. Capcom, 2006. Game.

Death of Wolverine. Marvel Comics, 2014. Web.

Deleuze, Gilles, and Felix Guattari. *A Thousand Plateaus*. Trans. Brian Massumi. New York: Continuum, 2004. Print.

Dendle, Peter. "And the Dead Shall Rise Again." In *Better Off Dead*. Ed. Deborah Christie and Sarah Juliet Lauro. New York: Fordham University Press, 2011. 159–162. Print.

_____. *Zombie Movie Encyclopedia*. Jefferson, NC: McFarland, 2010. Print.

_____. *Zombie Movie Encyclopedia*. Vol. 2. Jefferson, NC: McFarland, 2012. Print.

_____. "Zombie Movies and the Millennial Generation." In *Better Off Dead*. Ed. Deborah Christie and Sarah Juliet Lauro. New York: Fordham University Press, 2011. 175–186. Print.

Defoe, Daniel, and Paula R. Backscheider. *A Journal of the Plague Year: Authoritative Text, Backgrounds, Contexts, Criticism*. New York: W.W. Norton, 1992. Print.

Derksen, Craig, and Darren Hudson Hick. "Your Zombie and You." In *Zombies Are Us*. Ed. Christopher M. Moreman and Cory James Rushton. Jefferson, NC: McFarland, 2011. 11–23. Print.

Derrida, Jacques. *The Animal That Therefore I Am*. Ed. Marie-Louise Mallet. Trans. David Wills. New York: Fordham University Press, 2008. Print.

_____. *The Gift of Death*. Trans. David Wills. Chicago: University of Chicago Press, 1995. Print.

_____. *The Politics of Friendship*. Trans. George Collins. New York: Verso, 2005. Print.

_____. *Spectres of Marx*. Trans. Peggy Kamuf. New York: Routledge, 2006. Print.

Derrida, Jacques, and Elizabeth Rudinesco. *For What Tomorrow...* Trans. Jeff Fort. Stanford: Stanford University Press, 2004. Print.

Doc of the Dead. Dir. Alexandre O. Phillipe. Exhibit A Pictures, 2014. DVD.

Dodd, Michael. "Safe Scares: How 9/11 caused the American Horror Remake Trend (Part One)." Themissingslate.com. 31 Aug 2014. Web.

Drezner, Daniel. *Theories of International Politics and Zombies*. Princeton: Princeton University Press, 2011. Print.

Eliot, T. S. *The Waste Land*. New York, Norton: 2000. Print.

Emery, Amy Fass. "The Zombie In/As the Text: Zora Neale Hurston's Tell My Horse." *African American Review* 39.3 (2005): 327–336. Print.

Fido. Dir. Andrew Currie. Lionsgate, 2006. DVD.

Fitzpatrick, Kathleen. *Planned Obsolescence: Publishing, Technology, and the Future of the Academy*. New York: NYU Press, 2011. Print.

Flesch, William. *Comeuppance*. Cambridge: Harvard University Press, 2008. Print.

Foucault, Michel. "The Social Extension of the Norm." In *Foucault Live*. Ed. Sylvere Lotringer. Los Angeles, CA: Semiotext(e), 1996. 196–199. Print.

_____. *The History of Sexuality*. Vol. 1. New York: Vintage, 1998. Print.

_____. *The Order of Things: An Archaeology of the Human Sciences*. London: Routledge, 2002. Print.

Freaks of Nature. Dir. Robbie Pickering. 2015. Sony Pictures, 2016. DVD.

Freud, Sigmund. *Beyond the Pleasure Principle*. Trans. and ed. James Strachey. New York, Norton, 1989. Print.

_____. "The Uncanny." Trans. Alix Strachey. 1919. MIT. Web.

Friday the 13th. Dir. Sean S. Cunningham. Paramount Pictures, 1980. DVD.

Fürst, Martina. "Exemplarization: A Solution to the Problem of Consciousness?" *Philosophical Studies* 161.1 (2012): 141–51. Web.

Gerber, Richard J. "'Zombies! Ghosts! Cannibals! Whores!': A Report on the North American James Joyce Conference, College of Charleston, South Carolina, 11–15 June 2014." *James Joyce Quarterly* 49.2 (2012): 220–223. Print.

George: A Zombie Intervention. Dir. J. T. Seaton. Tarvix Pictures. 2009. DVD.

Gigante, Denise. *Taste*. New Haven: Yale University Press, 2005. Print.

Goldberg, Leslie. "The Walking Dead Dissection." *The Hollywood Reporter*. 18 Mar 2012. Web.

Gomel, Elana. "Invasion of the Dead (Languages): Zombie Apocalypse and the End of Narrative." *Frame* 26.1 (2013): 31–46. Web.

Gora, Joseph, and Andrew Whelan. "Invasion of the Aca-zombies." *The Australian Higher Education Supplement*. 3 Nov. 2010. Web.

Grahame Smith, Seth. *Pride and Prejudice and Zombies*. Philadelphia: Quirk Books, 2009. Print.

Grant, Mira. *Feed*. New York: Orbit, 2010. Print.

Gross, Doug. "Why We Love Those Rotting, Hungry, Putrid Zombies." CNN. 2 Oct. 2009. Web.

Grossman, Lisa. "Galactic Zombies Roam the Cosmos." *New Scientist* 225.3004 (2015): 8. Print.

Gunn, Joshua, and Shaun Treat. "Zombie Trouble: A Propaedeutic on Ideological Subjectification and the Unconscious." *Quarterly Journal of Speech* 91.2 (2005): 144–174. Print.

Hacker, Stephen. "Zombies in the Workplace." *Journal of Quality and Participation* 32.4 (2010): 25–28. Print.

Hall, Derek. "Varieties of Zombieism: Approaching Comparative Political Economy through *28 Days Later* and *Wild Zero*." *International Studies Perspectives* 12.1 (2011): 1–17. Web.

Hardin, Garrett. "The Tragedy of the Commons." *Science* 162 (1968): 1243–1248. Print.

Heraclitus of Ephesus. "B12." *Heraclitus Fragments*. Trans. Jonathan Barnes. http://www.heraclitusfragments.com/B12/index.html. Web.

Herne, Lily. *Deadlands*. Johannesburg: Puffin, 2011. Print.

_____. *Death of a Saint*. Johannesburg: Puffin, 2012. Print.

Hobbes, Thomas. *Leviathan*. Oxford: Oxford University Press, 2009. Print.

Hopkins, Gerard Manley. *Poems and Prose*. New York: Penguin, 1985. Print.

Horlacher, Stefan. "Taboo, Transgression, and Literature." In *Taboo and Transgression in British Literature from the Renaissance to the Present*. Ed. Stefan Horlacher, Stefan Glomb, and Lars Heiler. New York: Palgrave Macmillan, 2010. 3–21. Print.

Hughes, Jacob. "A Monstrous Pedagogy." *Rocky Mountain Review* 63.1 (2009): 96–104. Print.

Hurley, Kelly. *The Gothic Body: Sexuality, Materialism, and Degeneration at the Fin De Siècle*. Cambridge: Cambridge University Press, 1996. Print.

I am Legend. Dir. Francis Lawrence. Warner Brothers, 2007. DVD.

I Walked with a Zombie. Dir. Jacques Tourneur. RKO Radio Pictures, 1943. Web.

Inguanzo, Ozzy. *Zombies on Film: The Definitive Story of Undead Cinema*. New York: Rizzoli, 2014. Print.

Invasion of the Body Snatchers. Dir. Don Siegel. Allied Artists Picture Corporation, 1956. DVD.

Invisible Invaders. Dir. Edward L. Cahn. Robert. E. Kent Productions. 1959. Web.

Iron Man. Dir. Jon Favreau. Paramount, 2008. DVD.

Jones, Steve. "Porn of the Dead." *Zombies Are Us*. Ed. Christopher M. Moreman and Cory James Rushton. Jefferson, NC: McFarland, 2011. 40–61. Print.

Jonson, Ben. *The Alchemist*. New York: Hill, 1966. Print.

Keats, John. *Complete Poems*. Ed. Jack Stillinger. Cambridge: Belknap Press of Harvard University Press, 1982. Print.

Keats, John. *Complete Poems and Selected Letters of John Keats*. Modern Library: New York, 2001.

Kee, Chera. "From Cannibal to Zombie and Back Again." In *Better Off Dead*. Ed. Deborah Christie and Sarah Juliet Lauro. New York: Fordham University Press, 2011. 9–23. Print.

Keebaugh, Cari. "'The Better to Eat You[r Brains] With, My Dear': Sex, Violence, And Little Red Riding Hood's Zombie BBQ as Fairy Tale Recovery Project." *The Journal of Popular Culture* 46.3 (2013): 589–603. Web.

Keetley, Dawn. Ed. *"We're All Infected": Essays on AMC's The Walking Dead and the Fate of the Human*. Jefferson, NC: McFarland, 2014. Print.

Ke$ha. "Die Young." *Warrior*. RCA, 2012. CD.

King, Stephen. *Cell: A Novel*. New York: Pocket Books, 2006. Print.

_____. *The Gunslinger*. New York: Signet, 2003. Print.

_____. *The Stand*. New York, Anchor. 2012. Print.

_____. "Why We Crave Horror Movies." *Models for Writers*. Ed. Alfred Rosa and Paul Eschholz. 8th ed. Boston: Bedford, 2004. 460–463. Print.

Kirk, Robert. "The Inconceivability of Zombies." *Philosophical Studies* 139.1 (2008): 73–89. Print.

Kline, Jim. "Zombie Typology." *Psychological Perspectives* 55 (2012): 467–81. Print.

Krips, Henry. *Fetish: An Erotics of Culture.* Ithaca: Cornell University Press, 1999. Print.

Kristeva, Julia. *Powers of Horror: An Essay on Abjection.* New York: Columbia University Press, 1982. Print.

Lanci, Yari. "Zombie 2.0: Subjectivation in Times of Apocalypse." *Journal for Cultural and Religious Theory* 13.2 (2014): 25–37. Print.

Land of the Dead. Dir. George Romero. Universal Studios, 2005. DVD.

Large, Gerald. "Theatrical Physicality, the Gross-out Zombie, and Michael Chekhov Technique: Creating a Bridge from the Actor's Body to the Character's Body via the Zombie-Body." *Theatre Topics* 25.3 (2015), 295–303.

Lauro, Sarah Juliet. "Zombie (R)evolution." *Better Off Dead.* Ed. Deborah Christie and Sarah Juliet Lauro. New York: Fordham University Press, 2011. 5–8. Print.

Life After Beth. Dir. Jeff Baena. Abbolita Productions. 2014. DVD.

Lippit, Akira Mizuta. *Electric Animal: Toward a Rhetoric of Wildlife.* Minneapolis: University of Minnesota, 2000. Print.

Lushin, Guy. *The Living Dead: Alzheimer's in America.* Potomac, Maryland: National Foundation for Medical Research, 1990. Print.

Macpherson, Fiona. "A Disjunctive Theory Of Introspection: A Reflection On Zombies And Anton's Syndrome." *Philosophical Issues* 20.1 (2010): 226–65. Web.

Marder, Elissa. *Dead Time.* Stanford: Stanford University Press, 2001. Print.

Matheson, Richard. *I Am Legend.* 2nd Ed. New York: Tor Books, 2007. Print.

McCarty, Willard. "The Residue of Uniqueness." *Historical Social Research/Historische Sozialforschung* 37.3 (2012): 24–45. Print.

McGill, Natalie. "Student Zombies Overrun Michigan." *The Nation's Health* 43.6 (2013): 19. Print.

McGlotten, Shaka, and Steve Jones. *Zombies and Sexuality.* Jefferson, NC: McFarland, 2014. Print.

Miller, Arthur. *The Price.* New York: Penguin, 1985. Print.

Moreman, Christopher M., and Cory James Rushton, eds. *Race, Oppression and the Zombie.* Jefferson, NC: McFarland, 2011. Print.

_____. *Zombies Are Us.* Jefferson, NC: McFarland, 2011. Print.

Moretti, Franco. *Signs Taken for Wonders: Essays in the Sociology of Literary Forms.* London: NLB, 1983. Print.

Munz, Philip, Ioan Hudea, Joe Imad, and Robert Smith. "When Zombies Attack!: Mathematical Modelling of an Outbreak of Zombie Infection." *Infectious Disease Modelling Research Progress.* Ed. Jean Michel Tchuenche and C. Chiyaka. New York: Nova Science, 2009. Print.

Murray, Jessica. "A Zombie Apocalypse: Opening Representational Spaces for Alternative Constructions of Gender and Sexuality." *Journal of Literary Studies* 29.4 (2013): 1–19. Web.

Nasiruddin, Melissa, Monique Halabi, Alexander Dao, Kyle Chen, and Brandon Brown. "Zombies-A Pop Culture Resource for Public Health Awareness." *Emerging Infectious Diseases* 19.5 (2013): 809–813. Web.

New American Standard Bible. Biblegateway. Web.

Niehaus, Isak. "Witches And Zombies Of The South African Lowveld: Discourse, Accusations And Subjective Reality." *Journal of the Royal Anthropological Institute* 11.2 (2005): 191–210. Web.

Night of the Living Dead. Dir. George Romero. Continental Distributing, 1968. DVD.

The Omega Man. Dir. Boris Sagal. Warner, 1971. DVD.

Orwell, George. *1984.* New York: Signet, 1950. Print.

Owen, Wilfred. "Dulce et Decorum Est." *The War Poetry Website*. Warpoetry.co.ok. Web.

Paffenroth, Kim. *Gospel of the Living Dead*. Waco: Baylor University Press, 2006. Print.

Perry, Katy. "Friday Night." *Teenage Dream*. Capitol Records, 2010. CD.

Petri, Alexandra. "Zombie Apocalypse: Are Bath Salts to Blame?" *The Washington Post*. 07 Jun 2012. Web.

Pielak, Chase. *Memorializing Animals during the Romantic Period*. Burlington, VT: Ashgate, 2015. Print.

_____. "Wolverine's Fearful Symmetry." *The Comics Grid*. 7 Nov 2012. Web.

Pielak, Chase, and Alexander Cohen. "Archiving the Apocalpyse." *Midwest Quarterly* 57.3 (2016), 241–275. Print.

_____. "Yes, But in a Zombie Apocalypse..." *Modern Language Studies* 43.2 (2014), 44–57. Print.

Pielak, Chase, and Fanny Ramirez. "Growing Up Walking." *The Mid-Atlantic Almanack* 23 (2014), 37–57. Print.

Plan 9 from Outer Space. Dir. Ed Wood. Distributors Corporation of America. 1959. Web.

Planet Terror. Dir. Robert Rodriguez. Dimension Films, 2007. DVD.

Pokornowski, Steven. "Insecure Lives: Zombies, Global Health, and the Totalitarianism of Generalization." *Literature and Medicine* 31.2 (2013): 216–234. Web.

Poltergeist. Dir. Tobe Hooper. Metro-Goldwyn-Mayer. 1982. DVD.

Ponder, Justin. "Dawn of the Different: The Mulatto Zombie in Zack Snyder's Dawn of the Dead." *The Journal of Popular Culture* 45.3 (2012): 551–71. Web.

Quarantine. Dir. John Erick Dowdle. Sony Pictures, 2008. DVD.

Re-Animator. Dir. Stuart Gordon. Empire International Pictures. 1985. DVD.

R.E.M. "It's The End of the World." *Document*. I.R.S. Records, 1987. CD.

REC. Dir. Jaume Belaguero and Paco Plaza. Sony Pictures, 2009. DVD.

Redfield, Marc. *Phantom Formations: Aesthetic Ideology and the Bildungsroman*. Ithaca: Cornell University Press, 1996. Print.

Reich, Robert. Robertreich.org. Web.

Reinhard Lupton, Julia. "Re-vamp: A Response." *PMLA* 126.2 (2011): 467–471. Print.

The Return of the Living Dead. Dir. Dan O-Bannon. Orion Pictures. 1985. DVD.

Return of the Living Dead III. Dir. Brian Yuzna. 1993. Lions Gate. 2001. DVD.

Return of the Living Dead: Necropolis. Dir. Ellory Elkayem. Aurora Entertainment. 2005. DVD.

Return of the Living Dead: Rave to the Grave. Dir. Ellory Elkayem. Aurora Entertainment. 2005. DVD.

The Returned. Dir. Manuel Carballo. Ramaco Media. 2013. DVD.

Rihanna. "Right Now." *Unapologetic*. R Studios, 2012. CD.

Romdhani, Rebecca. "Hopkinson's Brown Girl in the Ring." *Research in African Literatures* 46.4 (2015): 72–89. Print.

Rushton, Cory James, and Christopher M. Moreman. "Introduction: They're Us: Zombies, Humans/Humans, Zombies." *Zombies Are Us*. Ed. Christopher M. Moreman and Cory James Rushton. Jefferson, NC: McFarland, 2011. 1–7. Print.

Russell, Jamie. *Book of the Dead: The Complete History of Zombie Cinema*. Surrey: FAB Press, 2005. Print.

Ryan, Suzanne. "Academic Zombies: A Failure of Resistance or a Means of Survival?" *Australian Universities Review* 54.2 (2012): 3–11. Print.

Sartre, Jean-Paul. *Being and Nothingness*. New York: Citadel Press, 1966. Print.

_____. *The Imaginary*. Trans. Jonathan Webber. New York: Routledge, 2004. Print.

_____. *No Exit and Three Other Plays*. Trans. Stuart Gilbert. New York: Vintage Books, 1989. Print.

Schlozman, Steven. "The Seductive Nostalgia of *The Walking Dead*." In *The Walking Dead Psychology*. Ed. Travis Langley. New York: Sterling, 2015, 20–30. Print.

Schwartz, Janelle A. *Worm Work: Recasting Romanticism*. Minneapolis: University Press of Minnesota, 2012. Print.

Scouts Guide to the Zombie Apocalypse. Dir. Christopher B. Landon. Paramount, 2016. DVD.

Seabrook, William. *The Magic Island*. New York: Harcourt, Brace, 1929. Print.

Serenity. Dir. Joss Whedon. Universal Studios, 2005. DVD.

Shaxson, Nicholas. "The Zombies of Mayfair." *New Statesman* 142.5164 (2013): 30–35. Print.

Sheldon, Lee. *The Multiplayer Classroom*. Boston: Cengage, 2012. Print.

Shelley, Mary. *Frankenstein*. New York: Norton, 1996.

Sigurdson, Ola. "Slavoj Žižek, the Death Drive, and Zombies: A Theological Account." *Modern Theology* 29.3 (2013): 361–80. Web.

Simmons, Thomas E. "What Zombies Can Teach Law Students." *Mercer Law Review* 66.3, 729–780. Print.

Slater, Jay. *Eaten Alive! Italian Cannibal and Zombie Movies*. London: Plexus Publishing, 2006. Print.

Smithies, Declan. "The Mental Lives of Zombies." *Philosophical Perspectives* 26.1, 343–372. Print.

Spencer, Edmund. *Faerie Queene*. Book 1. Indianapolis, IN: Hackett Publishing Company, 2006. Print.

Stanley, David. "The Nurses' Role in the Prevention of Solanum Infection: Dealing with a Zombie Epidemic." *Journal of Clinical Nursing* (2011): 141–51. Web.

State of Emergency. Dir. Turner Clay. Clay Bros. Motion Pictures, 2011. DVD.

Stoker, Bram. *Dracula*. Oxford: Oxford University Press, 2011. Print.

Struthers, William. "Comic Books, Mock Trials, and Zombies: Engaging Integrative Biopsychology Themes in the Classroom." *Journal of Psychology and Theology* 42.2 (2014): 188–199. Web.

Stutzky, Glenn. "SW 290: Surviving the Coming Zombie Apocalypse: Catastrophes and Human Behavior." In *Summer 2012 Online Electives*. 12 Aug 2012. Web.

Tanney, Julia. "On the Conceptual, Psychological, and Moral Status of Zombies, Swamp-Beings, and Other 'Behaviourally Indistinguishable' Creatures." *Philosophy and Phenomenological Research* 69.1 (2004): 173–186. Print.

Tenga, Angela, and Elizabeth Zimmerman. "Vampire Gentlemen and Zombie Beasts: A Rendering of True Monstrosity." *Gothic Studies* 15.1 (2013): 76–87. Web.

The Terminator. Dir. James Cameron. Orion Pictures. 1984. DVD.

Thoreau, Henry David. *Walden, Civil Disobedience, and Other Writings*. New York: Norton, 2008. Print.

Turan, Kenneth. "'World War Z' Gets a Rise from the Undead." *Los Angeles Times*. 20 June 2013. Web.

28 Days Later. Dir. Danny Boyle. DNA Films and UK Film Council, 2003. DVD.

2012: Zombie Apocalypse. Dir. Nick Lyon. The Asylum, 2012. DVD.

Van Valkenburg, Nancy. "USU Professor Uses Zombie Apocalypse to Teach Math and Biology." 23 Feb. 2012. *The Standard-Examiner*. Web.

Vials, Chris. "The Origin of the Zombie in American Radio and Film." In *Generation Zombie*. Ed. Stephanie Boluk and Wylie Lenz. Jefferson, NC: McFarland, 2011. 41–53. Print.

Verstynen, Timothy, and Bradley Boytek. *Do Zombies Dream of Undead Sheep?: A Neuroscientific View of the Zombie Brain*. Princeton: Princeton University Press, 2014. Print.

Walker, Childs. "Zombies Lumber into Curriculum at University of Baltimore." *Baltimore Sun* 6 Sept. 2010. Web.

The Walking Dead. Telltale Games, 2012. PC Game.

The Walking Dead. Dir. Frank Darabont, Greg Nicotero, et al. AMC, 2011–2016. Web.

Waller, Gregory. *The Living and the Undead: Slaying Vampires, Exterminating Zombies.* Urbana: University of Illinois Press, 2010. Print.

Walpole, Horace. *The Castle of Otranto.* Oxford: Oxford University Press, 2014. Print.

Warm Bodies. Dir. Jonathan Levine. Lionsgate, 2013. DVD.

Wasting Away (Ahhh! Zombies). Dir. Matthew Kohnen. Level 33 Entertainment, 2010. DVD.

Weisberg, Josh. "The Zombie's Cogito: Meditations on Type-Q Materialism." *Philosophical Psychology* 24.5 (2011): 585–605. Web.

Which Character Are You? AMC. 16 May 2013. Web.

White Zombie. Dir. Victor Halperin. United Artists, 1932. DVD.

Whitehead, Colson. *Zone One.* New York: Doubleday, 2011. Print.

Wilcken, Lois. "The Sacred Music and Dance of Haitian Vodou from Temple to Stage and the Ethics of Representation." *Latin American Perspectives* 32.1 (2005): 193–210. Print.

Williams, Craig. *Zombies and Calculus.* Princeton: Princeton University Press, 2014. Print.

Witkowski, Karen, and Brian Blais. "Bayesian Analysis of Epidemics—Zombies, Influenza, and other Diseases." Cornell University Library. 27 Nov 2013. arxiv.org/abs/1311.6376. Web.

Wood, Ellen Meiksins. "The Separation of the 'Economic' and the 'Political' in Capitalism." *Democracy Against Capitalism.* Ed. Ellen Meiksins Wood. Cambridge: Cambridge University Press, 1995. 19–48. Print.

Woods, Robert T. *Alzheimer's Disease: Coping with a Living Death.* London: Souvenir (Educational and Academic), 1989. Print.

World War Z. Dir. Marc Forster. Paramount, 2013. DVD.

Yeates, Robert. "The Unshriven Dead, Zombies On The Loose: African And Caribbean Religious Heritage In Toni Morrison's Beloved." *Modern Fiction Studies* 61.3 (2015): 515–537.

Z Nation. Syfy. 2014 TV Show.

Zani, Steven, and Meaux, Kevin. "Lucio Fulci and the Decaying Definition of Zombie Narratives." In *Better Off Dead.* Ed. Deborah Christie and Sarah Juliet Lauro. New York: Fordham University Press, 2011. 98–115. Print.

Zealand, Christopher. "The National Strategy for Zombie Containment: Myth Meets Activism in Post-9/11 America." In *Generation Zombie.* Ed. Stephanie Boluk and Wylie Lenz. Jefferson, NC: McFarland, 2011. 231–248. Print.

Zehr, E. Paul, and Stephanie Norman. "Inside the Head of the Walking Dead." In *The Walking Dead Psychology.* Ed. Travis Langley. New York: Sterling, 2015. Print.

Žižek, Slavoj. *Living in the End Times.* New York: Verso, 2011. Print.

_____. *The Sublime Object of Ideology.* New York: Verso, 1989. Print.

"Zombethics." *The Neuroethics Blog.* Web.

"Zombie Preparedness." Office of Public Health Preparedness and Response. CDC.Gov. 18 Aug. 2014. Web.

Zombieland. Dir. Ruben Fleischer. Sony, 2009. Film.

"Zombies in Popular Media." Columbia College Chicago. 12 Aug. 2012. http://www2.colum.edu/course_descriptions/52-2725J.html. Web.

Index

abhuman 51, 130–132
abject 48–52
abyssal cat 45
aesthetics 40–53; 63
Afro-Carribean origins 20, 23–24, 37–38, 176
Agamben, Giorgio 4, 8; *see also State of Exception*
agency 20, 47, 65, 158–159, 175
Alzheimer's Disease 26–27
"And the Dead Shall Rise" *see* Boon, Kevin
animal studies 4, 42, 44–46, 61
The Animal That Therefore I Am 44
Anthropocene 82
anthropology 33
apocalypse 3–9, 15, 40, 51, 57, 73, 77, 81–82, 156–170; causes 14, 89, 102–123; curing 140–155, 170; temporality 71–101
archive 157–161
Atwood, Margaret 26, 159
avenir 5; *see also* Derrida, Jacques

Ba'athism 24
bath salts 122, 178
Baudrillard, Jean 112
Benjamin, Walter 158–160
Birch-Bayley, Nicole 24–28
Bishop, Kyle William 1–2, 19, 22, 66; *see also How Zombies Conquered Popular Culture*
Blanchot, Maurice 161
Blanton, Robert 27
Blumberg, Arnold 104
The Book of Revelation 157
Boon, Kevin 36–37, 125
Boyle, Danny 27
brains 94–95, 118
Brooks, Max 3, 27, 59, 115
Brown, Raymond 5, 157
bureaucracy 143–145

Das Cabinet des Dr. Caligari 38–39
Cain, James *see Double Indemnity*
Canavan, Gerry 21
cannibalism 45, 86, 90, 105; *see also* taboo
Carl Grimes 125–139; *see also The Walking Dead*
cataclysm 73, 85, 102, 142
Centers for Disease Control 30
Chien, Irene 176
Christie, Deborah, 20
Cold War 106, 172
Collings, David 80, 82
communication 69–70
Communist Manifesto see Marx, Karl
consumerism 21–24, 42, 78, 111–112
consumption *see* consumerism
Cook, Denise 24, 78
cultural subjectivity 4–5

Dawn of the Dead (1978) 21–23, 39, 42, 78, 109–110
Dawn of the Dead (2004) 23
Day of the Dead 39, 113–115
Dead Alive 6, 60, 121
Dead Snow 2, 66–67, 77
Dead Time see Marder, Elissa
death drive 19–20
Dendle, Peter 18, 132
Derrida, Jacques 5, 40, 44, 47–48, 84, 125, 133, 153–161; *see also* abyssal cat; *The Animal That Therefore I Am*; *avenir*
Diary of the Dead 26
digital humanities 160
disease 25
Doc of the Dead see Blumberg, Arnold
Double Indemnity 172

Electric Animal 42
Eliot, T.S. *see The Wasteland*
Emerson, Ralph Waldo 180

Emery, Amy Fass 177
empathy 65
The Epic of Gilgamesh 21
Ezekiel 155

Facebook 159, 168–169
faces 43–50
Faerie Queen 52
fear 35, 65, 68, 108–110, 172, 177; of death 18–21
Fear the Walking Dead 72, 87–92, 143
Feed 2, 44, 59–60
Fido 27, 97–101, 150
Foucault, Michel 43
found footage 160
Frankenstein 117, 120
Freaks of Nature 36, 47, 57
Freud, Sigmund 19–20, 41; 74; *see also* uncanny

Generation Zombie 22, 25
globalization 24–26
The Gothic Body see Hurley, Kelly
Gothic tropes 7–8, 50–52, 75–76, 104–105, 119
Grahame-Smith, Seth *see Pride and Prejudice and Zombies*
Grant, Mira *see Feed*
Gunn, Joshua 177

Hall, Derek 28
head shot 61–62
hell 110
Heston, Charlton 150
historical materialism 159
homecomings 74–75
honor 114–115
How Zombies Conquered Popular Culture 1, 22
hubris 117
Hurley, Kelly 7, 51–52, 124; *see also* abhuman

I Am Legend (film) 120, 145–150
Ibsen, Henrik 180
Inguanzo, Ozzy 18
Instagram 159
Interview with the Vampire 19
Invasion of the Body Snatchers 106–107
iZombie 36, 72–73, 86, 93–95, 180

Kee, Chera 37–38, 176–177
Keebaugh, Kerry 27
Keetley, Dawn 20, 22

King, Steven 26, 42, 81, 169; *see also The Gunslinger* 169; *The Stand* 26
King of the Zombies 105
Kline, Jim 21, 24
Kristeva, Julia 50–51; *see also Powers of Horror*

Lacan, Jacques 20, 46–47
Land of the Dead 39, 49
law 88, 103, 140
Lestat 19
Levinas, Emmanuel 125
Lippit, Akira 42; *see also Electric Animal*
Living in the End Times see Zizek, Slavoj

magic 104–105
Marder, Elissa 79–83
Marx, Karl 180
Matheson, Richard 39
Mazzara, Glen 109
McCarty, Willard 160
Milgram, Stanley 180
millennials 27–29, 85, 160–162, 171–173, 180–181
Miller, Arthur 78
monsters 4, 18–19, 113–114, 172, 181
Moreman, Chrisopher 19, 103
Moretti, Franco 1
mourning 40–41

Nazism 38–39, 105, 117
Night of the Living Dead 7, 22, 39, 56, 65–66, 107–108
nostalgia 73–74, 81–82; 92, 95–96, 101, 107

objectivity 106
"Ode on a Grecian Urn" 79
The Omega Man 25, 148–150
oppression 23–24, 103–105
Orwell, George 180
Oryx and Crake see Atwood, Margaret

Paffenroth, Kim 19, 68
Petri, Alexandra 122
Pokornowski, Steven 25
The Politics of Friendship see Derrida, Jacques
Ponder, Justin 23
post–Millennial zombie 24–25
Powers of Horror 51
Pride and Prejudice and Zombies 52, 60–61, 179–180

R 35–36
race 22–24
reason 64
Redfield, Marc 12
Reich, Robert 6
relative nostalgia *see* nostalgia
Resident Evil 25, 119–120
responsibility 96, 153, 175
The Return of the Living Dead 118
Return of the Living Dead 3 118–119
revelation 5–6
Romantic Period 50
Romdhani, Rebecca 23
Romero, George 22–26, 39, 78, 107–8;
   see also Dawn of the Dead (1978); *Day
   of the Dead*; *Diary of the Dead*; *Land
   of the Dead*; *Night of the Living Dead*
rot 51, 63
Rudinesco, Elizabeth 5, 156
Rushton, Cory James 19, 103

Sartre, Jean-Paul 74, 104, 106, 109, 114,
   123
Schlozman, Steven 74–76
Schwartz, Janelle 46, 50; *see also* worm
science 145–147
Scouts Guide to the Zombie Apocalpyse
   57, 67, 89, 120
Serenity 21
Shaun of the Dead 93, 115–116
Shelley, Mary *see Frankenstein*
Sigurdson, Ola 20
slavery 33
Smith, Will *see I Am Legend* (film)
Snyder, Zach *see Dawn of the Dead (
   2004)*
space 107–9
Spenser, Edmund *see Faerie Queen*
state of apocalypse 78, 123; *see also*
   apocalypse
State of Emergency 13–15
state of exception 3–6, 140–142, 154
State of Exception 4, 8, 141
Struthers, William 28–29

taboo 86, 138, 141–142
Tenga, Angela 19

The Terminator 172–173
Tetsuro, Takeuchi 28
time 71
transgression 105, 121–122, 138
Treat, Shaun 177
trioxin 110, 118
Tumblr 161, 166
28 Days Later 21, 28, 49
Twilight 19
twilight state 5, 79, 156–159, 162; *see also*
   Derrida, Jacques
Twinkie *see Zombieland*

The Umbrella Corporation 25, 119; *see
   also Resident Evil*
uncanny 41, 74, 77

vampires 19
video games 175–6
vileness 46–47, 50–53

The Walking Dead 41, 46, 49, 75, 109,
   143–145; Carl Grimes 125–139
Warm Bodies 35–36, 44, 49, 51, 151–153
The Wasteland 83–84, 155
Westphalian state system 24
White Zombie 39, 104
Wild Zero 28
Wordsworthian Errancies see Collings,
   David
World War Z (book) *see* Brooks, Max
World War Z (film) 54–55, 64, 98, 154,
   160
worm 46
Worm Work see Schwartz, Janelle

Z Nation 55
Zimmerman, Elizabeth 19
Zizek, Slavoj 20, 177–178
zombethics 31–32
Zombie Burlesque 51
Zombieland 80–81, 97–98
Zombies on Film see Iguanzo, Ozzy
The Zombie as Other *see* Boon, Kevin
zombie galaxies 33
Zombie Movie Encyclopedia see Dendle,
   Peter